ANCIENT CAMBODIA

Text by
DONATELLA MAZZEO AND
CHIARA SILVI ANTONINI

Foreword by
HAN SUYIN

MONUMENTS OF CIVILIZATION
ANCIENT CAMBODIA

CASSELL
LONDON

Frontispiece:
Ta Som: The tower of this temple, an annex to the Preah Khan at Angkor, is carved with the face of the Bodhisattva Lokesvara. Dated to A.D. 1191, this tower belongs to the second phase of the Bayon style. The roots of a great silk-cotton (Bombox) tree enclose the stonework; this was the condition of many of the great monuments of Cambodia when they were rediscovered in the nineteenth century.

CASSELL LTD.
35 Red Lion Square, London WC1R 4SG
and at Sydney, Auckland, Toronto, Johannesburg,
an affiliate of
Macmillan Publishing Co., Inc.,
New York.

English translation copyright © 1978 by Mondadori,
Milano-Kodansha, Tokyo; originally published in
Italian under the title CIVILTÁ KHMER. Copyright © 1972
by Mondadori-Kodansha, Tokyo. Copyright © 1972 by
Kodansha Ltd., Tokyo, for the illustrations. Copyright ©
1972 by Mondadori, Milano-Kodansha, Tokyo, for the text.
Copyright © 1972 by Han Suyin for the Foreword.

First published in Great Britain 1978

ISBN 0 304 30210 4

Printed and bound in Italy by Mondadori, Verona

Editorial Director
GIULIANA NANNICINI
American Supervisor
JOHN BOWMAN
Graphics Editor
MAURIZIO TURAZZI

CONTENTS

FOREWORD

The afternoon forest held all the greens and yellows of the world among its leafy horizons; a small wind caught in the high branches made no song; and in that feathery moment I saw the four-headed crowned towers upon the gates of the wall of the city of Angkor Thom. Four faces stared benignly, each some 23 feet high; inside was the beautiful Bayon temple, and in the pink and gold sunset each stone was alive, or so it seemed. It was a wonderful moment, there in 1955, when I first came to know Angkor.

Faces silent and timeless, with knowing eyes and that extraordinary mouth, the curved, widely bowed, tucked-in-at-the-corners, smiling Khmer mouth, a characteristic of the Khmer people of today, a beautiful people, robust yet supple, humorous and earthy, gentle yet capable of fierce passion, skilled and clever, and intensely brave.

I had come for four days; I stayed five weeks. Then I returned—twelve times more. "Once you love Angkor, you have to come back; you will end your days in Cambodia." Thus Bernard-Philippe Groslier, the devoted French curator of Angkor, told me on one of my visits. He was one of those who eat, sleep, live, love, and dream only of Angkor. His father had been curator at Angkor; now he had become the keeper of these monuments, restoring them, loving them with deep passion.

No film, no photograph, nothing can prepare one for Angkor and its impact. It is even difficult to speak of it in other than superlative terms. For it is colossal, enormous, prodigious, startling, awesome . . . and one either loves it or else one hates it. Those who hate Angkor, or see "nothing to it," are those who cannot bear the outsize, the uncomfortably nonutilitarian. "What was it for?" they ask. The answer is that none of these temples or monuments was built for human habitation or human use: Angkor is neither the Parthenon nor the Colosseum. Angkor was built for the idea of divinity; for the setting down in stone of the divine power of the kings of Angkor. But the kings and the nobles and the people did not live in these stone structures. They lived in houses of wood, or thatch, in and around the temples. Angkor is therefore the greatest complex of temples and monuments massed together in the world; none of these was ever intended to be utilized by mere mortals. The king who built his monument might live near it; and the monument assured his power, his *linga,* his rule, his worship. It was his divine substance; his body was the mere human envelope.

But what formidable, what enormous, what impossibly incomparable monuments! Testimony to the greatness and beauty, the vast wealth and strength of the Angkorean civilization, which lasted for some five centuries. Here was the capital of a kingdom, one of the most powerful in Southeast Asia. The earliest Chinese travelers who came here called the Khmer empire Funan, and the Chinese indefatigable passion for recording has left valuable documents on the Angkorean civilization. But neither the Chinese nor the Indians were the builders. It was out of the flux and reflux of many cultures, but with a personality all its own, that the Mon-Khmer people built this prodigious memory in stone of centuries of wealth and power.

One night two thousand years ago, it is said, a god visited a youth in India and said to the young man, named Kaundinya: "Find a bow, board your boat, sail toward the rising sun." Kaundinya went to the temple next morning and there found, on the floor, a bow with a quiver full of arrows; he embarked and the god-driven wind blew him across the elephant-backed sea to a shore where Willowleaf, the beautiful queen and leader of the Khmer amazons, reigned. The queen launched her war canoe to repel Kaundinya, but the youth shot it through with his arrows, and she submitted to him. They were married, and thus was born the dynasty of the first Khmer kingdom.

"The men are small and black . . . but many women are white . . . they wash every morning and clean their teeth . . . ." The Chinese observed many things, but they were puzzled by the religion and by the strictly nonutilitarian, lavish stone sculptures and temples. In the twelfth and early thirteenth centuries, the kingdom was at the height of its power, under such monarchs as Suryavarman II and Jayavarman VII. The latter built many monuments, but his greatest undertaking was the Bayon temple at the center of Angkor Thom, which was supposed to be the center of the world, the umbilicus, the omphalos.

The Bayon is perhaps the most fabulous and strange monument in the world. It is a work of sculpture, not architecture, and it is a riddle until suddenly one looks at it and exclaims, "It is a lotus, a flower of stone!" For it is an enormous flower, with all its many towers, each bearing four faces. Four faces, eight eyes, multiplied by all the towers, looking to encompass the whole world, up to the farthest horizon; the visible and the invisible; as the sun's eye makes the harvest ripen, so the eyes of the Bayon keep the world in equilibrium, assure that the sun and moon do not change places; for sight is command and possession, sight is immortality through awareness. It is said that the heads and the faces are those of the great king Jayavarman VII, whose compassion was so great he suffered his subjects' woes, and thus his eyes multiplied many times to look to their welfare beyond death.

The Bayon is also an astrological monument; for today, as a thousand years ago, the Khmers believe in soothsayers and prophecies, in omens and in the evil eye, in a thousand and more ways of predicting the future and avoiding bad luck. The Bayon housed within it a huge replica of Jayavarman VII as Buddha; it had no other purpose than the commemoration of the king's divinity. Today, no Khmer will come by night to the Bayon, nor venture near it, for it is said that to do so is to tempt fate, and a swift death follows.

But the Bayon's impact upon me was indescribable. I climbed the staircases to the upper gallery. It is a crazy maze, a building squashed by rebuilding, a labyrinth of galleries and still smaller tunnels, an overwhelming abracadabra. And yet, in this efflorescent, overbuilt richness, there is also a mystic aspiration, a prayer in stone. Surrounded by all these faces under the Cambodian sky, one is back in history during the great days of Angkor, for those days are all here, carved in stone, in the galleries.

The galleries show the great wars that the wealth of the Angkorean civilization brought; and the carvings are robust and beautiful; the fine sandstone from which Angkor was largely wrought is excellent for carving. Along all the friezes runs the theme of those centuries: wars with the Chams; the great battles. But also the theme of peace, for the people who carved this extraordinary and beautiful extravaganza did not forget to put themselves in. As the builders of the European cathedrals, the masons and the carpenters, put their own faces peeping from under the feet of saints, so did the Khmers of Angkor carve their living, their laughter, their dying, alongside the great friezes of wars and triumphs, of battling elephants and warriors in chariots, of great hordes going to war, of nobles in palanquins.

And so along with the lordly processions we see the Khmers live and build houses, eat and drink, hold cockfights and buy and sell; women give birth; men fish and till, drive oxcarts, grill fish on bamboo skewers; they sit under parasols and watch a circus; there are tightrope walkers and wrestlers; an orchestra plays. And the musical instruments, the oxcarts, the fishnets, the scythes, the faces, the bodies, the gestures—all, all are still seen today in the villages and the fields of Cambodia. The Khmers of today are the true descendants of those who built Angkor; they still use the same implements as they did then, even though the transistor radio and the motorcycle, the permanent and the jeep, are changing the pattern of living.

Angkor Wat, the largest and the best proportioned and harmonious (at least by Western norms) of all the temples, is like a prodigious funeral pyre of a divine king. What a wealth of things to see, with its many towers, courtyards, and staircases: it defeats the most hardy tourist! And along the galleries, hundreds of yards long, are the scenes from the great Indian epics, the *Ramayana* and the *Mahabharata*. There is the superb Vishnu Churning the Sea of Milk to gain the elixir of life: a great serpent coils itself around a mountain, and the gods and demons pull and spin the mountain to churn the sea, and all sorts of wonderful things come out of the sea, all the creatures of the world, including Vishnu's wife, Lakshmi, born of the sea spray, like Venus. There is the great battle of the monkey army against Ravana, the evil king who kidnapped Sita. There are enormous battle scenes between the Khmers and the Chams (with the Chams wearing a flowerlike bonnet on their heads). There are so many sculptures that each stone on the outside is covered with carvings; some are delicate as lace, others are monumental. There are hundreds and hundreds of beautiful female figures carved along the walls and no two are exactly alike.

It took me almost five days to see all of the Angkor Wat; I was footsore many times; and I still do not know all of it. There are so many legends about Angkor Wat, but it is not a place to be feared like the Bayon. (Angkor Wat is where the Royal Cambodian Ballet used to perform.) Indeed, during the war that split Cambodia, Angkor Wat—like all the great Khmer monuments—because of acts of war, lack of proper maintenance, and pillaging of statues and carvings, had far more to fear from human beings.

One of the most popular of the Khmer monuments for many Westerners is Banteay Srei, "The Citadel of Women," a work much nearer to the Indian style. Personally, I do not feel so stimulated by it; it is too beautiful, too perfect—exquisite and small and charming in its pink stone. I first saw it in 1955, when it was only accessible by jeep; now there is a good road to it. Its extraordinary beauty makes Banteay Srei the most threatened temple of all, for it is isolated in the forest. Wild elephants used to roam about it, and I remember their odor lingered strongly as one sat to contemplate the sunrise upon the loveliness of the pink little Banteay Srei.

More than Banteay Srei I like Banteay Samre, which is like the Bakong, a temple exploding stone with a passion heedless of canons. My own imagination begins to ferment in its presence, to churn like a sea of milk. It is said that Banteay Samre was built by a gardener called "the cucumber king." This man was a poor peasant who could produce wonderful, sweet cucumbers; he was a Samre, or aborigine, whom the Khmer nobles despised. In one version of the story, he was chosen king when the royal white elephant (perhaps because of those wonderful cucumbers!) "knelt before him, trunk between his feet, and picked him up and placed him on its back." Thus selected, the cucumber king tried to rule, but the nobles would not honor him; they continued to do obeisance to the relics of the previous king—bowing even to the clothes of the late king. This enraged the cucumber king, who then built Banteay Samre as the "citadel of the Samre," and indeed it has a fortlike appearance. Of course, it was never any king's habitation; it was the temple, the receptacle of his divine essence. The story goes on to say that the cucumber king called the nobles to do homage here. Then, as he knew they would refuse to bow to him, he produced the late king's chamberpot; as they did obeisance to it, he had them beheaded, one by one.

This, of course, is legend; the land is rife with tales, many of them with a strong touch of earthy Khmer humor—an element often found, too, in the folk dances. There is an exquisite reserve about Khmer sculpture; it is never erotic nor sensual, although it is full of sensuousness. However, the Cambodians today like their pungent jokes; they are not lascivious, but they enjoy life enormously, and their songs of love are delightfully frank.

Ta Keo, the crystal tower; Pre Rup, the pyramid with the name of "the body turning"; the enormous Bakong—these and so many of the other great temples are representations of Mount Meru, the great cosmic, five-tiered mountain of the world, which is also symbolized in the five-roofed pagodas of Nepal, in the *gopuras* of India, the pagodas of China, and Barabudur in Indonesia. Mount Meru is the order of the universe, and we might trace its origin back to Babylon and its ziggurats; we find the form again in the temple of Jerusalem, in the pyramid-temples of the Maya. And wherever these temple-mountains appear, it is in celebration of the divine essence, the power and the glory, not in tribute to man. All the fabulous enormousness of Angkor is the tremendous expression in stone of man's will to live beyond himself, to govern time and space beyond the allotted span of his own days. Hinduism, Buddhism, the strong imagination and vivid skill of the indigenous Khmers—all combined to produce an order, a culture, which lasted many centuries, and died of its own profligacy, of its own lavish and heedless use of manpower to build for the gods, until no one was left for the wars or for the harvest.

For that is what happened. At the time of Angkor's greatest splendor, under Jayavarman VII, the Bayon was built. Yet parts of it have been left unfinished, as if some great war, some scourge, had stopped the sculptors' chisels in place. After the Bayon, no more great monuments were built—the Bayon marks the end.

The quantities of gold and silver required, the numbers of laborers conscripted to quarry the stone out of Mount Kulen, to drag it to the site, and to erect and carve the monuments, stagger the imagination. No cement was used, and relatively few metal joints and crampons hold all these structures together. Most of the great monuments were built by placing one block of stone on top of another and then sliding the top one back and forth until through the erosion produced by this friction its bottom surface achieved an almost perfect fit with the top surface of the lower block. And after the great monuments were erected, virtually every stone, from the foundation right to the top, had to be carved with some sort of decorative element. Think of the work that meant, of the many thousands, hundreds of thousands, who spent years and years at such labor— probably up to sixty or seventy years for some of the largest ones. Consider the gold and silver, the pearls and precious stones, dedicated to the service of the divine essence of the kings.

Thus Angkor died: it died of its own splendor, magnificence, architectural megalomania. In 1432 it was abandoned as the capital of the kingdom. The irrigation system that had kept it alive fell into disuse. Then another invader came—the jungle: trees ate into the heads and stones; they smothered Angkor. But Angkor was not forgotten by the Khmer peasants, although it appeared lost to those who knew only a later capital city, Phnom Penh. In the sixteenth and seventeenth centuries, various Europeans who found themselves in Cambodia were aware of some of the monuments, but it was not until the nineteenth century that an adventurous Frenchman made his way through the jungle, perceived the cone-shaped towers of Angkor Wat, and then wrote about the Khmer monuments to bring them back to general public awareness.

The prophecy had predicted, the peasants said, that after 500 years Angkor would rise again. And it was in the twentieth century, almost exactly five centuries later, that the French School of the Far East, which had many eminent members, helped to reconstruct a large part of Angkor and made it the wonder and pride of Cambodia, a marvel of the world, an unbelievable, enriching experience for all those who are sensitive to beauty and great art.

"As the grace of spring on the gardens, as the night of fullness for the moon, thus, ravishing in its splendor the beauty of your body . . . and like the bees gathering at the hive, the eyes of men have turned toward you, to quench their thirst for beauty."

Alas, though, war came to Cambodia—as the soothsayers had predicted. A year or more before the coup of March 1970 against Prince Sihanouk—the ruler of Cambodia, the king descended from the Khmer kings, who abdicated in order to govern democratically—the soothsayers had found omens of tragedy and sorrow. Sihanouk and his kingdom would fall on evil days; a foreign invader would come and the people would suffer as under a great scourge; Sihanouk would have to leave, and that would mean calamity and death to many: all this was being predicted a year before the events actually happened. I was there and I heard the soothsayers.

But the prophecy continued: Sihanouk would travel eastward, toward the rising sun—not west, for west is the orientation of death for the Khmers; and from the east, after one thousand days, Sihanouk would return, and the kingdom would be at peace once more, and the glory of Angkor would be restored to the Khmer people.

That was the prophecy. Let us hope that, by the time this is read, the country and the people and the monuments are once again united and in peace.

Han Suyin

INTRODUCTION

To write about the ancient Khmer civilization of Cambodia is a more difficult undertaking than it might appear to be to anyone who glances through one of the many long bibliographies on Southeast Asia studies. For despite the books on Cambodia in general, and the numerous monographs on particular aspects of the history and art of the Khmers, there remain many problems that still require clarification and that, by sheer size alone, threaten to cast doubt on the conclusions experts have already reached. There are several reasons for this apparent contradiction—the long bibliographies, yet the many questions—and it is pertinent to mention a few of them before plunging into our own study.

First and foremost—and this pertains not only to the Khmers but, to a greater or lesser extent, to all Asian civilizations—there is the way the subject was so long approached. We refer to the attempt, at times carried to the limits of the absurd, to render the Oriental civilization comprehensible to the Western world by using critical yardsticks typical of the West. Symptomatic is the fact that when Spanish and Portuguese missionaries and travelers of the sixteenth and seventeenth centuries discovered the monuments of Angkor, they expressed astonishment both because they found themselves in the area pursuing other than cultural interests and because of a genuine inability to understand what they were seeing. They thus tended to describe the remains by saying they equaled those of the Western Classical world—even that they must have been creations of Alexander the Great or the ancient Romans. (See pages 181–82 for a fuller account of this phenomenon.)

This is, to be sure, an extreme case. And it would be misleading to claim that centuries of Oriental studies have gone by in vain, leaving such gross cultural chauvinism intact. The fact remains, however, that a "Europeanism"—all the more insidious for being disguised—still lurks within a discipline that purports to understand historical and cultural premises different from those of the West, as well as recognizing Oriental scholarship that has itself matured. These remnants of Western bias have kept the danger of critical distortion alive to this day.

Beginning in the middle of the nineteenth century, a new group of Westerners—mostly French this time, and undoubtedly better informed—discovered the monuments of Cambodia once again. These men guessed that the monuments were linked to the culture and religion of India, and in so doing, they shifted the terms of comparison, leaving the Western world aside and drawing much closer to the reality of this ancient civilization. Studies began to focus on the historical background of such links; confirmation was sought in written sources that had come to light and in archaeological finds. Yet we feel that all this led to another error: bypassing research into the autonomous characteristics of the Southeast Asian cultures themselves. In other words, scholars paid insufficient attention to the cultural and geographical world extending from Burma to the border of southern China and down to Indonesia—and including, of course, the territory of Cambodia.

The result of this new shift of focus was that all of Southeast Asia became known as "Indochina"—a territory where the two great Oriental civilizations known at the time, those of India and China, had succeeded in exporting their ideas or sending their armies, or in some way leaving clear evidence of their influence. We can hardly deny the importance of such influences in this area: to cite but two, there is the fact that the plastic arts of the Khmers are related to those of India's Gupta and post-Gupta periods, and the fact that most of the great Khmer towers are derived from the architecture of India's Pallava dynasty. But to admit this is not to deny that numerous local factors contributed to the molding of the art of Southeast Asia (even when it is called "Outer India" or "Greater India"), beginning with the religions that emerged from the autochthonous substrata and ending with the cultural exchanges between the various peoples of this area. It is accepted, for instance, that the kingdom of Champa, which rose in the southeastern region of what is now Vietnam—and which was mentioned by Chinese sources in the early centuries of our era—

gave rise to an art and a culture that, as we shall soon see, influenced the Khmers themselves. Some scholars have even found the origin of the temple-mountain—the most significant architectural and symbolic structure of the Khmers—in Java; they trace it to Barabudur, Java's great Buddhist temple.

There are still other reasons, some quite specific, for the methodological short-comings in Western studies of the Khmers—what we might call quite literally a "disorientation": a Western inability to view things from an Eastern angle. Part of the problem stems from the direction taken by the first students of the culture in the early part of this century. Most of them happened to be French, and they concentrated on two approaches. First, they sought for the data—the actual physical remains, in most instances—and then they analyzed them. And there is no denying that they arrived at many valuable results, often obtained through great personal sacrifice. But because of the large number of the finds, their extreme state of deterioration, and the way archaeology was understood in those years—all too often concentrating on "works of art"—most efforts were dedicated to the search for monuments in the intricate tangle of vegetation and their subsequent restoration. What these first men did not do was to excavate, to dig, for the less-than-monumental.

It was only relatively a few years ago that the terrain became subjected to systematic explorations, aimed at investigating a past more remote than that "related" by the monuments and also aimed at collecting the supplementary materials necessary for a more accurate interpretation of the major monuments. Even now, the scarcity of such materials and the fact that the secular or lay architecture (that is, royal residences and civic structures) of the ancient Khmers were made almost exclusively of perishable materials, renders us unable to document, except sporadically, the daily life of the Khmers from the seventh through the twelfth centuries. The objects of everyday use—handicrafts, pottery, utensils, and all such objects necessary for a reconstruction of daily life—still lie buried beneath the soil of such great cities as Angkor, Roluos, and Angkor Borei.

Still another problem is that presented by the inscriptions. The Cambodian epigraphy is, on the one hand, one of the richest of Asia; given the lack of historiographic and literary sources—and also of numismatics—it was thought that the steles (pillars, often inscribed) in the interior of temples and the inscriptions on the doorways would fill this gap. But the inscriptions' historical data are often vitiated or distorted by a number of factors—primarily, by the symbolical-metaphorical language used, based as so many of the inscriptions are on religious themes. Another distortion has been the panegyrical preoccupation of so many inscriptions. The inscriptions, however, have yielded such things as religious elements, genealogical lists of sovereigns, chronological references, and some hints as to the culture and literary education of their authors.

But in analyzing this material, modern scholars have often made serious errors of interpretation. Moreover, the concerns of traditional historiography, focused primarily on the great military and political developments, led to the neglect of elements that the epigraphy was especially adapted to furnish—particularly those in the Khmer language (as opposed to those in Sanskrit and Pali, that is). We refer to such matters as the mores of social life, information about donations to the temples, the transference of property, or the functions of various personages.

Inevitably some of these errors, uncertainties, distortions, and historical and archaeological gaps will affect this work. All that we will say, though, in conclusion is that what might appear to be one gap here is in fact quite deliberate: that is, the fact that various notable monuments and other remains are missing from both the text and the illustrations. There are so many Khmer remains that might qualify as "great" that we had to base our selection on several basic criteria. The first was that of presenting the reader with works that are as representative as possible of the evolution of the Khmer civilization from the artistic, social, and political points of view. The second, of a more didactic nature, was that of illustrating various types of architecture. Finally, there is an effort to suggest the extent of the Khmer expansion beyond the Angkor nucleus by showing at least some of the more widespread structures. In the end, without claiming to make a new scholarly contribution to the subject, the volume does make accessible to a large public a civilization that, because of its intrinsic values, and despite its remoteness, deserves to be better known.

Pagan

Irrawaddy River

B U R M A

Chieng Sen

Salween River

HANOI

Hoa-binh

Gulf of Tonkin

Prome

Chieng-mai

Lampun
(Haripunjaya)

Mekong River

Dong-son

Pegu

RANGOON

Thaton

Martaban

Say-fong

VIENTIANE

Sukhotai

L
A
O
S

Hainan

Pass of
Three Pagodas

T
H
A
I
L
A
N
D

Meyom

Menam

Mepinc

Namsak

That Tu
Panom

Namsi

Quang-tri

Hue

Si-Tep

Nammun

Phimai

Buriram
Surin

Basak
Wat Phu

Tra-Kiu

Mi-son

Dong-duong

Lopburi

Korat

Dangrek Hills

Preah Vihear

Banteay Chmar

KOH KER

Mlu Prei

Kontun

Binh-dinh

V
I
E
T
N
A
M

Ayudhya

Nakon Pathom
(Dvaravati)

BANGKOK

Sdok Kak Thom

Banteay Srei

ANGKOR

Rpluos

Thara
Botivat

Stung Treng

Battambang

Tonle Sap Lake

Sambor Prei
Kuk

Koh Krieng

Kratie

Cape Varella

Pursat

Kompong Thom

Vo-canh

Chanthaburi

Kompong
Cham

C   A   M   B   O   D   I   A

Prei Nokor

Lovek

Wat Sithor

PHNOM PENH

Prei Veng

Ta Kev

Xuan-loc

Angkor Borei

Ba Phnom

Plain of Reeds

Phnom Da

Kampot

Chau-doc

SAIGON

Phan-thiet

Gulf of Siam

Ha-tien

Oc-Eo

Rachgia

C
H
I
N
A

S
E
A

Isthmus of Kra

Chaiya

Bandon

Takuapa
(Takkola)

Ligor

Patani

Kedah

Kuta Radja

M
A
L
A
Y
S
I
A

S   U   M   A   T   R   A

Strait of Malacca

Malacca

SINGAPORE

ANCIENT CAMBODIA

✴ **Archaeological sites**

▲ **Sacred mountain sites**

0   5   100   200   300   400 Km.
3.11   62.5   125   250 miles

FM

The Pre-Angkorean Period

PREHISTORIC AND PROTOHISTORIC TIMES IN CAMBODIA

Those who encounter the masterpieces of the Khmer civilization for the first time, or who have had the extraordinary good fortune to penetrate into the Cambodian forest and find themselves facing the monuments preserved there, are usually too overwhelmed with amazement and admiration to ask about the cultural and ethnic roots of the people who erected them. As it happens, the name of this people, the Khmers, has in recent years come to be more familiar because of contemporary political troubles in Southeast Asia. For the Khmers who centuries ago gave rise to a powerful and prosperous civilization still represent some nine-tenths of the population of the nation of Cambodia. (The Khmers are also present as a more or less conspicuous minority in the bordering lands of Vietnam and Thailand.) In fact, modern Cambodians are essentially Khmers, and the reason the distinction is made is simply to avoid having to use the adjectives "ancient" and "modern" when referring to the inhabitants of this territory.

But it is also a fact that the Khmers themselves were not the first inhabitants of this region. And since their civilization could not have reached the levels it did without the contributions of those who preceded them, we must first review even more ancient epochs, examining at least briefly the progress of the Indochinese peninsula from prehistoric times.

The two essential factors interacting on the Indochinese peninsula were, at the outset and as everywhere, nature and man. From the Gulf of Tonkin to the Bay of Bengal, from Mandalay to Singapore, the physical geography of the region can be seen as fitting several patterns. Here we need only consider two: the principal mountain chains that cross it on the north-south axis—namely, the Arakan Mountains, the Indo-Malaysian and the Annamite chains—and the rivers—Irrawaddy, Saluen, Menam, and Mekong—that cut through it in the same direction, some flowing into the Bay of Bengal, the others into the China Sea, forming deltas of vital importance to the inhabitants' economy.

Cambodia in particular is hemmed in on the north by the Dangrek Hills and on the south by the Cardamom Mountains, while the vast basin of the Tonle Sap Lake opens out the central plain. Mountain ranges in Indochina have to some extent determined the direction of the migratory flows of humans, since it is certainly easier to follow the course taken by a mountain than to cross it. The same can be said of the rivers of Indochina, not all of which are completely navigable; the Mekong, for one, is often interrupted by rapids and falls. But the mountains also provided protection, and the rivers were a godsend to the first groups of people who became sedentary in this region, particularly to the growers of rice, who were already familiar with the beneficial fertilizing effects of floods. Indochina, like Egypt, has been called "the daughter of its rivers."

The most ancient bones of *Homo sapiens* so far known on the Indochinese peninsula were found among other remains at Tam-Pong and Tam-Hang (both in Laos). Their date has been put at somewhere around 5000–4000 B.C., and the material culture of these people has been assigned to the Lower Hoabinian (from Hoa-binh, a site near Hanoi), a Mesolithic culture. The transition from the Mesolithic to the Neolithic in this area saw the development of the Hoabinian and the success of the Bacsonian (a culture that also takes its name from a locale in North Vietnam). Both cultures were characterized by an "industry" that shaped stones and made semipolished axes (which has led, in fact, to some disagreement as to whether both should not be classified as Neolithic).

By about 1000 B.C., the people of Indochina became acquainted with metal, although it at first was employed only marginally alongside the stone utensils. By approximately 500 B.C., though, metal's use had become widespread, and in most cases the workmanship was exceptionally

Angkor Wat: The characteristic towers loom above the thick vegetation (first half of twelfth century). Although compared to everything from wings to pineapples, the towers were actually shaped to represent lotus buds, a flower with many symbolic associations for the Khmers.

good. (The site where this evolutionary process has been best followed is Samrong Sen, in Cambodia.) The appearance of metal leads Indochina into its protohistorical phase, during which the region experienced the flourishing of two cultures—the megalithic and the Dongsonian—and the emergence of three linguistic groups—Thai-Vietnamese, Champa, and Mon-Khmer. Like the language groups, the speakers of these languages were certainly closely related. As to their ethnic origins, various theories have been proposed, but it is enough to say that they were probably basically an offshoot of the Mongoloid race usually called Austro-Asian to indicate the mixture of peoples in this area.

But rather than becoming involved in the problem of origins, it is more useful to look at the nature of the two cultures mentioned, particularly the megalithic. This term is borrowed from the Bronze Age culture that spread across much of the Mediterranean and Europe approximately from 3000 to 500 B.C. (depending on the site, of course). Based on the Greek words for "large stone," the megalithic culture's characteristic relics are the menhirs, large stone slabs fixed vertically in the ground to form "avenues" or circles (of which Stonehenge is the best known), and dolmens, chambers formed by large stones. The original significance of most of these great stone constructions was perhaps connected with funeral rites. Another characteristic of this culture are large covered vases or urns, often found to have held human bones and so clearly indicating that these, too, had ties with funeral practices.

Now the megalithic culture of Indochina shares these characteristics with that of Europe, but the former lacks many of the other elements that allow the latter to be so well documented. On the basis of archaeological data, it can be stated only that the megalithic culture in Indochina spread across an extremely wide area, reaching from India to Sumatra, with the stone structures particularly numerous along the Mekong. The presence, along the middle and lower course of the Mekong, of more complex constructions—with a circular design and provided with enclosing walls and moats—suggests dwellings conceived as fortified centers; unfortunately their contemporaneity and connection with the rest of the megalithic complex in this region remain to be demonstrated.

We have focused on the megalithic culture for two principal reasons. First, because its area of diffusion appears to correspond to that of the Mon-Khmers; secondly, because the theories put forward concerning the religious interpretation of the great stone complexes relate to the monuments this book will be exploring in such detail. There is the theory, for instance (advanced by Heine-Geldern, an Austrian scholar), that the megaliths constituted not only the commemoration of the dead but also the materialization of the tie binding the living to the world beyond and the agent through which the magical power (or eternal life) of the dead was transferred in part to the person(s) who had the monument erected. An English scholar, Quaritch Wales, has taken this theory up and gone on to claim that the worship of the dead person (having become the ancestor, par excellence) fused, in the China of the Shangs, with that of the god of the soil. As a result, says Quaritch Wales, the megalith was the seat of the god himself, with whom man could communicate thanks to the mediation of the ancestor. The eventual shift from the megalith to the mountain and then to the artificial mountain, or pyramid-temple, as well as the shift from any dead person to the king, would then seem rather easy. If this was, in fact, the process—albeit oversimplified here—then the religious practices of megalithic Cambodia could provide an original explanation—above all, one bound up with autochthonous elements—of the creation of the Angkorean temple-mountains many centuries later.

Menhirs and dolmens also had another function, one that the French scholar Paul Mus, in his study of the indigenous religions of Champa, described as "cadastral"—that is, pertaining to, focused on, the ownership of land. The stones were erected in the center of a site chosen for

construction, and this in itself indicated that the god of the soil, represented by these stones, gave the erector(s) virtual ownership of the land. This cadastral aspect appears to resemble closely that assumed by the *linga,* the phallic symbol of Shiva, the Hindu deity, which the Khmer sovereigns erected after they had conquered or acquired new territory.

The megalithic culture in Indochina seems to have been somewhat influenced by the other culture mentioned, the Dong-son, and presumably they overlapped in time. The Dong-son culture, however, was concentrated on the eastern coastal strip of the peninsula (the name itself coming from a site near the Gulf of Tonkin), and it was evidently more advanced, at least in the elaboration of artistic motifs. The most typical product of the Dong-son culture are the celebrated bronze drums (page 17), whose top surface bears etchings of scenes depicting propitiatory rites connected with work in the fields, and which, in fact, were used by wizard-magicians to implore the gods for beneficial rain. The large quantity of bronze objects in common use among the Dong-son people testifies to the vitality of this culture and enables us to single out the close relationships with, even dependence on, the Chinese bronze output of the same period.

Despite the fact that the Chinese influence was without question predominant, some scholars have expressed the view that this Asian production also received some cultural contributions from the West. This theory would tie Dong-son works to those of Hallstatt (an early Iron Age center in Austria), and its chief proponent is Heine-Geldern, who bases his views on analogies between weapons and knives. He postulates a migration from the European center to China and Southeast Asia through Central Asia. Then, at a later time, he traces an influence from Hellenistic art due to the objects that arrived from the West by sea. Whatever the extent or degree of such specific influences, it must be admitted that by the outset of the Christian era, the Indochinese peninsula had begun to occupy a place in the network of commerce growing more and more complex as it stretched from the Graeco-Roman world to the Far East, and thus incorporating the East Indies and Indochina. (See map, page 19.)

THE INDIANIZATION OF SOUTHEAST ASIA

We have been following the inhabitants of the Indochinese peninsula up to about the beginning of the Christian era, by which time they had already reached a relatively high level of culture. They practiced an agriculture based mainly on rice and millet, they raised livestock (particularly the buffalo), and they were adept at using metals. They were also capable navigators. As for the sociopolitical structures and the mythological worlds these Southeast Asians had created, there is little that can be backed up by solid documentation. (Only a study of legends and Chinese sources of the by then Indianized kingdoms of a later period enable us to formulate hypotheses.) We know, however, that Indian commerce and expansion began in earnest about this time, and since this phenomenon is of primary importance in understanding the Khmer civilization, we must examine its chief characteristics.

To explain the origin of the Indianized kingdoms in Southeast Asia it has seemed necessary to some to postulate the arrival of an exceptionally large mass of people from the Indian subcontinent. As a result, Indian history of the centuries around the beginning of the Christian era has been carefully sifted in an attempt to find an event that could have determined the exodus of such a population toward more hospitable lands. But because the theories formulated to date have never found sufficient data to back them up, we prefer the theory of the French authority on the Khmers, George Coedès. He claims the causes of the Indian expansion come down to two factors: commerce and the quest for gold. As for commerce, this is substantiated not only by Indian sources but by the presence of commercial ports along the navigation routes and by im-

THE CINNAMON TRADE

The cargo is carried across the vast sea on rudderless rafts, without oars to propel them or any other kind of navigational aid. Alone at the helm is a man and his courage. He is sent out to sea in winter, moreover, at the time of the winter solstice, when the winds from the east blow more strongly, carrying him in a direct line from gulf to gulf.

Cinnamon is the chief item of their trade, and they say these seagoing merchants take at least five years to return, many of them perishing on the way. But they come back loaded with objects of glass and bronze, clothing, pins, bracelets, and necklaces. It is a commerce based primarily on the constancy of women.

Pliny: *Natural History* (XIII: 87–88)

CHINESE COMMERCE

When the Chin dynasty moved toward the south, it was separated from the Yellow River and the Kansu by a great distance. Barbarians blocked all the roads and the foreign regions had become as remote as the sky. Ta Chin and India lay extremely far off in the vastness of the west. Even when the two Han dynasties had sent out expeditions, those routes were found particularly difficult, and some of the goods on which China depended were brought in from Tonkin. The merchants had sailed on the waves of the sea, following the wind and traveling from far-off places all the way to China. There are also chains and chains of mountains. There are numerous tribes with different, oddly-sounding names. Precious things come from the mountains and the sea along this route. This is merchandise such as the horns of rhinoceroses or the feathers of kingfishers, and such rarities as serpent or pearls. There are thousands of varieties and are all ardently desired by kings. And so it is that the ships come and go in a steady stream, carrying merchants and ambassadors.

Liu-Sung Shu (Chap. 97)

BARBARIANS FROM THE SOUTH

Of all the precious things in the world, none is better than those of the barbarians to the south. Hidden from view in the mountains and in the sea, they are without number. Merchant ships arrive from afar and carry them to the southern provinces [of China]. Thus it is that Tonkin and Kuan-tung are rich and have an abundance of well-stored goods, which are included in the imperial treasure.

Nan-Chi Shu (Chap. 58)

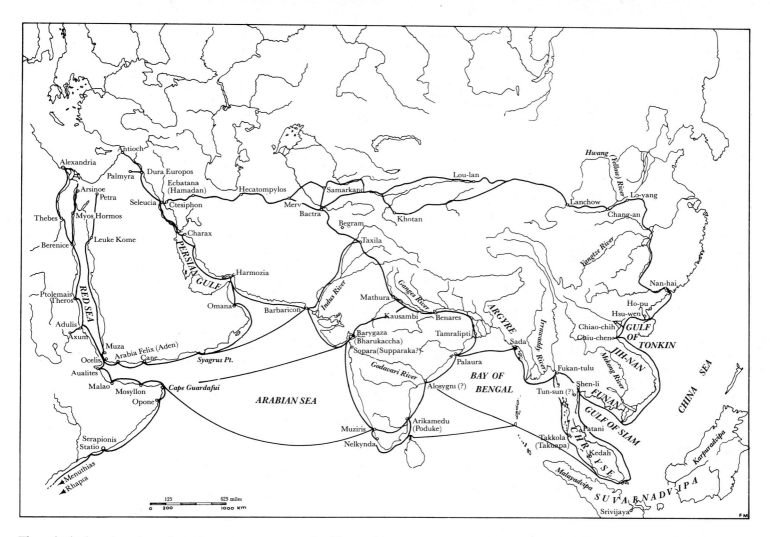

The principal ports and sea lanes for commerce in the early centuries of the Christian era. The map is based on data from Indian works *(Mahaniddesa, Milindapanha)*, Pliny's *Natural History, the Periplus of the Eritrean Sea,* and *The History of the Later Han Dynasty,* a Chinese text.

ported objects found in great quantity in the lower levels of the city of Funan, in the southwestern corner of the peninsula. And it seems reasonable that the merchant vessels might have carried a number of men forth to find gold, drawn to these distant lands by tales of their wealth of precious metals.

But if we wish to understand how it was that such factors, evidently already in effect, suddenly took on such a great importance as to transform what had been superficial contacts between two peoples into a new political-cultural unit, it is necessary to consider a variety of other elements affecting not only the Indian subcontinent but the entire civilized world of the time. One example would be the discovery by Hippalus (c. A.D. 50),of the alternation of monsoons, the periodic winds of this region, which enabled ships to sail more swiftly, thus making voyages safer. Contacts between India and the West by sea were quick to draw a great boost from this, for the exotic tastes of imperial Rome prompted the capital's merchants to undertake trade with India to procure the desired spices and other goods. This then induced the Indians to make ever more frequent trips still farther east to supply this market. And since ships were obliged to wait in one port or another for a monsoon to blow from the east to take them home to India, their crews settled down for months at a stretch, thus establishing close ties with the local populace. Becoming frequent and drawn-out, such contacts facilitated the transmission of Indian ideas on a large scale, although we must also accept that such ideas could not have been absorbed if the local population had not already attained a high enough degree of civilization to understand them.

Another, and perhaps even more important, reason for the increase in contacts between Indians and the people of Southeast Asia was the spread of the Buddhist faith. This in no way conflicts with the factor of trade, for Buddhism, in wiping out the rigid caste divisions prescribed by the Hindu religion, fostered the development of such activities as com-

THE PRE-ANGKOREAN PERIOD   19

merce. Heretofore this occupation had been considered improper for persons belonging to the high castes, people who might otherwise have the resources to engage in such an activity. Buddhism, moreover, in admitting the possibility for each and every individual to achieve truth through the "eightfold path," had surmounted the barrier of ethnic purity and isolation erected by Hinduism. Finally, Buddhism had inspired a missionary vocation that induced its monks and faithful to set out in all directions to spread the teachings of Buddha.

It seems safe to conclude that several factors played a part in bringing Indians toward Southeast Asia—a process that was, by the way, to involve a series of waves during the first five to six hundred years of the Christian era. Once these Indians arrived and settled, their success likewise depended on several factors—involving both the persistence of the newcomers and the receptivity of the natives. During these centuries, many principalities rose and fell among the people at the southern end of the Indochinese peninsula. One of these, the one that most concerns us because it was perhaps the major predecessor of the Khmer kingdom, was the kingdom of Funan.

THE REALM OF FUNAN

The Funanese were evidently a tribe of the Mon-Khmer group; they lived in the lower Mekong River valley, where they established a relatively prosperous and active kingdom in the first centuries of the Christian era. Much of what we know of the history of life of the Funanese comes from the works of Chinese historians of a later date, who made use of the

The Bayon: This bas-relief of a cockfight is in the outer gallery of this temple at Angkor Thom (first half of thirteenth century). The scene is marked by both a remarkable vivacity and the artist's ability to fit the various figures into a limited space. The custom of training animals for combat was common even in Funan times, and it has remained a custom in Cambodia into our own age.

information brought back by travelers and ambassadors. The oldest such work in which the name Funan appears is the *San kuo chih,* which mentions a Funanese diplomatic mission that took tribute to Lu Tai, the governor (on behalf of the Wus) of Kuan-tung province and Tonkin. The event is dated to about A.D. 225–230. This was followed some time later (243) by a diplomatic mission the Funanese sovereign Fan-Chan sent directly to the Chinese court. We thus come to realize that by the middle of the third century Funan was already a sufficiently important kingdom to have friendly relations with its powerful neighbor.

The *Chin shu (Chronicle of the Chins)* was compiled in the sixth and seventh centuries to narrate the events of the Chin dynasty (265–419). Alongside a number of passages merely providing data on the diplomatic missions that carried tribute to China (between 268 and 375), the work contains an entire paragraph dedicated to Funan. In this, Funan is described as being "found at more than 3,000 *li* west of the Lin-yi, in a great bay. Its territory is 3,000 *li* wide." This description was also repeated in other dynastic histories—such as the *Sung shu (History of the Sung),* the *Nan-Chi shu (History of the Southern Chi),* and the *Liang shu (History of the Liang)*—with slight variations and additions, such as facts about the presence of a river or the nature of the terrain. The Chinese sources also include descriptions of cities, palaces, and two-story homes, and the *Chin shu* in particular notes the physical characteristics of the inhabitants.

From the various passages in these books, it has been possible to deduce two important points: the name of the state and its geographical location. The modern Mandarin pronunciation renders Funan with an

The Bayon: Another bas-relief from the outer gallery of this temple, this one representing a dogfight (first half of the thirteenth century). As an episode from everyday life, it is similar to the one on the opposite page, but it has been executed with less liveliness. It is interesting for such details as the personages' clothing and certain architectural elements.

ideogram, the sound of which in ancient times was *biu-nam,* close to the ancient Khmer *bnam* (*phnom* in modern Cambodian speech), which means "hill" or "mountain." It is believed, therefore, that the early Chinese visitors to Funan heard of a "mountain king" (*kurum bnam* in Khmer), and that they drew the name of the kingdom from this royal title (the Chinese *biu-nam* becoming our Funan). This interpretation has been accepted by most if not by all scholars, as has been the location of this kingdom—across the southern end of the Indochinese peninsula, including possibly the territory of the Khmers.

As for the question of the origin of the Funan state, the *Chin shu* tells the story of a foreign "worshiper of genii" (or spirits), Hun-hui, who arrived in Funan, drawn there by a prophetic dream, married the local princess, Yeh-liu, and began to rule. To understand what is involved here, we must consider a few of the variants of this story in texts of a later date. To begin with, the name of the Hindu—for this is assumed to be what was meant by the phrase, "worshiper of genii—got passed on in a different type of writing that changed his name to Hun-tien. This Chinese version is traced by modern annotators to the Sanskrit name Kaundinya. (Sanskrit, of course, was ancient India's sacred language, taken over by the Khmers for their religious, historical, and formal inscriptions.) The detail of the dream is the same in the three texts that mention it, but this is not the case with that of the meeting with the local princess. The *Chin shu* and *Nan-Chi shu* tell us that Yeh-liu issued forth from her city to resist the foreigner, while the *Liang shu* asserts that the princess and her people "saw the boat arrive and wished to seize it."

This and other details in the sources confirm the fact that Funan was located on the sea lanes of merchant ships (and in fact, the Hindu arrived there by joining a group of merchants). But we do not agree with the theory of most scholars that these accounts point to a peaceful penetration of the territory in question by a small group of foreigners. Hun-tien, in fact, is armed with a bow, and he uses it, while Yeh-liu does not wait for the newcomers to arrive at the gates of her capital but goes out to meet them with a show of hostility, accompanied by an armed guard. More in line with the theory of the peaceful penetration is the legend handed down by a Sanskrit inscription of Mi-son (in Champa), dated to 658. According to this, the Hindu Kaundinya, having received a javelin from the Brahmin Asvatthaman, hurls it into the air to mark the point where his capital was to be built, and afterwards marries Soma, daughter of the king of the *nagas,* the mythical serpents that inhabited, and symbolized, the waters. In this version, then, there is a wedding, an absolutely legal succession to the throne by the foreigner, with no mention of struggles.

If King Naga and his *nagas* obviously belong to myth, Kaundinya represents the first step towards historical reality by these people, a humanizing of their semiprimitive culture. And if we further accept that this legend is nothing more than a repetition of the Indian one on the origin of the Pallava dynasty (which ruled eastern India from the fifth to ninth centuries), this assumption seems fully confirmed. The Funan kingdom, for instance, is less advanced than the homeland of Kaundinya. Indeed, the *Nan-Chi shu* includes the detail that the Hindu, unable to bear the sight of the princess going naked, folded a piece of cloth "through which he made her thrust her head." From these tales, too, emerges the image of the newcomer, the Hindu, who is to establish order and spread more advanced customs among the people. In the end, the two cultures merge, more or less peacefully.

The composition of this picture would be perfectly balanced were it not for two elements that can be included only on the basis of theories that have never been confirmed. The first of these discordant elements is represented by the figure of Kaundinya himself. Presumably he is a high-caste Brahmin or Kshatriya (warrior caste). Now we have already mentioned that the impetus for the Indian expansion toward Southeast

Angkor Wat: This many-headed crest of a *naga*, a mythical serpent-god, forms the end of a balustrade that is, in fact, the long body of the *naga*.

THE TUN-SUN KINGDOM

More than 3,000 *li* from the southern border of Funan one finds the kingdom of Tun-Sun. . . . The territory reaches out 1,000 *li*; the capital is 10 *li* from the sea. There are five kings, all of whom call themselves vassals of Funan. The eastern border of Tun-Sun is in communication with Chow-Chou [Tonkin], the western border with Tien-Chou [India] and An-Hsi [Parthia]. All the countries beyond its frontier come and go for commercial reasons, for Tun-Sun extends out into the sea for more than 1,000 *li*. The Chung-hai [Gulf of Siam] is extremely broad and even seagoing junks have never sailed directly across it. This market is a meeting place for east and west, bringing innumerable persons together each day. Precious goods and rarities of all kinds—there is nothing that cannot be found.

Liang Shu (Chap. 54)

The *Nan-chou I-wu Chih* [a work of the third century A.D.] states that Tun-Sun is more than 3,000 *li* from Funan. Once it was an independent kingdom. An old-time king of Funan was full of courage; he seized and subjected it. Now it is under Funan. . . . The *Funan Chi* of Chu-Chih states that the kingdom of Tun-Sun comes under the jurisdiction of Funan. Its king is called Kun-lun. In this country there are five hundred Hu, families from India, two *fo-tu* [Buddist relic mounds, or *stupa*], and more than one thousand Indian Brahmans. The inhabitants of Tun-Sun follow their doctrine and give them their daughters in marriage. As a result, many Hindus do not leave the country. They study their holy books, bathe with essences and flowers, and practice piety incessantly, day and night.

Tai-Ping Yu Lan (Chap. 788)

Asia seems to have come primarily from the Buddhist merchants. Hindu canons, however, called for rigid caste divisions, making it impossible for a Hindu like Kaundinya not only to marry but even to have the slightest contact with an "impure" person. Moreover, there was a Hindu prohibiton against crossing over the "dark water"—that is, to cross the sea in search of undiscovered lands. And since this is exactly what had to occur for Indians to make contact with Funan, the chances are that the canonization of such rules and prohibitions came in an epoch after the one referred to in the legend of Kaundinya. It may also be that the legend reflects the fact that the *vaisya,* the third of the Indian castes, at first made up of farmers and later of artisans and merchants, drew even members of the higher castes into the new activities.

But why was it that the Indians succeeded so easily in imposing their culture, technology, religions, and civil institutions on the Funanese (and, by extension, on so many of the peoples of Southeast Asia)? The legends present the foreigner as one who naturally comes out on top, owing to his self-evident superiority. Yet as we have seen, the cultures of the megalithic and Dong-son people of Indochina were not all that barbarous. So it has been generally agreed that the assumption of power by the Indians resulted from their supremacy in the techniques of regulating water. That is, the Indians taught the native Indochinese how to set up a network of irrigation ditches, canals, and reservoirs that freed them from the nightmare of alternating floods and droughts.

According to one legend, King Naga had drunk the waters covering part of the territories of his reign in order to give them, thus reclaimed, to his daughter as a dowry. Certainly the problem of keeping water off arable land existed. What must be established is whether this was solved in Southeast Asia in the centuries that preceded the Indianized kingdoms, or whether these latter were the first to accomplish this. Archaeology has been able to confirm the existence of a far-flung network of irrigation ditches in the southern part of the Indochinese peninsula, but it is not yet possible to assign definite dates to these works. Yet there is no contradiction if we speculate that lands were artificially irrigated in relatively ancient times, and then accept that Indians introduced superior techniques to extend and maintain the system.

The later history of Funan was treated in the *Liang shu,* compiled in the first half of the seventh century. In this work we learn that, after a series of legitimate sovereigns and the reign of a king of foreign origin, a Hindu from India, prodded by a supernatural voice, arrived at Pan-pan to reign over Funan, and "the entire kingdom rose up in joy, went before him, and elected him king." This Hindu restored the political structure the people had been accustomed to, according to the Chinese source: "The king once again changed all the rules to make them accord with the methods of India."

The extraordinary events that accompanied the coming of this second Kaundinya—inspired, note, like the first, by the heavens—suggest an intensification of the Indian influence, and the period of his reign is usually called "the second Indianization" of Funan. For this phase, as for the first, an effort has been made to find the causes in the internal events of India, but we have already had occasion to point out how inconclusive are such links. We should be content, rather, with noting that at the outset of the fifth century the cultural life of Funan was revitalized by new influences from India, which this time is confirmed by archaeological data and artistic works alike.

FUNAN'S SECOND PHASE

The story told by the Chinese sources, after mentioning several Funan sovereigns of minor importance, focuses on a king Jayavarman, who ruled from about 480 to 514. He is remembered mainly for having sent two diplomatic missions to China. The first, in 484, was entrusted to an

The Krishna Govardhana of Wat Koh (Style A) of the Phnom Da style, first half of the sixth century; sandstone, 63 inches high. The statue represents Krishna, an incarnation of Vishnu, in the act of raising Mount Govardhana to provide shelter for flocks and shepherds during a raging storm unleashed by the god Indra, who was angry with them for failing to offer him sacrifices. The effort necessary to lift the mountain is sustained almost entirely by the raised left arm and rigid left leg. The curly hairdo and Krishna's garment reveal the influence of Indian sculpture of the post-Gupta epoch. (National Museum, Phnom Penh)

HUN-HUI (KAUNDINYA) BECOMES KING OF FUNAN

The sovereign was originally a woman named Yeh-Liu. Then there was a foreigner, Hun-Hui by name, a worshipper of spirits. This foreigner dreamed that a spirit gave him a bow and at the same time ordered him to board a trading junk and set out to sea.

One morning Hun-Hui went to the temple where he found a bow. Then, with a group of Indian merchants, he boarded a vessel and put out to sea. He arrived at the gates of the city of Funan. Yeh-Liu put herself at the head of her troops to repulse him. Hun-Hui took her as his bride and seized the kingdom. In time his descendants grew weak and his lineage ceased to reign. General Fan Hsun gave rise to a new hereditary line of the king of Funan.

Chin Shu (Chap. 97)

THE INHABITANTS OF FUNAN

The men are all dirty and dark, with curly hair. They go naked and barefoot. They are good-natured, they dedicate themselves to farming; their country has a great wealth of silver, pearls, and perfumes. They have books and warehouses with archives and other things. Their handwriting resembles that of the Hu.

Chin Shu (Chap. 48)

Indian monk, Nagasena; it aimed to obtain from the Chinese emperor military aid for a war against Champa, the kingdom to the east (southern Vietnam), where a former "slave" of Jayavarman had seized power. Indications are that the quarrel was of limited proportions, and the real interest of the passage lies in its account of the religious practices and customs of Funan's inhabitants. From the account of the diplomatic mission of 503 we learn that the Chinese emperor, in exchange for the numerous gifts he had received, conferred on Jayavarman the title "general of the South Pacific region and king of Funan." The emperor's appointment undoubtedly helped boost the sovereign's prestige, since in practice it amounted to an official recognition on the part of the Celestial Empire of his sovereignty.

The extensive space the Chinese sources devote to descriptions of the customs and practices of the Funanese of the period in question complement this image of an important kingdom. The people enjoyed a comfortable standard of living, and resided in raised houses built of wood and tree branches. Their handicrafts were flourishing, and they were capable merchants and shipbuilders. Life at the court of Funan was not without splendor. The king with his concubines lived in a two-story palace amid ease and affluence. When the sovereign and his womenfolk decided to go out, they were carried by elephants. Public amusement was assured by cockfights and pigfights. Justice was entrusted to the system of "trial by ordeal"—that is, to the divine judgment that inevitably condemned the guilty and rewarded the innocent. The latter were expected to come forth unharmed from the terrible trials prescribed, such as carrying a red-hot chain seven steps, extracting objects from a cauldron full of boiling oil, or jumping into water and remaining dry.

As for the religion of the Funanese, the *Nan-Chi shu* stresses that among the various gifts sent by Jayavarman were two ivory reliquaries. This account also has the emissary Nagasena say: "The custom of this country is to worship the god Mahesvara. The god constantly descends on Mount Motan." The *Liang shu* asserts that the Funanese worship the "spirits of heaven," images of whom they fashion from bronze; these strange divinities can have two faces and four arms, or even four faces and eight arms. Such images were evidently too far from the orthodox Buddhism of the Chinese chronicler for him to be able to grasp their significance. In fact, the images were probably representations of the divinities of the Hindu pantheon, further testimony to the diffusion in Indochina of India's religious currents.

To round out the picture of Funan's religious life at this time, we might refer to two inscriptions of Hindu inspiration, whose execution was ordered by Queen Kulaprabhavati, wife of Jayavarman, and by her son, Gunavarman. There is also the report that Rudravarman, successor to Jayavarman on the throne of Funan, sent a mission to China, and this mission revealed the existence in Funan of an important relic, a hair of Buddha. Now the Mahesvara referred to by Nagasena has been claimed by some commentators to represent a Bodhisattva, which would be another indication of the prominence of Buddhism. But it is more generally accepted that the Mahesvara is to be identified with Shiva and that Shivaism was the most widespread religion during the reigns of Jayavarman and Rudravarman, although Vishnuism was also practiced. (Shivaism and Vishnuism were merely Hindu "denominations" that emphasized, respectively, Shiva or Vishnu.)

So far our picture of the kingdom of Funan has been drawn largely from Chinese texts or inscriptions from Funan. The archaeological finds of the last few years add little to the reports of the first visitors to the region. But the excavations of Malleret in the city of Oc-Eo and his extensive survey of the delta region provide a fairly exact idea of what the life of the times was like. The city of Oc-Eo was rectangular (some 2 miles by 1 mile) surrounded at the perimeter by a series of moats and mounds and subdivided internally into ten sectors by canals. These latter—four of them laid out perpendicularly to a canal that evenly divided the area lengthwise and continued on outside the city's bounds—made up the city's main network of "streets." The houses and palaces were built of wood on pilelike pillars along the edges of the canals. But wood, it goes without saying, cannot stand up to water and time; as a result, there is little more left of this city—as is the same with the other cities of Funan—than the remains of a few special buildings. These were built of more lasting materials, presumably because they were used for religious functions. At Oc-Eo, these edifices include monuments A and K; their exact function is not easy to determine. The reconstruction of monument K proposed by Malleret—who also dates it to the fifth century—suggests it was a sanctuary made up of a chamber within a porch and of an upper portion that, thanks to the use of great slabs of stone, simulates a grotto. It might be classified, then, as a building intended to emulate the type of Indian temple carved in solid rock and which, owing to the nature of the local terrain—low-lying land, devoid of peaks—demanded the artificial construction of such an environment.

Also brought to light at Oc-Eo has been a great quantity of objects of various kinds: pottery, glasswork, bronzes, gold pieces, etc. Many of the objects were unquestionably imported, and as a result afford highly useful data, both because in many cases they represent the source of inspiration for contemporary and subsequent Funanese art and because they indicate the extent, direction, and intensity (ascribed to a particular epoch) of the city's commerce. It should not be forgotten that this commercial activity was always the source of prosperity for the kingdom of Funan and an occasion for contacts with whatever societies happened to be flourishing at the time. While the jewels, seals, and amulets with religious symbols are clearly of Indian origin, inscriptions on hard stone and the medals of Antoninus Pius and Marcus Aurelius testify to relations with the West in a period running from the second to fourth centuries A.D. The fragment of a Han mirror and a medal with the image of a Sassanid sovereign suggest the extension of Funan's relations with, respectively, China and Persia.

These cultural contacts gradually became a stimulus for local production, which in some fields sets out timidly following models from abroad, then little by little breaking away to express religious or political attitudes the Funanese came to feel confident of as their own. The figure of the personage seated under a canopy wearing a strange pointed hat, or the all-but-naked native with his hair done up in braids—both obviously derived from Chinese models—are typical results of this process. Nevertheless, indications are that up to the outset of the sixth century, stone statuary was virtually unknown in Funan. Chinese sources mention statues of divinities sculptured in Funan, but they were evidently images of small proportions and of wood or bronze. The few relics of stone found within the walls of the city of Oc-Eo cannot be considered certainly as the work of local artists or as contemporaneous to the site. This absence of stone in Funanese sites is explained, among other reasons, by its scarcity in the southern territory where Funan was centered.

THE DECLINE OF FUNAN

After the death of Jayavarman in 514, Rudravarman, the son of a concubine, slew his younger brother, son of his father's legitimate wife, and himself usurped the throne. Rudravarman, who was to rule for some twenty-five years, is known as the last king to govern a unified Funan, and the only one to be remembered in the inscriptions of the later Khmer sovereigns. He also sent many diplomatic missions to China from 517 to 539. During his reign, the political center of the nation shifted to the

KAUNDINYA AND THE DAUGHTERS OF THE NAGA KING

XV. Then the illustrious Sri Jagaddharma, a man of great courage, went to the city known as Bhava.
XVI. It was there that Kaundinya, Brahman bull of this city, drove into the ground the javelin he had received from the eminent Brahman Asvatthaman, son of Drona.
XVII. There was the daughter of the Naga king, by birth who founded on earth the race by the name of Soma; having adopted this state, a remarkable thing, he took up residence in a human abode.
XVIII. The bull of Munis, Kaundinya by name, took her as his bride in order to fulfill the rites. With regard to the nature of events to come, the action of fate is indeed incomprehensible!
XIX. The leader who, having been born to royalty by an uninterrupted transmission of pure blood, is still the pride of his people because of his excellent works.

Inscription III A of Mi-son

Funan Kingdom: The network of canals (visible today by aerial observation):
1 Óc-Éo
2 Angkor Borei
3 Chau Doc
4 Triton
5 Mop-van
6 Ta Kev
7 Da-noi

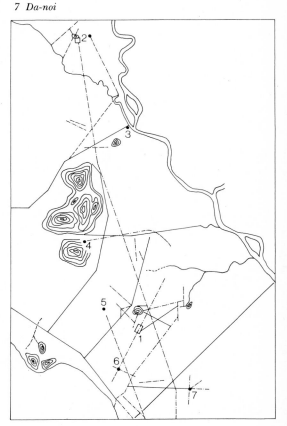

The Harihara from the Ashram Maharosei (Style A of the Phnom Da style, middle of the sixth century; sandstone, 70 inches high). Harihara is one of the best-known divinities of Khmer iconography and bears witness to the religious syncretism of Cambodia. This god unites the characteristics of Shiva and Vishnu. The former is represented (on the statue's right) by such typical features as the high curly hairdo, the eye in the middle of the forehead, the trident (only the end of which is preserved), and the garment, the skin of a feline whose head is etched on his right leg. Vishnu is represented (on the statue's left side) with a cylindrical miter on his head; he holds the *cakra*, or sun-symbol wheel; and he is clad in the typical garment, draped and knotted at the waist with folds dropping in the front. (Guimet Museum, Paris)

BRAHMA'S WORDS TO THE SAGE MARKANDEYA

On the slopes of Mount Mandara, in the Na-lini, O Brahman, I saw in a dream during the night Bhava and Kesava, Hara and Acyuta, Hari in the aspect of Hara, Hara in the aspect of Hari; Hara covered by a yellow garment, with the shell, the disk, and the club in his hands; Hari clad in a tiger skin, with trident and lance. As an insignia Hara bore the *garuda* while Hari used the bull.

Harivamsa (II: 4)

THE WORDS OF KRISHNA, INCARNATION OF VISHNU, TO SHIVA

You can see, O Sankara [a name for Shiva], that you are no different from me. What I am, you are too, in the same way, and I am this world inhabited by gods, demons, and men. Those who perceive a difference are beings whose souls are blinded by ignorance.

Vishnupurana (V: 33)

Left:
A close-up of the figure of Harihara from the Ashram Maharosei, pictured on the previous page. More clearly visible here are some of the elements that characterize Shiva (statue's right) and Vishnu (statue's left). (Guimet Museum, Paris)

north, and Rudravarman founded his capital at Angkor Borei; this was farther from the sea but connected to Oc-Eo and other nearby towns by a network of artificial canals (see page 26). The exploration of Angkor Borei, although limited, has revealed that most of the buildings have disappeared, except for the foundations of the wooden structures and a brick sanctuary that was never completed. On the Phnom Da hill, a few miles north of the capital, however, are the remains of an artificial grotto and one of the oldest stone buildings known in Cambodia (its date is still not fixed—somewhere between the sixth and seventh centuries), the Ashram Maharosei, a small temple.

What has been found both at Angkor Borei and in sanctuaries at Phnom Da is a considerable number of stone (schist and sandstone) statues, some of sizable dimensions. These have been divided into two groups: Style A of Phnom Da (corresponding to the Rudravarman period) and Style B of Phnom Da (a slightly later period, from middle of the sixth into the early seventh century). For the most part, the works are images of the Vishnuite pantheon or Shivaite *lingas*. The anthropomorphic portrayal of Shiva is rare, and in practice appears only in images of Harihara, the divinity who was half Shiva and half Vishnu, so characteristic of Khmer iconography.

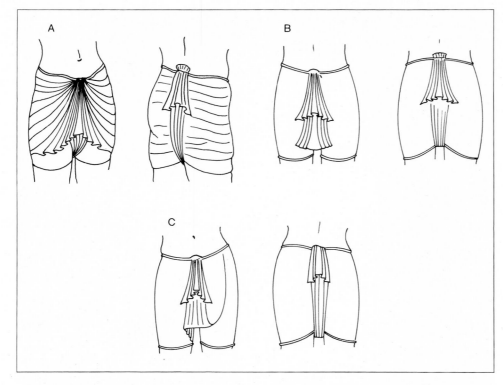

Ways of representing the sampot in the Phnom Da style:
Style A:
A Balarama of the Phnom Da
Style B (double anchor motif, with or without pocket):
B Harihara from the Phnom Da
C Vishnu from Tuol Dai Buon

Works belonging to the Phnom Da style of sculpture have several stylistic and iconographic features in common, which might be summed up as follows: the hairdo with close-fitting locks, over which a miter is worn; wide, flat faces, narrow eyes with eyebrow arches close together; muscular bodies (although in time this feature was less accentuated); nude bodies without ornaments (but with apertures in which jewels could be set). The lower part of the body is covered with a *sampot,* a rectangular-shaped piece of material that circles around the waist and is fixed at the center with a buckle. The leftover edges of cloth (as can be seen in the first pair of drawings on page 30) are passed between the legs and tied at the waist in back so as to form an "anchor" drape. Other variants include a double "anchor" drape in front (set B), and the hint of a baglike fold or pocket on the left side (set C), which in time would become more pronounced. In making statues intended to be fully in the round, the sculptors had recourse to supporting arches and narrow strips for the upper members and the head. If this testifies to the uncertainty of the sculptors, it also shows their originality compared to the models from Gupta India, where sculptors simply rejected sculpture in the round and worked on steles. That some detachment from the Indian models was intentional is suggested by the fact that the chief images created—such as the Krishna Govardhana of Wat Koh (page 24)—resemble steles.

Deserving separate mention is the Buddhist statuary, about the chronology of which scholars voice different opinions. Some of them have ascribed dates between the fifth and the beginning of the sixth century to such works as the wooden image found at Oc-Eo, the Buddha of Romlock, and those statues found at Angkor Borei. Others have held that the statuary of the southernmost part of the Indochinese peninsula cannot be dated back earlier than the sixth century and that the earliest Funan works must be considered imports. Allowing the question to remain open—since the few examples known can scarcely resolve it—we may take note of certain characteristics common to the sculptures in question. From a technical standpoint, we see that the supporting arch has been eliminated; but it must be said that the image of Buddha does not entail the same problems, since his garment drops all the way down to his feet, thus providing the lower part of the statue with a sufficiently stable mass, and Buddha does not possess the numerous hands of the Hindu deities, with their various attributes. The iconography is otherwise

Gold rings from the Oc-Eo excavations. The upper one (A) is decorated with a bull, perhaps intended as Nandi, the vehicle (vahana) of Shiva. The other two bear Sanskrit inscriptions, here reproduced upside down because they were to serve as seals.

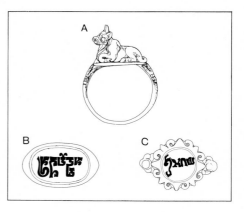

This image of a woman is thought to have portrayed Uma, the goddess-wife of Shiva. It is from the N₁ sanctuary of Sambor Prei Kuk (Sambor style, seventh century) and is one of the first female images from pre-Angkorean times. Worthy of note is the movement given to the figure by the slight twisting of the bust, and the draping of the garment achieved by incised double lines that converge from the sides toward the center, where the material is gathered in a knot. (Guimet Museum, Paris)

Wooden Buddha from the Plain of Reeds. (National Museum of South Vietnam, Saigon)

traditional: Buddha, standing, wears a long, close-fitting tunic *(uttarasanga)*, which at times leaves one shoulder bare; he has a hairdo characterized by large, flat curls; and he has elongated ear lobes. The untraditional elements, however, include two important details: the slight importance given to the *ushnisha,* the cranial protuberance usually attributed to Buddha, and the omission of the *urna,* the "third eye" between the eyebrows: elsewhere in Asia these were considered essential in portraying the master.

As for the style of this Buddhist statuary, there have been suggestions of Indian influence (emanating from Amaravati in India and Gupta and post-Gupta plastics), and also Singhalese influence (from Anuradhapura, Sri Lanka), which is said to be found primarily in the manner of dealing with the drapery and a latent dynamism within the images. This latter characteristic, it has been noted, may also have stemmed from a more pronounced Western influence, specifically of the Hellenistic sort. In conclusion, it may be said of Funanese sculpture, as of Funan in general, that many aspects are not yet clearly defined, and only more intensive excavations of the delta region will clarify them.

THE EMERGENCE OF CHENLA

If Funan lacks definition, the same must be said of Chenla. Like all the names used for the earliest political and geographical subdivisions of the Indochinese peninsula, Chenla cannot be defined precisely (although the ancient Chinese seem to have used Chenla as almost synonymous with the

This female divinity from Popel has been tentatively identified as Lakshmi, consort of Vishnu; it is in the Prasat Andet style (seventh century; sandstone; 41 inches high). The high attainments of this Prasat Andet style may be seen in such elements as the subtle smile and the body enlivened by the slightest hint of a bend in the torso on the left. The garment is tied at the waist to form a drape in relief, while the draping is suggested by incised lines; at the bottom, the draping breaks into a zigzag at the center to function decoratively. (Guimet Museum, Paris)

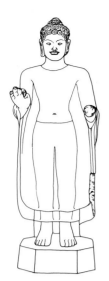

This statue of a Buddha, from Tuol Preah That, portrays Buddha with his right hand raised (although now broken) in the gesture of imparting a lesson. The left hand holds the edge of his mantle. On the back of the statue is an inscription in Pali, an Indic language used by Buddhists, dating from the seventh century. (Guimet Museum, Paris)

THE KINGDOM OF CHEN-LA

The kingdom of Chen-la lies southwest of Lin-yi. It was originally a vassal kingdom of Funan.... The family name of the king was Kshatriya, his personal name was Sitrasena. His forefathers had gradually increased the country's power. Sitrasena seized Funan and subjected it. When he died, his son Isanasena succeeded him, taking up residence in the city of Isana.

Sui Shu

region we know as Cambodia). It seems to have been another Indianized state, slightly north of Funan and including at least part of modern Cambodia. Its inhabitants were presumably of the same Mon-Khmer group as the Funanese and judging from later inscriptions and Chinese texts they had their own kings from the fifth century A.D.

Then, about 550—after the death of Rudravarman of Funan, note—Bhavavarman, a member of the Funanese royal family (and perhaps even a grandson of the king) married a princess of Chenla and ascended to the Chenla throne (thus achieving a union of the solar race of Cambodia with the lunar race of Funan). Not content with ruling Chenla, Bhavavarman decided to attack Funan, and he assigned his cousin (or possibly brother) Sitrasena to lead the military campaign. Evidently it was not that successful, though, because in a later Chinese text, the *Siu Tang shu (New History of the Tangs)* it is recorded that a later king, Isanavarman, "subjected Funan and seized its territory." In fact, what all this reflects is that these years were a time of indecisive conflicts and uncertain victories, and no king of Chenla probably had that much power over that much territory.

Bhavavarman, however, founded his own capital at Bhavapura, on the northern shores of the great central Tonle Sap Lake, not far from the ruins of Ampil Rolum; he also left inscriptions in the areas of Mongkolborei and Si Tep. Then, about 600, he was succeeded by Sitrasena, who took the name Mahendravarman on ascending to the throne. Little or nothing is known about his brief reign, although he did leave several inscriptions. By this time, Funan had ceased to exist as a true state, although this was not entirely due to the pressure from Chenla. Indeed, some scholars contend that the decline of Funan resulted primarily from the terrible floods of the fifth and sixth centuries, which caused irreparable damage and compelled the inhabitants to abandon part of their lands to the waters. Moreover, the kingdoms along the Indochinese coast were gradually losing their commercial prominence to Indonesia, where the seventh century was to witness the consolidation of the power of Srivijaya, the Sumatra kingdom that dominated the straits and thus the sea lanes.

Sitrasena's son, Isanavarman, succeeded him on the throne in 616 (or possibly in 611); he is known to us from the Chinese sources as the founder of the city of Isanapura, which has been identified with Sambor Prei Kuk, where archaeological remains of great interest have been found. Aerial observation of the area made it possible to distinguish traces of a great square city at least 1 mile on each side, enclosed by a double wall and supplied with a large reservoir of water on the south. To the east is the religious complex, made of three groups of temples; these are indicated by the letters N, C, and S, depending on their location (north, center, south), and with numerical exponents to distinguish individual temples within a group—as N_1. Only the north and south groups are considered contemporaneous with the founding of the capital. Each group was surrounded by walls with either two or four portals, and it may be that walls surrounded the entire complex. The pivotal element of each group is the central sanctuary (N_1, S_1, C_1). S_1 is accompanied by a portico, five sanctuaries inside the first circle of walls, and by another eight sanctuaries in the space between the first and second circles. Group N, which was extended and restored in Angkorean times, includes a central sanctuary built in the middle of a terrace with four corner temples (N_2–N_5) and another four sanctuaries outside.

It all seems quite ambitious, considering the probable modesty of Isanavarman's power and reign. What most concerns us, however, is the part these sanctuaries play in the evolution of structures that were to culminate in the great Khmer temples. The sanctuaries at Sambor Prei Kuk were essentially towers *(prasats),* with a lower section that was a cell, or chamber, to hold the sacred image, and an upper part formed by a series of terraces of diminishing dimensions. Within the framework of this basic form, two variants are to be seen: outside walls of cells may be enlivened by slightly protruding pillars, and a roof of regular steps might be added. This latter variant was the more complex, particularly when every step repeats the motif of the facade on a smaller scale; its design might also be more varied, due to the inclusion on each side of a false door and a greater number of pillars. Sanctuary S₁ at Sambor Prei Kuk is of this type. And it should be noted that many of the structures of this period do not fit into this pattern: there is a sanctuary at Han Chei that has a flat roof, and at Sambor Prei Kuk itself N₇ has an octagonal tower.

Just as the Sambor sanctuaries constitute the prototype of the later Angkorean architecture, the architectonic decoration contains many elements that we will encounter in the centuries to follow. The lintels in particular deserve our attention (see page 35). They are made in the form of an arch interrupted by three medallions with images of divinities shaped in relief. The ends of the arches are "swallowed" by the yawning jaws of two *makaras*—crocodilelike monsters clearly reminiscent of Indian motifs—from which a lion with wings and horns is emerging. On the back of the *makara* sits a small person. The space underneath is filled with carved garlands, pendants, and leaves, all tending toward extreme stylization. There are also variants. Sanctuary S₁ has a lintel replacing the *makara* with human figures riding fantastic mounts, and the ornamental relief with a scene populated by a number of persons in high relief.

The Sambor Prei Kuk complex has also yielded examples of sculpture in the round—a statue of Harihara, another of Uma (page 31)—that, together with others of the period (a head of Vishnu, a Harihara of uncertain origin, the *devi* of Koh Krieng) form a stylistically homogeneous group. Masculine images sculptured in the "Sambor style" have a slim, muscular body, narrow waist, wide face with the hint of a stylized smile, and a garment with a double pocket on the side. For the first time, female figures appear; they are characterized by rather heavy physiques with heavy breasts, and a garment (the *samrong*) that, beginning at the sides, forms a cascade of dense folds in the center. The unusually high chignon hairdo calls to mind the images of Shiva. In conclusion, it may be said that the Sambor style constitutes a prolongation of that of the Phnom Da B style, but it added female figures to the repertoire and extended over a wider area.

But if the artistic physiognomy of Isnavarman's reign (c. 616–635) is well delineated, the same cannot be said of other aspects of his kingdom. He seems to have expanded beyond the central highlands and left inscriptions in the provinces of Kompong Champ, Prei Veng, Kandal, and Takeo—mainly in the south, in fact. An inscription at Svay Chno mentions his conquest of three "capitals"—that is, three kingdoms, formerly vassals of Funan. An inscription found at Wat Sabat (a place on the Siamese coast) indicates the probable maximum expansion toward the west and the sea. But no inscriptions have been brought to light in northern territories, the very region where Bhavavarman I had begun his conquests that pushed Chenla into power. If we were to base our conclusions on inscriptions, therefore, we should have to presume that Isanavarman had lost control of the very territory that initially comprised Chenla. But such a theory would be premature, since so much material still waits to be uncovered and studied (despite the enormous efforts of the French School of the Far East).

The inscriptions dating from the kingdom of Isanavarman, however, hold further interest for us—both sociological and linguistic. On the steles of Angkor Borei (Takeo) and Wat Vihear Trabh (Kandal), the Khmer language is used for the first time. This is not to say that it has replaced Sanskrit, which was still used in that part of the inscription that praised the sovereign and in the dedication to the divinity. Khmer was used to annotate administrative questions: the number of slaves or quan-

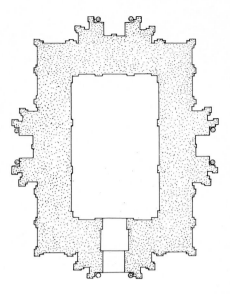

Sambor Prei Kuk: Plan of sanctuary number 1 of the south group.

Below and right:
Main types of pre-Angkorean sanctuaries:
A Prasat Preah Theat Toch
B Prasat Preah Theat Thom

In the former (A), the plan is a simple quadrangle, emphasized by outer pillars; the roof is formed by diminishing terraces. The plan of the latter (B) presents great corner pillars and sharply jutting doorframes; the roof repeats, on a diminishing scale, the complete design of the facade.

A

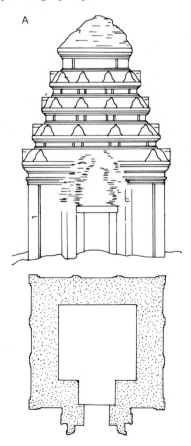

tity of land donated to the sanctuary by the sovereign or by the high-ranking dignitary who sponsored the foundation. This makes it plain that the local language was now commonly used by the royal bureaucracy, while Sanskrit was becoming a purely ceremonial or ecclesiastic language.

THE END OF CHENLA

The last known date for the kingdom of Isanavarman is actually 628—the year of a diplomatic mission to China—but it is usually assumed he ruled for several more years. Meanwhile, the first mission of his successor, Bhavavarman II, as indicated by the Takeo province stele, is 639. Possibly the eleven years separating one from the other indicate a period of interregnum and struggle. In any case, Bhavavarman II seems to have initiated a new dynasty, or so it appears from the epigraphic sources of later times. The Kolei Ang inscription of 667 provides a genealogical list of preceding sovereigns beginning with Rudravarman—evidently included to demonstrate the dynastic continuity of Chenla with ancient Funan. But the name of Bhavavarman II is not mentioned, so we might assume that he ruled over only a part of the region of Chenla. Two other elements characterize the reign of Bhavavarman II, at the same time creating a connection with his successor, Jayavarman I. One was the fact that he declared himself to be a descendant of the "lunar family"; the other is that he was designated with a posthumous name. After his death, in fact, Bhavavarman II was remembered as the one who had departed for *Shivaloka* ("Shiva's Heaven"); his son, Jayavarman I, after his death, went on to *Shivapura* ("Shiva's city").

The period of Jayavarman I's reign comprises the years from 657 to 681, but as with all these kings little else is known about him or his reign. He did not seem to have ordered any foundations—as the various temples, sanctuaries, or other structures are known—and we do not even know for certain where his capital was located. Some scholars have suggested the area of Banteay Prei Nokor; others nominate the submerged part of the West Baray at Angkor, which has yielded an inscription of Queen Jayadevi, the young wife of Jayavarman I. Dated to 713, this inscription focuses attention on the instability of the times. But the same sites tend to be suggested as the capital for Jayavarman II, so all theories about Jayavarman I's capital remain inconclusive.

We have more solid evidence, however, for the artistic production of the times of Bhavavarman II and Jayavarman I, particularly in the ongoing developments of the lintel and sculpture. The Sambor style is first

succeeded by that of Prei Kmeng, where the lintels still employ the central motif of an arch with medallions; however, the figures of animals on the sides have been replaced by human figures, and the garland motif has become even more stylized. The false tympanum beneath the arch sometimes has the image of a divinity—usually Vishnu resting on the waters. As for statuary, it is enough to note here that the Prei Kmeng style reached its zenith about the years 640–645, and that it is documented in the entire territory of Chenla. In the matter of iconography, there were three significant innovations. One was the production of small Buddhist bronzes. The second was the portrayal of Brahma in Hindu sculpture. And lastly, the many images of Bodhisattvas, particularly Avalokitesvara and Maitreya, seem to indicate a diffusion of Mahayana ("Great Vehicle") Buddhism, a less pessimistic form of Buddhism that at times almost merged with Hinduism.

Of still greater significance are the works belonging to the next phase, the Prasat Andet style, which constituted both a synthesis of the preceding styles and a model for its successor, the Kompong Preah style. In the Prasat Andet style, the decoration of the lintel changed considerably, conceding more and more space to the foliage of the arch, which in the end supplants the figurative elements altogether. As for the sculpture, the images are all drawn from the Hindu pantheon, and so the most representative subjects are Vishnu, Harihara, and Devi. Male faces are portrayed in a somewhat "dry" manner, with thin moustaches; the human figure remains tall and slender, with broad shoulders, intent on a forward movement scarcely perceptible to the beholder. The males wear a short garment, draped in such a way as to form on the left side a large pocket that represents one of the distinctive features of the style. The female figures still wear a garment that descends all the way to the feet, spreading out in bell fashion with a drape indicated by thin lines inscribed on the sides.

With the death of Jayavarman I (681), an epoch came to a close: the whole region split into principalities, and no unanimously recognized sovereign was to emerge for over a century. The *History of the Tang* records that the Cambodian territory broke up into two kingdoms—

Chenla of the Land and Chenla of the Water, names that clearly allude to their geographical position. But if we are to understand the complex political events of the eighth century, we must first go back to the beginning of the seventh century and glance at the history of the southernmost part of the Indochinese peninsula, where a vassal state known as Aninditapura was ruled by a minor king, Baladitya. We have noted that the conquest of Funan by Chenla was never that thorough; as a result, the slow disintegration of the Funan region had undoubtedly left a power vacuum that was filled with able governors. Baladitya was perhaps one such; in any event, he succeeded in founding a "dynasty" that ruled Aninditapura for more than a century. In addition to this founder, we also know the names of the last two sovereigns in this region, Nrpatindravarman and Puskaraksa; their reigns probably coincided with that of the legitimate sovereigns of Chenla, Bhavavarman II, Jayavarman I, and Jayadevi (Jayavarman's wife, who seems to have survived him and held power for at least a brief time). We have already referred to the inscription of Jayadevi, and it is virtually coeval with that of Puskaraksa, found in the Kratie region and dated 716.

This Puskaraksa actually assumes some significance beyond the minor kingdom of Aninditapura, for two kings of Angkor, Indravarman and Yasovarman, in their claims to descent from the kings of Funan, actually mention him in their inscriptions. Puskaraksa himself must have been aware of some special role, since he had a royal *linga* erected, in which his name was joined with that of Shiva. And an inscription of the Angkorean period confirms all this by stating that Puskaraksa "had taken over the kingdom at Sambupura." The studies of the French scholar Dupont have placed this city in the present-day region of Kratie, which would bring Puskaraksa's authority considerably farther north; moreover, Dupont has advanced the theory that the ascension to the throne referred to in the Angkorean inscription did not refer to a normal transference of power from father to son but to an attempt by Puskaraksa to proclaim himself king of all Cambodia—in effect, to usurp the throne that, at least until 713, Jayadevi had been able to hold.

Following Dupont's reconstruction of this period, the split into Chenla of the Land and Chenla of the Water did not occur until after the appearance of Puskaraksa. In any case, Chenla of the Land seems to have comprised essentially the same territory as the original Chenla, and in its own way it functioned throughout the eighth century—as witnessed by data on the diplomatic missions sent to China throughout the century. But Chenla of the Water failed to remain united, except for the period when Puskaraksa reigned; its subsequent history was marked by at least five different dynasties at the head of as many small states, none with much power. The territory they divided among themselves comprised essentially the ancient kingdom of Funan, particularly the Kampot region in the southwesternmost corner of the peninsula. Furthermore, these southwestern territories were almost certainly subjected to a protectorate of Java, whether of a formal nature or otherwise.

Such territorial and political instability hardly favors the development of art, and that is why the production in the Kompong Preah style of this period was not only scanty but also not of a very high quality. Examples of this style include seven statues representing Shiva, Devi, Harihara, and Maitreya, which merely repeat the elements typical of previous styles— the rounded face, the cylindrical miter, the pocket of the garment emerging from a maze of etched folds. But there were some positive elements. One instance is the attempt to produce sculpture in the round without any supporting arches, a technical achievement that was to enable the more gifted artists of the ninth century to create works of true value. Indeed, for all the limitations of these early centuries in Cambodia, we must recognize that they served as the seedbed of what would become the great kingdom of the Khmers and the monuments of Angkor.

Harihara of Prasat Andet in the Praset Andet style (mid-seventh to early eighth centuries); this is considered one of the finest examples of pre-Angkorean statuary, possessing all the characteristics of the style from which it draws its name. The face is oval, the upper lip marked by a thin moustache, the anatomy of the body barely hinted at. Great care, however, has been taken in the execution of the garment: part of it passes between the legs and fastens in the back, while the other part folds to form a drape or side pocket on the left thigh before returning to the middle and falling in front in thick and rigid folds (sandstone; 77 inches high). (National Museum, Phnom Penh)

A detail of a lintel with the image of the lingodbhavamurti *from the Wat Eng Khna, in the Prei Kmeng style (seventh century). The* linga *is in the center, where the visage of Shiva appears, surrounded by stylized flames. On the right, bottom, amid the floral decoration, is a bear; on the left, a goose. On the two ends of the lintel, but not visible in this drawing, are images of Vishnu (on right) and Brahma (left) in an attitude of veneration. The images allude to the myth of the* lingodbhava: *while Brahma and Vishnu disputed for primacy among the gods, a column of fire appeared before them. Brahma and Vishnu sought to reach its ends, one rising into the air in the form of a goose, the other burrowing into the ground in the form of a bear. Both failed. They then prayed to Shiva, who manifested himself to them by appearing amid the column of fire, which was his* linga, *and proclaimed the unity of Brahma, Vishnu, and Shiva. This same representation of the myth has been found in Champa as well. In the lower register of the lintel (not visible) is one of the rites for the consecration of the king—a sprinkling rite. The joining of these two episodes on a lintel unquestionably reflects the desire to establish a parallel between Shiva, king of the gods, and the human king. (National Museum, Phnom Penh)*

Angkor: The Classic Period

JAYAVARMAN II AND THE FOUNDING OF KHMER KINGSHIP

The political situation in the Indochinese peninsula in the closing years of the eighth century, as we have seen, was extremely unstable. Although we lack almost any documentation for the period, it is not difficult to imagine that the principalities found themselves hard put to maintain their own borders, let alone to resist any states that were more powerful. One such state was the Javanese kingdom of Srivijaya, which in fact reached its acme in the eighth century. We have already had occasion to refer to this and other Indonesian kingdoms in connection with the role they played in maritime commerce. But now, to understand the history of Cambodia, we must focus somewhat more closely on their political and cultural aspects. For the name Java is, in fact, closely bound up with that of Jayavarman II, the sovereign that Khmer writings of a later date extol as the founder of the dynasty that reigned at Angkor.

This Jayavarman must undoubtedly have been a personality of the first order, although probably not quite as great as his successors sought to make him appear, inclined as they were to build him up for obviously selfish political motives. Since none of Jayavarman II's inscriptions has come down to us (or, to be more exact, none yet known can be ascribed to this king), the only way we can describe various events of his reign is to turn to testimonials of a later period, particularly to the inscription of Sdok Kak Thom (the ancient Bhadraniketana). This stele had been ordered by a high official named Sadashiva to commemorate the foundation of a personal *linga* in 1052. From the inscription we learn that Jayavarman (also cited by his posthumous name, Paramesvara) had come from Java, where he had spent many years at the court. There is no indication as to whether he first went there as a guest, hostage, or prisoner. But there is no question that he assimilated local traditions, practices, and, most crucially, the Javanese sovereign's lust for power and conquest and the desire to impose his own ideas of "good government." The kings of Java, meanwhile, considered themselves heirs to the realm of Funan, and Jayavarman II, who felt that he had blood ties, however distant, with the Indochinese dynasty, came to feel that he should return to his homeland and lead it in a new political direction.

Indications are that he arrived in Cambodia around the year 790 and conquered his first bit of territory halfway up the Mekong; immediately afterwards he founded a capital at Indrapura, which is tentatively identified with the locality known as Banteay Prei Nokor. Then Jayavarman moved further west to the province of Purvadisa—the area where Angkor would later rise; from there he moved to found another city, Hariharalaya (near the site of Roluos); subsequently he moved and founded still another, Amarendrapura, which may be the submerged ruins of the West Baray. The most significant event of his reign, however, seems to have come next—at least it is the event that his successors chose to emphasize: Jayavarman II took up residence at Mahendrapura, which has been identified as Phnom Kulen, the hills just north of Angkor. There he had himself consecrated king, freed himself of any ties still binding him to Java by proclaiming himself "universal sovereign," and initiated the worship of *devaraja* (Sanskrit for "god-king"). This occurred in 802, the date usually taken as the founding of the Khmers' kingdom of Angkor. According to the Sdok Kak Thom inscription, Jayavarman's wanderings ended shortly afterwards with his return to Hariharalaya (Roluos), where he remained until his death in 850.

All this seems clear enough, but the fact is that a number of contradictions emerge from the reign of Jayavarman II. For one, how was it that such a king left no inscriptions (assuming, of course, that this is not merely a gap in modern archaeology)? Or why did he feel the need to

Banteay Srei: This relief depicting Shiva on Mount Kailasa is on the west pediment of the south "library"; it is in pink sandstone and dates to 967. Shiva, whose arms and chest are guarded by serpents, sits in a "royal position" atop a step-pyramid, a symbolic representation of Mount Kailasa. On his right is Parvati, his *Sakti*—or his creative force as a female consort—kneeling as she holds the rosary. To his left is Kama, the god of love, in the act of aiming at him with a bow and arrow; at Kama's side, one step lower, is his wife, Rati. On each step of the pyramid is a row of personages. On the step just below Shiva are a group of *rsis*, or ascetics: Shiva is the penitent par excellence. Below them are personages with heads of animals; similar figures (sculptured in the round) are at various points around the temple's perimeter, serving as guardians. At the base of the pyramid—in a livelier composition than the two rows above—are several ascetic Hindu youths; on opposite sides are two great deer, while in the middle is the bull Nandi, the "vehicle" of Shiva.

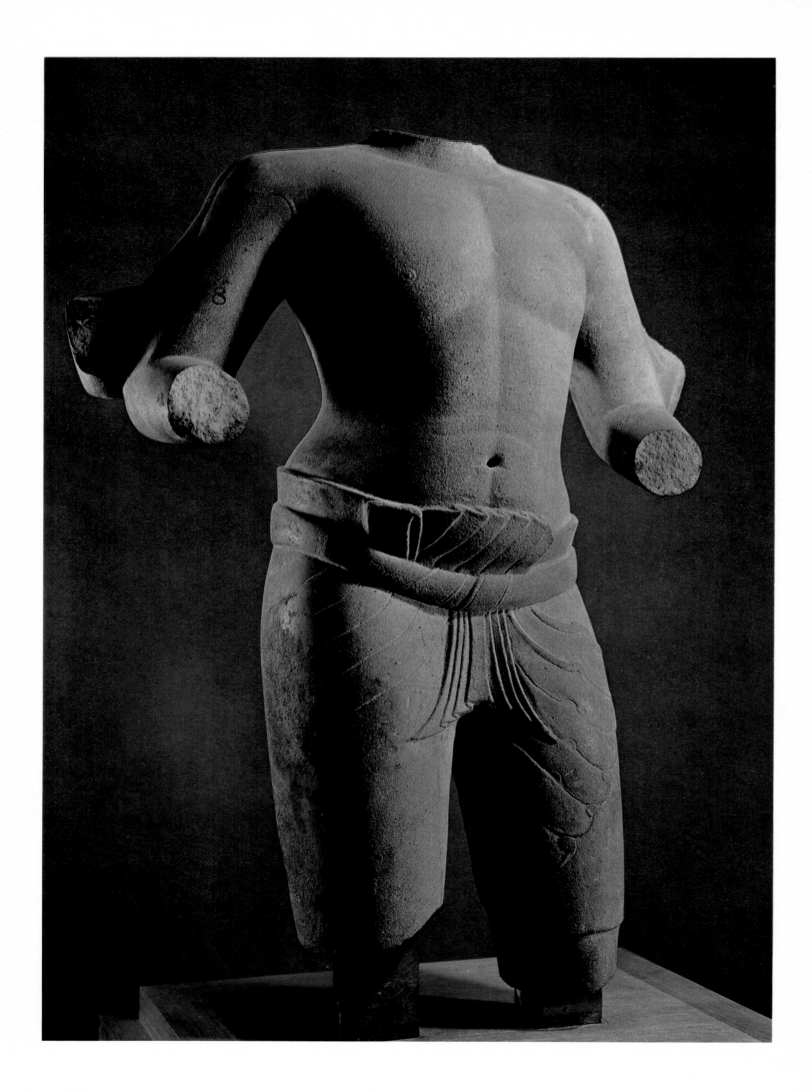

change his residence so often? And why did he choose Phnom Kulen on which to celebrate the rites connected with his consecration and sovereignty? The most convincing answer to the first question appears to be that of Dupont, who argues that Jayavarman II must be viewed in the historical context in which he lived: Indochina of the eighth and ninth centuries, when the land was divided into a number of warring principalities. The new king then assumed a role within this framework and founded a kingdom perhaps only a bit larger and more powerful than the others. It is logical, hence, that at least at the outset he turned his attention to annexing new territories and that like the other sovereigns of his time he paid no heed to new foundations or commemorative steles.

An obvious objection to this explanation is that Jayavarman II's kingdom was characterized by the many capitals he founded. But suppose the cities that appear in the Sdok Kak Thom inscription really only represent stages in Jayavarman's territorial conquests. This would perhaps explain why Hariharalaya was mentioned twice as his residence—a sign that the place was not decisively captured the first time—and that many of the towns identified with Jayavarman's capitals reveal, in the light of modern stylistic analyses of their monuments, that they had in fact been founded at least a century later.

If this version is at least close to the truth, then once Jayavarman concluded that he had established some measure of political stability throughout his conquered territories, he then selected a special place, Mahendrapura, as his true capital and had himself proclaimed king there. Or, to be more exact, he had himself proclaimed not king but "universal sovereign" *(cakravartin).* The inscription says explicitly that the solemn ceremony was aimed at assuring the country's liberation from Javanese tutelage, not at affirming the Cambodian king's sovereignty, but this latter would follow as a consequence of the liberation from foreign domination. And Jayavarman II at least achieved this liberation, even though it did not produce all the results he must have expected; indeed, it did not substantially change his political and territorial position. Some commentators have even considered the Phnom Kulen episode as an "abortive ploy," but it seems rather to have been of fundamental political importance for the future of the Khmers. (One person fully aware of this, and who therefore exploited his predecessor's intuition, was Indravarman I, who came to rule in 877.)

For one thing, the choice of this site for the ceremony was by no means haphazard. Mahendrapura is the "city on the mountain" (Great Indra Mountain), a holy city, situated on the high plateau of Phnom Kulen some 25 miles northeast of Angkor. The sanctuaries of Jayavarman II's period found here are all of brick and in a poor state of preservation. The collapse of some of them resulted from the deterioration of the materials by natural atmospheric agents and also from the fact that, in order to bring them to light, the tangle of roots in which they were enmeshed were cut—thus destroying the prime cause of their deterioration but also their chief support. In spite of all, enough of these sanctuaries on the Kulen plateau have survived to allow for a reconstruction of the basic design: a square tower, a cell with an entry and three false doors, a high roof of superimposed levels decreasing in size, each of which reproduces the facade in ever-smaller dimensions.

In addition, the French scholar Philippe Stern, who has devoted himself to stylistic questions, has defined the "Kulen style" as an original phase in the evolution of Khmer art, despite the apparent disunity of the works of which it is comprised. Stern lays particular stress on the exuberance and variety of motifs of this style—the result, in his view, of the number of historical forces at work and the receptivity of the artists of the time to new trends. Prompted by a strong desire for innovation, they accepted all suggestions, creating works that to all appearances were quite

different from one another: only a thorough study of these works has revealed their common denominator.

It is with the statuary and the architectural decoration that the Kulen style is most clearly definable, in part because the statues, lintels, and small columns were made of stone, a material more substantial than the brickwork of the structures. A number of different patterns were used in making lintels. In one pattern, the decorations were exclusively floral motifs—a continuation, to be sure, of a style already introduced at Prasat Andet; another pattern drew even older motifs back into service. Examples of this latter are the medallion arch with human figures (although this structure now assumed a lobed form); and that of the *makara,* facing both the inside and the outside of the lintel itself. Leaves—or, more exactly, series of leaves and pendants—are of a more elaborate type, although they still alternate with the typical floral pendants: in a word, the basic composition remains unchanged. Leaves, or series of leaves and pendants, are also the chief decorative motif of the small rectangular or octagonal columns that support the lintels. These columns serve as a significant characteristic of the Kulen style; simultaneously they constitute a differentiating element with respect to previous styles, which used small round columns. The diminutive columns—sometimes known as colonnettes—of Kulen are constructed symmetrically in four or eight sections, separated respectively by rings or thin ribbing. The middle zone is stressed by a ringed element of slightly greater proportions.

Statuary of the Kulen style, freed once and for all of supporting arches, appears to want to continue along the road taken by the artists of the Prasat Andet toward a type of image that was refined, abstract, and of an ever more pronounced religiosity. The faces of statues of Harihara and Vishnu are still wide, marked by lines determined by the eyebrows; the head is covered with a high cylindrical miter whose lower edge terminates behind, with a broad neckpiece, while on the two sides it descends in a pointed shape to the lower extremity of the ears. The *sampot* extends down as far as the knee, forming a voluminous pocket on the left thigh; the edge is held by a thin belt at the waist, over which it folds, ending on the right side or in the middle with a dense "anchor motif" drape. No female figures have been found in the Kulen style, although other subjects include a number of animals sculptured in the round, particularly the lion and the *garuda,* the birdlike monster that was Vishnu's "vehicle."

Of major monuments, some twenty-eight structures are included as representative of the Kulen style; these have been further subdivided into three phases of execution. Among the first edifices whose construction was ordered by Jayavarman II, we must mention sanctuary C1 of Sambor Prei Kuk, the Ak Yum temple of West Baray (although this is tentative), the Khting Slap, the Phnom Sruoch, the Pam Kre, and the Prasat Damrei Krap on the Kulen plateau. This last-named is particularly well known, both because it is fairly well preserved and because of its extraordinary resemblance to the monuments of Champa. The Prasat Damrei Krap is a vast terrace with three tall brick towers; only the middle one is complete with upper levels. The Champa influence is visible primarily in its decorations. The north and south towers seem never to have been completed, despite the fact that the temple was undoubtedly used for worship, as evidenced by a sculpture of Vishnu in the central cell.

In the second phase of the Kulen style of architecture are the Prasat O Paong, the Rup Arak, and the Prasat Neak Ta, where enough sandstone elements—lintels and small columns, that is—have survived to make it possible to delineate the phase's stylistic characteristics. The third phase includes Kraham I and II, Thma Dap, and possibly Anlong Thom. But it must also be admitted that other sanctuaries of the Kulen period cannot be fitted into this three-phase context, even approximately. Under this heading we must, in fact, include the most important monument of the Phnom Kulen plateau, the temple-mountain of Kruh Preah Aram Rong

INSCRIPTION OF THE GURU SHIVASOMA IN HONOR OF INDRAVARMAN

XIV. As if out of fear of drought, he placed in the heart of all creatures the ambrosia of his charm, which the eyes of women drank insatiably.

XV. After having contemplated his lasting refulgence, which surpasses that of the bright stars, the Rudra of destructive fire still today bows his head in fright.

XVI. Fearful all at once that his arm—this Mandara—might stir it up again so as to draw forth good fortune, the ocean granted him as tribute its depth.

XVII. "The dust raised by his marching army, drifting away to the four cardinal directions, diminishes my bulk to the same extent." It was with this thought that the earth some way or other received the ocean as one of its members.

XVIII. As if out of fear of having to pay him tribute, inimical Fortuna—that courtesan—followed this king, whose hand toyed with the pearls that began to break off from the forehead of the elephants during the fray.

XIX. From the slopes of Mount Meru it was as though this king of the entire earth, which he had conquered with his unparalleled power, were making fun of the receding sun.

XX. On the haughty heads of the kings of China, Champa, and Yavadvipa, his order was like a stainless crown, made of jasmine garlands.

XXI. The long series of smoke gusts rising into the air from the offerings made to Agni during his sacrifices shone in the sky like banners heralding his fame as he was about to march through heaven.

XXII. Flooded by the copious waters poured on the occasion of his donations of gold and other riches, the earth, although burnt with the fire of Kali, would think nothing, it seems to me, of the deluge from the clouds.

XXIII. His fame, tirelessly spreading its luminescence through the world, seems to make fun of the sun and the moon, which alternate in spreading their light.

XXIV. This king, who had satisfied his cravings to the point of satiation, nevertheless was wont to fret over the fact that he could not find an adversary capable of measuring up to that great club, his arm.

XXV. Although he had hidden in the dark forest, the enemy, enlightened by the lamp of his glory, came to seek refuge at his feet, for fear of being captured anew.

XXVI. Having crossed the ocean of virtues, joyous in his possession of the earth, he constantly held up Fortune like another four-armed Vishnu.

XXVII. Having heard the praises of this king sung wherever he went, Svayambhu now has a high opinion of the excellence of his creation.

XXVIII. Although he had kept his promise to serve up the leftovers, he devoured this delicious morsel, the entire conquest, sharing no part of it with the others.

XXIX. He had a mentor by the name of Shivasoma, whose lessons deserved the veneration of all teachers versed in the sciences.

XXX. This was the son of the son of King Sri Jayendradhipativarman, maternal uncle of the king who settled on Mount Mahendra.

XXXI. His feet, rising like an aurora over the large groups of bending ascetics, shone as though it had been licked by the flame generated by the fire of the meditation of former ascetics.

XXXII. Drinking the entire ocean of *sastras,* humiliating the mountain of passions, he always behaved with rectitude. He was like another Agastya, who was born in a pitcher.

XXXIII. Although his spirit was without desire of profit, he practiced a highly profitable profession. Although swollen with knowledge, he grew thin with asceticism.

XXXIV. The dazzling rays of light that came from his head when he practiced yoga shone like the flame of the fire of knowledge, purified from inner obscurity by combustion.

XXXV. Forever hanging on his lips, the portals of much sage advice, Sarasvati [eloquence] seemed desirous of acquiring an extreme holiness.

XXXVI. Upon merely touching the dust of his two lotus feet, men gathered the same fruit they would have acquired by bathing in all the holy pilgrimage sites.

XXXVII. In this inconstant world the pure spirit of this sage, who had dedicated himself completely to the public welfare, was constant like the light of the moon rising into the sky.

XXXVIII. It was to serve as a sole receptacle for the virtues of compassion, generosity, constancy, patience, the purity of truth, and other virtues, that he was brought into being by the Creator.

XXXIX. He learned the *sastras* from the mouth of the one known as Bhagavad Sankara, whose lotus feet are feathered by these garlands of bees that are the heads of all the sages.

XL. His mentor was Bhagavad Rudram, the sole receptacle of all the sciences, a Veda scholar, born of a Brahmin family like a second Rudra.

XLI. Having since youth served the other sages versed in knowledge, he acquired a clear intelligence, based on logic, rhetoric, and other branches of knowledge.

XLII. He was an expert in the *sastras, Puranas, Mahabharata,* grammars, and all the other treatises, as though he had written them himself.

Inscription of Prasat Kandol Dom (Chap. 809)

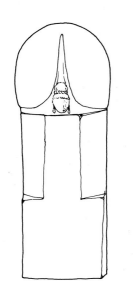

This linga *with the head of Shiva (a* mukhalinga) *was found at Oc-Eo. This view shows the hairdo with its characteristic knot.*

Following page:
The Bakong (Roluos): A view of the temple-mountain built by King Indravarman I in 881.

Chen. This is in the form of a step-pyramid, composed of four superimposed terraces of earth held in by walls of laterite (although in the two upper levels there is also some brick filling); at the top was a pedestal (which has survived) that was probably topped by a *linga*.

COSMIC SYMBOLISM OF THE KHMERS

At this point, it seems desirable to digress for a consideration of several of the elements that we have encountered as part of the accumulating symbolism of the Cambodian sovereigns—the *linga*, the temple-mountain, and the *devaraja* cult. If it is not already clear, mountains early came to be crucially important in the symbolism of the peoples who inhabited these early states of Cambodia. The best known aspect—of Indian derivation, to be sure—is the earthly mountain as equivalent of Mount Meru, the mythical dwelling of the gods ruled by Indra. And since Mount Meru marks the axis of the world, the mountain represents the focal point of the city and the kingdom, the only site worthy of the residence of a sovereign and of the raising of temples in honor of the gods. And as a mountain was virtually synonymous with a holy place, mountains naturally came to be chosen as the sites for establishing religious centers—as at Phnom Da or Phnom Kulen. But the time came when the natural terrain seemed inadequate, when it seemed necessary to provide a temple for the gods or the sovereign of the gods. Inevitably this was made in the form of a small mountain—such as the small sanctuaries we have seen at Sambor or at Phnom Kulen. Then, as economic conditions and the means of production changed, the cities were built down on the plains, and the elevated temple was supplanted by a step-pyramid—an artificial mountain, that is—atop which was placed the symbol of divinity. From this time on, the temple-mountains, atop which a *linga* was placed, began to appear throughout Cambodia. The mountain their builders intended to reproduce was no longer Mount Meru but Mount Kailasa, the abode of Shiva; but all the other cosmological implications were preserved. The link between the mountain and the step-pyramid is confirmed by at least one known relief carving—Mount Kailasa itself is represented in this form.

Still remaining to be demonstrated is the originality of such Khmer monuments vis-à-vis the temples of India, as well as the specific associations binding these monuments to Khmer royalty. As for the first of these two problems, it should suffice to point out that India never erected this type of step-pyramid. Or if, as some have contended, the Indians did, its proportions were extremely small and its meanings less complex. Furthermore, we should not forget the striking parallels between the Khmer structures and the works of the megalithic culture of Cambodia, previously described. The elements necessary for an indigenous birth and development seem present in Cambodia.

Moving on to the second problem—namely, the relationship between the temple-mountain and the *linga*, and between this latter and the sovereign—we must start with a few basics. From the first half of the ninth century to the end of the twelfth—the period of the "classic" Angkorean civilization—each capital had its temple-mountain; in most cases, this housed a *linga* that bore the name of the sovereign and that of Shiva (Isvara: "supreme deity") joined into one. For example, after his death, Indravarman I became Indresvara. This was nothing original, of course, and the conception of the king as an incarnation of a divinity is typical of India and of other ancient civilizations. In pre-Angkorean times, too, the king was considered an incarnation of Shiva; later the king became not just a symbol of the god but the actual substance of the god.

All this might easily have remained in the field of metaphysics, and probably would have, had not steps been taken to substantiate, by means of a tangible symbol, the union between the Khmer king and the god. Such a symbol could only be a *linga*—that is, the phallus of Shiva, itself emblematic of his life-giving force; this *linga* was the god himself and simultaneously the most intimate essence of a king. It also represented that which the given sovereign and Shiva had in common: royalty.

The credit for having first satisfied this need in Cambodia seems to belong to Jayavarman II, the king who had the first step-pyramid built, who proclaimed himself universal sovereign, and who set up the cult of the *devaraja* among the Khmers. And although the concept of the sacred mountain and that of the royal *linga* were already implicit in the construction of Indian temples and in pre-Angkorean edifices, the step-pyramid is a new departure. And does not the fact that this architectural form appeared at the same time as the cult of the *devaraja* indicate some close connection? The Sanskrit term *devaraja* has been translated as "god-king" but the corresponding term in ancient Khmer makes it more explicit: *kamraten jagat ta raja*—"The Lord of the Universe, who is king." The term *devaraja* doesn't appear until the Sdok Kak Thom inscription of 1052, where it is told how Paramesvara (or Jayavarman II) called to the city of Mahendraparvata the Hindu priest Hiranyadama, who was from Janapada. This priest performed the "magic rites bearing the name of *devaraja*," basing the ceremony on four Sanskrit texts, cited by the inscription (all but one of which are mentioned in a text in a Nepalese library).

One apparent contradiction between the archaeological and epigraphical evidence has been resolved by Philippe Stern. The inscriptions distinguish among three types of temples: that dedicated to an ancestor; that of the *linga*, in which the name of the king and Shiva are joined; and that of the *devaraja*. Yet the monuments so far known seem to be of only two types: the tower dedicated to an ancestor; and the temple-mountain, with the royal *linga* on its summit. But Stern has rightfully observed that to identify the temple-mountain (with its *linga*) with the shrine of the *devaraja* not only resolves the clash between epigraphical and archaeological data but also provides answers to other minor problems. Nevertheless, rather than consider the *devaraja* a full-fledged divinity, Stern prefers to recognize in this name a complex of consecration rites associated with the royal *linga*. This interpretation, which effectively replaces one put forward by certain French scholars some time ago—to the effect that there was only one *linga*, carried from city to city and from temple to temple—still cannot be accepted in its entirety.

But the deeper significance of the theory remains valid; that is, the *linga* designated with the name of the king, merged with that of Shiva, gradually becomes the essence and symbol of royalty through the consecration rite. We have seen earlier that the term *devaraja* first appears in the Sdok Kak Thom inscription (1052). But inscriptions at Preah Ko (877) and the Prasat Thom of Koh Ker (first quarter of the tenth century) already bear witness, respectively, to a Sanskrit *devaraja* and to an ancient Khmer *kamraten jagat ta rajya,* with which the concept of "divine royalty" is expressed. In the second instance, for that matter, Coedès feels it is possible that the Khmer expression refers to Tribhuvanesvara ("Lord of the Three Worlds"), the god venerated in the Prasat Thom sanctuary (as we learn from another inscription found there).

Another inscription, at Prasat Khna, refers to *kamraten an ta rajya* in a list of divinities to whom offerings are made. And it can hardly be considered mere chance that this same inscription includes a place name, Janapada, which corresponds to the locality from which came the Hindu priest Hiranyadama (identified, it will be recalled, in the Sdok Kak Thom inscription). It appears reasonable, therefore, to conclude that this Hindu had officiated at a ceremony at Phnom Kulen that was customary in the region of his origin and in honor of a known entity, the essence of deified royalty. Worship of Shiva *devaraja,* for that matter, was not unknown in southern India, which considered this divinity the sovereign of the country where "the mountain," his abode, was located. This circumstance, mentioned by Filliozat, is extremely useful in that it permits us to as-

SRI JAYAVARMAN IV

XVII. Shiva, the three-eyed god, having down through the ages seen the world defiled over long periods by the filth of the Kali era, went to earth to protect it, this resolute king who was a part of his own being.

XVIII. Even the masters of language were incapable of enumerating completely, word for word, like sages of a supernatural time, the majority of his miraculous qualities.

XIX. Sri Jayavarman, victorious, erected this *linga* of Shiva, aimed at obtaining an adequate treatment in the afterworld for his elder brother, who was born of the same mother and who bore the fortunate and significant name of Rajendravarman, the first of those who possess in abundance fame, virtue, intelligence, and wealth.

XX. Out of devotion, the king gave Shiva every sort of wealth. He erected a stucco-covered abode that resembled the highest peak of the king of the mountains, thus making the old indivisible Bull a sovereign worthy of homage, a friend of fortunate persons, living with him in great affluence.

Inscription of Prasat Damrei (Chap. 677)

sociate with Shiva the attribute *devaraja* formerly believed to pertain exclusively to the god Indra.

Judging by the evidence in our possession up to now, the cult of the *devaraja* appears to have been associated with certainty only with one temple, the Rong Chen. This observation is less surprising if one considers the fact that the Sdok Kak Thom inscription associates the *devaraja* only with four sovereigns: Jayavarman II and III, Indravarman I, and Jayavarman IV. Dupont links to this the no less significant fact that no worship was accorded the royal *linga* during the reigns of Jayavarman II and III; he deduces from this that the cult of the *devaraja* may have been practiced only by those sovereigns whose hereditary legitimacy was in some doubt. The others, whose right to the throne could not be contested, are believed to have transformed the cult into, or associated it with, personality cults—so important during the Angkorean period.

In conclusion, we are inclined to feel that the first ceremony on the Phnom Kulen, involving Jayavarman II and the Hindu priest Hiranyadama, had a clear political purpose. In effect, Jayavarman wanted to concentrate in the cult of the *devaraja* all the meanings implicit in the concept of royalty, which had previously been expressed by the rites involving the "sprinkling" of the sovereign and the consecration of the royal *linga*. It was, in substance, a solemn stressing of the parallel, or more precisely the identity, between the divine sovereignty and human sovereignty, so that the latter could avail itself of the former. The "message" was understood in these terms by those of his successors with a more acute political intuition, but particularly by those who stood most in need of consolidating such authority in themselves.

INDRAVARMAN I AND THE BIRTH OF THE CITY

Although Jayavarman II was succeeded by his son, Jayavarman III, who reigned between 850 and 877, the next truly important king of the Angkorean period was Indravarman I. According to the most recent studies, he was the true founder of Khmer power, from both the territorial and political standpoints. In climbing to the throne, Indravarman—born of a younger branch of the reigning family, his father perhaps being the uncle of Jayavarman III—inherited the lands of his predecessors, the fiefs belonging to his parents and to his wife's family. The size of his kingdom, insofar as it is possible for us today to know its precise confines, must have been relatively large. (And incidentally, it was during Indravarman I's reign that for the first time inscriptions began to refer to the kingdom of the Khmers as Kambuja, or Kambujadesa, or Kambupuri—all based on a mythical being, Kambu, from whom the Khmers claimed to have descended—the origin of our modern name for their land, Cambodia.) Indravarman I's privileged position and prestige must have led him to hope he could succeed in unifying a country that by then had been without true cohesion for centuries. These and other factors—such as the king's clear thinking and innate political abilities—provided the basis for the genuine progress achieved in the country during the last quarter of the ninth century. Signs indicative of the change are the commissioning of royal foundations—that is, religious and ceremonial structures—important both for their beauty and their value as symbols, and a return to the custom of honoring royal foundations with inscriptions.

Indravarman I reigned only twelve years (877–889), but during this brief time he initiated—and probably completed—a series of innovative works. The first of these seems to have been the digging of the Indratataka, a vast artificial lake that, thanks to a system of dams, collected the waters of the Roluos and the runoff of the region. This water was then channeled into the irrigation ditches in the fields below, and was also used to replenish the moats that surrounded the temples, the royal palace, and the municipal aqueducts. Any surplus water moved on into the natural lakes south of Angkor. Compared to the hydraulic works of the Funanese—whom the Khmers must have considered as their mentors—those built by Indravarman incorporated changes demanded by the different geographical conditions. The lowlands of the delta, where the Funanese had been, essentially required drainage. In the region of the Great Lakes around Angkor, it was a problem of providing for the regular irrigation of the rice paddies, both during periods when the river was in flood and when it was running shallow.

It seems superfluous to point out how beneficial this work must have been to the development of urban life. The abundance and planned distribution of water led to a series of positive consequences: a boost in agricultural productivity, demographic expansion, increased transportation facilities, trade, and building activity (public as well as religious-monumental works). In a word, the hydraulic works brought prosperity. As a result, the city spread out in all directions, and a modern scholar such as Groslier does not hesitate to nominate the organization of the Angkorean city as the crucial achievement of Indravarman I's reign, with the hydraulic system considered the prime cause of the capital's progress.

Having brought this vital task to completion, or at least seen it well underway, the king turned his attention to building a temple to be dedicated to his ancestors, thus initiating a tradition that was to endure down through the centuries. Preah Ko, as the temple has come to be known, is made up of six brick towers built on a raised platform, two boundary walls with entrance pavilions (gopuras)—the space between the two walls

Fortune, success, happiness, victory! Honor to Paramesvara!

I. Honor to Shiva, the supreme Lord, the supreme soul that, being by nature indivisible, assumes forms of its own will.
II. Honor to the god that carries the javelin, and who though indivisible, is ceaselessly decomposing, dwelling in innumerable beings.
V. The right arm of this prince [Indravarman], long and round, terrible in battle when it brought its vibrant sword down on the heads of the enemies, vanquisher of the kings of all the cardinal points, invincible.
VI. It was through the rite with which Svayambhu consecrated the Mahendra, elevating it to divine royalty [that is, establishing the cult of devaraja], that Sri Indravarman, endowed with all the virtues, including an irresistible heroism, received a consecration that was not indivisible.
IX. His step raised him to a height so prodigious that even the step of Vishnu Trivikrama could go no higher.
XI. How can these two objects be distinguished? It is clear that after having created the visage of this king, the creator, precisely in order to render a difference perceptible, marked the moon with the imprint of the gazelle.
XV. Although in his profundity he was like the ocean, it was the jewel of virtue that was seen to rise to the surface and not the foam of vice.
XIX. If the creator placed the earth and the sky with the moon in the ocean, it was because he feared the effect of the dust produced by the armies of this king and that of the smoke rising from the sacrifices from his abode.
XX. It is certainly for shame of having been vanquished by its beauty that the one who carries the makara [Love] as insignia is hidden still today in the spirit of men.
XXI. It was for fear that the earth might disintegrate under the weight of his marching elephants that the Creator bound it tightly together, using the king of serpents as a rope.
XXII. In that ocean so difficult to cross, battle, he used the decapitated heads of his enemies to build an embankment so that his troops could pass.
XXIII. As if out of a wish to guard the treasure of knowledge stored in the warehouse of his spirit, Sarasvati [eloquence] remained constantly at the threshold of his mouth.
XXIV. The virgin of the east, having fallen in love with this king whose ornament was his own glory, and overcome by the force of his spells, spontaneously presented him with tribute.

Inscription of the Preah Ko Stele (Chap. 713)

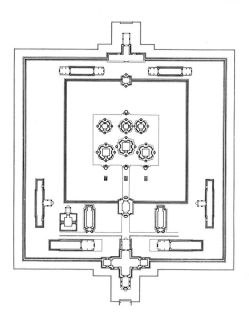

Preah Ko (Roluos): Ground plan of the temple.

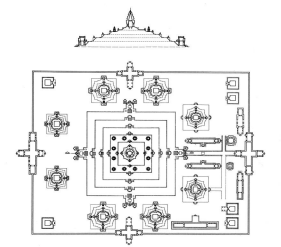

The Bakong (Roluos): Ground plan and elevation of the temple.

Following page:
The Bakheng (Angkor): A view of the upper sections of two towers at this temple (late ninth to early tenth centuries).

being occupied by several rectangular structures with a portico in front—and an outer moat. The towers, arranged in two rows and facing east, were erected in honor of the king's ancestors, the three front ones for the males, the three rear ones for the females.

At Preah Ko, the middle tower of the first and second rows contained, respectively, an image of Jayavarman II and his wife; and this central sanctuary was called the "Paramesvara," the king's posthumous name. By building such a temple, Indravarman again proved his adroitness as a politician, in that the dutiful act of homage to Jayavarman II (and which in theory should have been the concern of the latter's son and successor, Jayavarman III) tended to establish a direct link, even of spiritual descendance from this sovereign—to whom he was perhaps not related at all. Indeed, on an inscription listing his blood relatives, Indravarman I omitted the name of Jayavarman II, even though he gave him the place of honor in the Preah Ko temple.

In the history of the monuments of Khmer art, Preah Ko marks an important turning point, while simultaneously giving its name to the style characterizing the architectural and sculptural works of the period. The sanctuary's towers were built of brick, although this material was soon to be replaced by sandstone and laterite. But the architectural decoration is particularly striking. By now the lintel was dominated by leafy ornamentation, with two branches that reach out horizontally from a middle element (such as a *garuda,* with or without gods; a *kala,* a three-headed elephant with Indra; flowers). These branches bend outward, changing into the curious image of a *makara*-elephant holding a garland (or pendant) by the trunk, or an image of a *naga* with spread crests, or simply into a cluster of foliage. The originality, vivacity, and dynamism of these lintels—which Mme. de Coral Remusat has called "perhaps the most beautiful works of all Khmer art"—are expressed in particular by the fanciful inventiveness of the artists that places a host of tiny human figures in the very thick of the floral decoration.

Above the lintel is a sculptured frieze—a characteristic of this Preah Ko style—which functions as a transition element between the tympanum above and the lintel itself; such a frieze became necessary because of the lack of alignment between the upper molding of the pillars that support the pediment and the lintel itself. The *makara* and *naga* heads appear again on the lobed pediments, reminiscent, according to some experts, of the horseshoe arch of India (the *kudu*), while the tympanum bears the images of divinities accompanied by men in prayer, placed inside veritable miniature edifices.

The next important step taken by Indravarman I, at least as a builder, was the construction of the temple-mountain, the Bakong. The design of such a monumental complex, in which the temple is the fulcrum, appears at first glance to be quite obvious: an initial group of walls enclosing a five-step pyramid, eight main sanctuaries, a few buildings (towers or "libraries") of lesser importance, a strip of land with the lodgings of those assigned to staff the temple, and all this set off by another group of walls. Outside is a broad moat, broken only by four axial crossings—that is, they constitute an extension of the ideal axes, whose point of junction is at the very center of the pyramid-temple. Then comes another group of walls, and a large space of some 370,000 square yards, set aside perhaps for the buildings—of perishable materials—that composed the city proper. The entire complex, finally, was surrounded by a narrow moat, spanned like the first by a number of axial causeways.

Such a description makes it all seem easy to have designed, as we have said, but there is far more to it than meets the eye. The key to understanding the structure of this type is the interpretation of its symbolic structure. The Angkorean city, like those of India for that matter, follows rigorous laws of a cosmological and mystico-religious nature, admitting few variations to be dictated by the local terrain or conditions. First, as we have seen, the overall design is quadrangular—that is, it has the form of a

mandala, or "cosmogram, an entire universe in its essential makeup, in its process of emanation and reabsorption," as the Italian Orientalist Tucci puts it. "It is the universe not only in its inert spatial expanses but also as temporal revolution; it is one and the other as a vital process based on an essential principle and rotating around a central axis, Mount Meru, the *axis mundi* that holds up the heavens and sinks its foundation into the mysterious subsoil." The enclosing sets of walls, therefore, represent the successive stages in the progress of the initiated toward knowledge, the culminating point, the moment of direct contact with the divinity (in the design of the city, the approach to the temple-mountain, and the symbol of the divinity). Beyond this, on the cosmological level, the walls represent the mountains that surround the earth (which they believed to be square), while the moats symbolize the oceans. "The fundamental divisions of the internal surfaces of the *mandala,*" Tucci goes on to say, "are drawn following two main lines." And in fact, the city, like the temple, is rigorously divided into four parts by the principal axes, along which the entrance to the central sanctuary runs as well. The temple stands at the point where the two axes come together, so that it becomes the center of the world (as well as of the city), not only horizontally but also vertically, since the edifice follows an ideal axis uniting heaven and earth (zenith and nadir). The presence of a subterranean Meru in a position corresponding to this axis is symbolized, in the architecture, by a deep well, or shaft, dug exactly down from the middle *prasat,* or tower.

In the last analysis, the Khmer city was a microcosm that, by virtue of its perfect adherence to the image of the macrocosm, rendered possible a magical relationship between the two. Respect for the cosmic pattern therefore becomes necessary when there is a desire to guarantee, to the sovereign and to the people, the benevolence of heaven. Bearing all these elements in mind, we should then find it easier to understand why certain structures were used and the reason, too, why the Khmer artists—who certainly cannot be accused of a lack of ability or imagination—continued to repeat the same patterns, adapting them from time to time to specific needs but never changing them substantially.

But let us look more closely at the Bakong itself, particularly at the buildings within the inner circle of walls. At the center is a five-step pyramid, built of sandstone, almost perfectly square in shape (the foundation measuring some 220 feet by 215 feet) and about 45 feet high. Note the use of sandstone, which up to this time had been employed most sparingly, the architects having preferred small bricks. Sandstone, a soft stone with delicate nuances ranging from gray to rose, was to become especially suitable for the realization of the splendid bas-reliefs of this monument. On the top level of the step-pyramid is the sanctuary (although the one we view today was built in the twelfth century to replace the original one, somehow destroyed). The twelve towers of the fourth level and the eight towers at the foot of the pyramid (two on each side) belong to the time of Indravarman I. The towers rest on a low terrace with four approaching flights of stairs; they are square and have roofs of diminishing levels that repeat on a smaller scale the motif of the facade. The monotony of the design, based on layers of the same geometrical form, is broken by bringing into play the vertical elements offered by the high pediments that rise one above the other. On each of the four sides of the towers, the doors (or false doors) and the small columns and pilasters draw the eye upward, while the molding of the columns and pilasters and of the various levels mitigates the dryness of the horizontal lines. The empty spaces between the pilasters of the door and those of the corner are filled with images of *dvarapalas* ("guardians of the doors") and *devatas* (female divinities) arranged in large niches. The lintels are supported by small round or octagonal columns, richly decorated with floral motifs, as are the pediments and tympanums, all consistent with the Preah Ko style.

THE SRI INDRESVARA *LINGA*

III. He was a master of the earth, who became king in the designated years. The king of kings, Sri Indravarman, who possesses the power of Mahendra and Upendra.

XIX. Love who arms himself with flowers could not dwell in his heart, as if he feared the nearness of the god carrying the half-moon, jewellike, on his head [Shiva].

XXIII. In the indicated year of the [8] Vasus, the sky [0], and the [3] fires, this godlike king, dispenser of wealth, erected a *linga* named Sri Indresvara, here, on the jewel of the heads of the three worlds.

XXIV. And here, at the court of Sri Indresvara, for the joy of those who contemplated him and causing the unreserved wonder of the Tvastar himself.

XXV. He erected the eight bodies of the Lord, indicated as the royal use, which are the forms of the earth, the wind, fire, the moon, sun, water, ether, and of the sacrificer.

XXVIII. For these gods he built a number of stone *prasats* decorated on top in a pleasant form resembling seeds of religious merit.

XXIX. He erected an Isvara named Umagangapatisvara, with the hollow of the kidneys closed in by the vines of the arms of Uma and Ganga.

XLIV. "When I shall have obtained happiness, may this edifice become the joy of the world." It was with this thought that, full of compassion, he had a *nandika* made.

XLV. At the urging of Amratakesvaraswami, he erected there in the ashram of the gods a *linga* of Shiva extracted from the water.

XLVI. He made the Indratataka, mirror of his glory, like the ocean, having surrounded his residence with buttresses as if in fear of underwater fire.

Inscription of the Stele of Bakong (Chap. 826)

Inside each tower—at least as far as we can tell today—was a pedestal for the statue of the divinity. The ceiling of these interior cells rested on wooden beams, and the walls were lined with red plaster. The use of the towers is known to us thanks to an inscription found in a pavilion built here especially to house it. After an invocation to Shiva, the inscription states that the monument was erected by the sovereign in 881 to receive the *linga* Indresvara, while the towers symbolized the eight forms of Shiva—or, more exactly, the manifestations of the god through the eight elements: the sun, moon, wind, earth, water, fire, ether, and *atman* ("breath of life").

The text of this stele then enumerates the statues the sovereign ordered for this monument. Two of them—a Harihara, and a group with Shiva between Uma, his consort, and Ganga, her sister (see pages 50 and 51)—were found during the restoration of this monument. An analysis of such works and others belonging to the period has led to the conclusion that the representation of the human figure in the round differs from the previous models not so much through changes in iconographic details as in stylistic factors. The masculine garment, for instance, while maintaining the pocket on the left leg, converges toward the center in three groups of separate folds; the female garment preserves the cascade of folds in front, the edge folded over the belt, but brings a new touch by adding a fanlike drape that, descending from the waist, adorns the left side. The headdress is made up of a finely wrought diadem, topped by a smooth, conical, or bell-shaped, chignon, with superimposed circles.

Also typical of the Bakong are the lions at either side of the pyramid's stairway. Pleasing to the eye, with their exceptional vivacity, they were to become the prototype of lions that, in an ever more stylized form, were to flank Khmer temple stairways for centuries to come.

Public works, ancestor temple, temple-mountain: Indravarman I fulfilled his duties toward his subjects, his predecessors, and the concept of royalty by establishing an order, a "rhythm"—to use Stern's expression—that was to be maintained by his successors as well. It was not until the time of Rajendravarman II, in the second half of the tenth century, in fact, that the clear distinctions between the functions of the various temples were lost. But Indravarman I's son and successor, Yasovarman I (889–900), varied the rhythm somewhat by building an ancestor temple on an island in the middle of the artificial reservoir of Indratataka, which his father had built. All that remains of this monument, the Lolei, are the ruins of four towers erected on a raised terrace of not especially large dimensions. Evidently Yasovarman fulfilled his duties of filial piety at once because he realized his stay at the ancient Hariharalaya was to be brief. He must have begun early to think of emulating his predecessors by establishing his own capital—indeed, of surpassing them in grandeur. And it was due to this sovereign, Yasovarman I, in fact, that the city of Angkor developed where it did.

YASODHARAPURA: THE FIRST CITY AT ANGKOR

"Then His Majesty Paramasivaloka [Yasovarman] founded the royal city of Sri Yasodharapura and led the god-king [*kamraten jagat ta raja*] from Hariharalaya to this city. This His Majesty Paramasivaloka erected the central mountain [*vnam kantal*]. The Lord of Shivasrama placed a holy *linga* in the middle." With these words, the Sdok Kak Tmon stele tells us of the foundation by Yasovarman (here indicated by his posthumous name) of his new capital, Yasodharapura, situated a few miles northwest of Roluos, in the Angkor plain that constitutes the approximate geographical center of the kingdom. The choice was a particularly fortunate one because this area remained the site of the capitals of future kings—except for an interval at Koh Ker—for over three centuries.

After first deciphering this crucial inscription, by the way, the task of students of the Khmer civilization was to find the site of the royal city and the ruins of this "central mountain." The identification of this latter with the Bayon—the great temple-mountain at the center of Angkor Thom—at first appeared incontrovertible, and for many years Yasodharapura was believed to have been located within the walls of Angkor Thom. Finot advanced the first doubts that the Bayon, a temple in which the bas-reliefs were largely inspired by Buddhism, could be the temple-mountain of a Shivaite sovereign. And then Stern demonstrated through careful stylistic analysis that those same bas-reliefs dated to an era long after Yasovarman's reign (889–900). It became necessary, therefore, to resume the quest for the remains of the city of Yasodharapura.

The credit for having found the site goes to V. Goloubew, who began his search by making a painstaking study of the maps of the region, from which he drew the first indications of the layout of the city's ancient boundary walls; then he located the center of the city itself and also of the building that had been erected there. The careful reconstruction of the monument made it possible to identify what had at first seemed a heap of ruins as the Phnom Bakheng, the temple-mountain of Yasovarman I.

We know today, therefore, that after having built the ancestor temple, the Lolei, at Hariharalaya, the city associated with his predecessors, Yasovarman moved on and dedicated his efforts to a project that even a few details will convince us was colossal. On the Angkor plain he had constructed the great reservoir, the East Baray, measuring about 8,000 by 2,000 yards—four times as large as the Indratataka. This great reservoir is fed by the Siemreap River, the course of which at the mouth of the Baray is regulated by a series of dams and which runs along the eastern side of the city. As for the moats surrounding this latter, only two have been identified—that on the south, and the lower half of the one on the west; it has been impossible to locate the others because of subsequent construction on this area (such as the walls of Angkor Thom). The city of Yasodharapura was inside the area we have indicated and, like the Khmer cities that preceded and followed it, was built of light materials. The temple-mountain of the Bakheng, carefully sited in the middle of the town, was erected after the public works—that is, the reservoir.

The Bakheng deserves to occupy a place among the "great monuments" of the Khmers, and it also qualifies as one of the most interesting ones. Standing on a vast rectangular base is a square, five-step pyramid; the first step measures some 250 feet along each side, the last step some 155 feet. In the middle of the top step a platform, also square, supports five towers distributed in such a fashion as to occupy the corners and the middle: this pattern, repeated with so many of the Khmer temples, is sometimes known as the quincunx design, but we find it more vivid to refer to it as a five-towered sanctuary. The stairways to this central sanctuary are laid out to coincide with the four cardinal directions. The whole structure, by the way, sits on a small natural hill, and it is quite likely that this hill was the determinant factor in Yasovarman's choice of this site for his capital.

On the structure built on this hill, the architect had constructed a series of twelve towers on each of the five steps, while another forty-four towers decorate the great base. Along with the five that comprise the main sanctuary, the total number of towers thus comes to 109, and like virtually everything to do with the Khmers' architecture, this has its own symbolic significance. To understand this, we must first consider how the towers have been arranged. On the five levels, they are at either side of the stairway and in line with the corners; on the base, however, four towers in two rows flank the entrances to the pyramid, with another eight, of smaller dimensions, flanking these entrance pairs. The result (and the plan on page 58 makes this all clear) is that anyone viewing the temple from the middle of any side would see thirty-three towers.

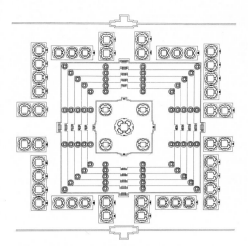

Phnom Bakheng (Angkor): Ground plan of the temple.

Now, to the ancient Khmers, such sequences as 33, 12, 60, or 109 all had specific meanings. And because Western commentators on ancient Cambodia have too often in the past explained artistic and cultural phenomena exclusively through religious and symbolic elements, we have been emphasizing up to now the practical usefulness and the social and economic aims behind certain works and actions of the various sovereigns. But with the Bakheng, we may admit that the predominant stimulus seems to have been precisely this religious-symbolic desire to re-create a perfect Mount Meru, a cosmogram exemplifying spatial and temporal meanings in every architectural detail.

Drawing on the symbolism inherent in the concept of Mount Meru—which we have previously discussed—a leading authority on Indian cosmology and astronomy, Jean Filliozat, interpreted all the numerical elements in the Bakheng. The 109 towers represented the axis of the world—the central one—and the 108 cosmic revolutions around the polar axis itself. In calendrical symbolism, 108 was also arrived at by multiplying 27 by 4—the lunar phase having twenty-seven days, with four such phases. The sixty towers on the five levels correspond to the cycle of revolutions of the planet Jupiter, while their division into twelve per step recalled the cycle of twelve animals, a typical Khmer motif. In order to represent a true Mount Meru, the Bakheng also had to express its role as the dwelling of the thirty-three gods, guided by Indra, who lived on the sacred mountain at the center of the universe. This explains why thirty-three towers were visible from the cardinal points. Mount Meru, moreover, supports the cities of Brahma, Shiva, and Vishnu, and is usually described as a mountain with five peaks. Filliozat rightly points out that the Bakheng thus becomes "the seat of the divine assembly, which under the principality of Indra and the sovereignty of Brahma, Shiva, and Vishnu, watches over the Order of the World. The role of the mountain is in keeping with the Indian ideal of royalty and with the panegyrics of Yasovarman found in the inscriptions," which in fact compare the sovereign to Indra, Brahma, Shiva, Vishnu, and even to Mount Meru. The circle thus closes again, establishing a link between the cosmic order, which comprises heaven and earth, the world of the gods and that of man, and divine and human royalty.

During his brief reign, Yasovarman had no occasion to build more works of such monumental nature. Despite an inscription's claim that this sovereign had five more temple-mountains erected, only three temples found can be dated to this era (late ninth to early tenth centuries)—the Phnom Krom, the Phnom Bok, and the Phnom Dei. From these, as from the Bakheng, elements have been extracted that have led to the designation of a style that takes its name from the Bakheng. In fact, this Bakheng style broke no new ground, but rather confined itself to the development of a number of motifs already noted at Preah Ko. In the realization of the lintels, for example, there is an impression of stagnation, of a lack of movement, stemming in part from the cramming of tiny figures among the foliage and in part from the increased heaviness of the central motif, which tends to drop toward the lower limit of the lintel and thus to make the two branches converge toward the center. The pediments, with broken or many-lobed arches, always end in a *makara* head, while a thick floral ornamentation, which will attain its full development at Koh Ker and in the Banteay Srei, appears in the tympanums, where it surrounds the main figure. The sculpture of the Bakheng style, however, brought interesting technical innovations, such as the use of a double stroke to stress the shape of the eyes and the mouth, or the thin line (in relief or etched) marking the contours of the moustache and the beard ending in a point on the chin. Other features on the face and the drapery of the clothing repeat the elements of previous periods, with perhaps a more pronounced stylization.

Left:
Prasat Kravanh (Angkor): This relief is from the interior of the central tower (dated to 621) and depicts Vishnu on the shoulders of Garuda, his "vehicle." In a change from the technique usually used with brick reliefs, the layer of plaster covering the relief is extremely thin. The Garuda was a mythical beast, a tamer of serpents, and had a human torso but the claws and other bodily parts of a bird. With its raised arms, Garuda supports the knees of the god, who is seated "Javanese style." Vishnu, in his lower right hand, holds the earth; in the upper right hand, the sun symbol; in his upper left hand, the shell; and in his lower left hand, a club. All these are the attributes with which Vishnu is usually represented in Cambodia. The Prasat Kravanh relief marks the beginning of a period when Garuda was often represented, and not only as the "vehicle" of Vishnu. Later the Garuda would be sculptured in the round and with large proportions, as at Koh Ker.

THE GREAT HYDRAULIC WORKS AND AGRICULTURE

In the foundation stele of Preah Ko and the Bakong, erected by Yasovarman's predecessor, Indravarman I, the sovereign is compared to Indra; to the moon; to Hari (Vishnu) drawing forth Sri (Prosperity, good fortune) from the "Churning of the Sea of Milk"; to Vishnu Trivikrama, who with three steps encircles and measures the world; and to Govinda (Krishna). Above and beyond the exaggerations of the panegyrist, we recognize in these comparisons the functions and powers that the Indian texts—with which the Khmer epigraphists obviously had both extensive and intensive familiarity—attributed to the king. Indra was the king of kings; the dispenser of rain, he thus presided over the fertility of the soil. The moon was bound up with vegetation as well, and was often identified with Soma, "god of plants."

The "vegetation theme" was recognized, at least from one point on, in the composite divinity of Krishna. The sway of the king over the land was expressed through Vishnu Trivikrama. This was also the meaning of the image of the "long arm" of the king—this, too, being an attribute of Vishnu—subjugating the sovereigns of all the cardinal points of the world. The scholar Gonda—who collected the data on Indian royalty— has underscored the importance the texts assign to the concept of space, vastness, extension: "Only if there is space can the blessings of heaven, light, and rain reach the ground; only then can the earth produce food;

Baksei Chamkrong: This is a view of the east facade of this stepped pyramid. The pyramid is of laterite, and measures some 80 feet along its base sides and is 43 feet high. The crowning tower, of brick and stucco, is another 36 feet high.

only then has man sufficient *Lebensraum*." The adversary of Indra in the great battle that was essentially a creation myth was called Vrtra (he who limits, covers, encloses). The space that Vishnu Trivikrama creates with his three steps renders possible the combat that is at the origin of the world and the power of the gods. The king, similarly, extending his territory and regulating the distribution of waters, determines the fertility of the soil, and hence the survival and prosperity of his subjects.

Let us now see how all this fits in with the realities of the Angkorean world. In the Angkor plain the irrigation system necessary for growing rice, the chief food, was highly complex. Bernard-Philippe Groslier, who has studied this subject closely, says that the drainage techniques developed earlier by the Funanese were used in conjunction with the distribution of water by the exploitation of the natural slopes—a technique tested in the more mountainous region of Chenla. Since the rains, brought by the southeast monsoons, are copious but concentrated in a brief period of the year—four months, compared to eight months of total aridity—and since the irrigated rice paddy has permanent need of abundant water that must be continuously renewed, it became necessary to create great basins or reservoirs—in other words, to collect all excess water and assure its regular distribution during the dry months.

The first great reservoir known to us today was the one that Indravar-

East Mebon (Angkor): Three of the five towers (the central and the two western towers) that belong to the main sanctuary; this temple is dated to 952. The temple base is of laterite, the towers are of brick.

man I had built, the Indratataka; it measured some 2¼ miles in length and ½ mile in width, occupying a position perpendicular to the slope descending to the Great Lake and hence along the course of the Roluos River. Stierlin, to whom we owe a particularly lucid description of the irrigation system employed in the Angkor plain, observes that the relationship between length and width and the position in relation to the slope made it possible to store a maximum quantity of water in the minimum space of excavated earth. This is a sign that the Indratataka reservoir was the crowning effort of a series of attempts that had probably begun during the reigns of Jayavarman II and Jayavarman III.

We also note that the water was found at a higher level than that of the surrounding plain, and this was the far-reaching innovation of the Khmer irrigation system. The earth dug on each side of the periphery of the reservoir was accumulated to form a wall along the same side. This wall-dam held back the water and made it possible for it to reach the higher level. Then, through a system of sluices and narrow ditches, water flowed downward by gravity to irrigate the fields, without a complex and costly system of pumps. The plain irrigated by this reservoir was rigidly subdivided; the various plots were surrounded by small dams that permitted perfect control of the levels and constant circulation of renewed water; each element in the system was bound up with all the others and was indispensable to the proper functioning of the whole.

This work of Indravarman represented the maximum exploitation of the Roluos site. Yasovarman, to create something similar, had to move farther north, and there he dug, as we have seen, the East Mebon, with a surface area four times that of the Indratataka. The two reservoirs together contained some 7 million cubic yards of water. Providing the necessary space, clearing the tropical forest, digging the great peripheral moats, building dams, creating the network of canals running out of the reservoirs, maintaining the systems (for waters heavy with slime, while valuable for their fertilizing properties, often cause clogging)—all this demanded coordinated and collective labor, a "superior cooperation" that only a centralized state could ensure.

The sole proprietor of the land was the king. Inscriptions proclaim him "master of the lower surface," and the king was requested to confirm all land transactions. Each time such a request was made, the detailed history of the plot in question was set forth, it being made clear who had used the land previously, often with a reference to the royal grant on which this use was based. Nor does the fact that the land was bought and sold (in reality, exchanged for other possessions: money did not come into general use in Cambodia, in fact, until fairly recent times) clash with this concept of royal property. The king's claim was on "superior property," attributed to the sovereign in that he embodied the entire collectivity in its state organization.

This very concept is to be found, for that matter, in Indian writings as well. Manu, author of the celebrated Indian "treatise on good government" (the *Dharmasastra*), seemed to contradict himself when he asserted that "the owner of the land is the king," and later said that "whoever was the first to clear a piece of land of the jungle became owner of that land." But it has been shown that there was no real contradiction, if along with the use of the land by those who farmed it we consider this "royal property," which was at the basis of all individual grants. This was a living concept until only recently in Cambodia and Thailand, in fact: it was the king who saw to the distribution of land. (And in Vietnam, as the scholar Chesneaux noted, the French tried to exploit precisely this deeply rooted concept of "superior property," to take land away from the village communities and hand it over to the great colonial companies.)

When we concentrate on Angkorean society, we note that at the outset of each new reign—or so it appears—the assignment of lands during the previous reign had to be confirmed. A careful analysis conducted by

East Mebon (Angkor): One of the four elephants placed at the corners of this temple-mountain; they are *dinnagas*, guardians of the four cardinal points, and were installed in temple-mountains from the Bakong on, until at the end of the tenth century the elephants were replaced by towers. The elephant was closely connected with royalty, as well as being a symbol of the earth; the "vehicle" of Indra, king of the gods, was the elephant Airavata.

Dupont on the epigraphy of Angkorean times showed that the most ancient land assignments do not date back further than Jayavarman II (the early ninth century). It is true that his reign was preceded by a period of political splintering. But none of the royal concessions made in earlier times (as recorded by inscriptions of the seventh and early eighth centuries) appears to have been confirmed in Angkorean times. It is therefore probable that Jayavarman II ordered a major redistribution of land.

THE POLITICAL AND SOCIAL SYSTEM

From the outset of the Angkorean period, the various principalities, known to have existed in the seventh and eighth centuries, were gradually converted into provinces *(pramans);* later the term *visaya* was used along with *praman.* Each province was ruled by a governor *(khlon visaya)* and was subdivided into *sruks,* an administrative unit corresponding to villages (with the terms *sruk* and *grama*—"village"—being used synonymously). In Angkorean epigraphy the terms *dasagrama* ("ten villages") and *satagrama* ("one hundred villages") appear in accordance with an Indian custom, as though indicating administrative units.

The control of the territory was exerted by the king through the bureaucratic apparatus, which had begun to take shape in its fundamental characteristics in the pre-Angkorean period but which over time be-

I. Homage to Shiva! His first energy is united to the *purusa* [original man], the second lies in *prakriti* [material], and both penetrate the universe.
II. This energy, Sambhavi [Durga], protects the world, through which Shiva, though indivisible, is seen in his various manifestations, like the moon through its image.
III. There was a supreme master of the earth, who had seized a stretch of land as far as Sindha, called Sri Suryavarmadeva, protected by the sun as by a jewel.
VI. There was a devoted slave, driver of the holy oxen, celebrated in this world as the shepherd Nanda, husband of Yasoda.
VII. Devoted to the well-being of the king, constantly honoring Shiva, he also concerned himself with Buddhists and other sects.
VIII. At the age of eighteen, Udayadityavarman appointed him to an office in the service of the gods and the Hindus.
IX. Later, on the occasion of the consecration of Sri Harsavarman and the other kings, he drove the sacred cow at the head of the procession around the royal palace.
X. Named head of the royal cattle drivers by Sri Suryavarmadeva, he also enjoyed the confidence of King Sri Dharanindravarman.
XI. Thanks to the favor of King Sri Suryavarmadeva, he restored the cow territory that had been damaged by the weather.
XII. Having received a bit of land among the treasures received through the favor of the king or obtained in some other way, and having drawn out their boundaries, he erected a number of divine images [Shiva, Vishnu, Devi].
XV. Desirous of obtaining the fruit of his merits, and having propitiated these gods with sacrifices, he installed a basin of water, a moat, around the temple, and a number of bridges along the road.
XVI. For the worship of the gods, during the last month, he assigned servants and fields. From the land he drew the supports of the *hetar* [fire priest], the sacrificer, and the servants.
XXVI. The lands, the *khnum*, the fields of the gods are under the jurisdiction of a man of my family who is *pandit* [priest] for the divine worship: the lands can be used for no other purpose.
XXVII. Thus having spoken, he cursed in these terms all those who destroyed his foundations: "Anyone who destroys this foundation will be as guilty as one who commits an offense against his spiritual mentor."

Inscription on the Trapeang Don On Stele (Chap. 254)

came more and more complex. During the course of the tenth and eleventh centuries we see the multiplication of administrative positions and the extremely subtle nuances in titles, a spectrum not always easy to separate. Nor do we have sufficient data to be able to draw a clear picture of how positions were assigned; we can only say that some of them were undoubtedly hereditary. Only a comparative study of the inscriptions, the following of a word through various epochs, and a consideration of its use in various contexts, could throw light on many such problems and supply indispensable data on the ramifications of the bureaucratic apparatus of Angkorean times.

A careful comparative study of the inscriptions would also be necessary for a more thorough knowledge of the makeup and organization of Khmer society. In this field, as in so many others involving the ancient Cambodians, many fundamental problems remain to be solved. The term *varna*, for instance—which in Sanskrit means "color"—refers to caste in its Indian context. And it sometimes had this meaning in Cambodia as well. But more frequently it indicated a group of persons with the same function; for instance, the *varna* of fan bearers, of temple guards, or of those assigned to take care of sacred vestments. Of the four traditional castes of India—namely, the *brahmana* (priests), *kshatriyas* (warriors), *vaisyas* (farmers, and later also artisans and merchants), and *sudra* (serfs)—it was the two top castes that were represented in Khmer society. The first of these, believed to have stemmed from a group of Indian priests, enjoyed exceptional power and numerous privileges. The one with the highest authority, the first among the priests—known as the *vrah guru*—actually consecrated the king and celebrated the ceremonies that assured a harmonious relationship between the real world and cosmic order, the basis of the reign's prosperity and stability, the well-being of its inhabitants, and a defense against disorder and destruction.

Numerous inscriptions were the work of priests, ostensibly glorifying the king but also serving to glorify themselves. The best known is that of Sdok Kak Thom, which we have had frequent occasion to cite. It was ordered by a great priestly family, the descendants (in the female line) of Shivakaivalya, a priest of the time of Jayavarman II. These descendants clung to the privilege of celebrating the *devaraja* rite for 250 years. The inscription is highly valued today because it gives us a good impression of the ceremony with which the royalty of Angkor was initially established, the succession of kings, and the vicissitudes of the reigns. But undoubtedly the motive behind the inscription was to underscore the privileges of the family itself, to furnish a complete list of the lands and religious foundations assigned by various sovereigns.

Probably the need arose to stress acquired rights in this solemn fashion. Indeed, we know that while the drafter of this inscription, Sadashiva Jayendravarman, was *vrah guru* during the reign of Udayadityavarman II (1050–1066), who conferred on him another title, almost equal to that of king, the ceremony for the consecration of the next king, Harshavarman III, was celebrated by Sankarapandita, who belonged to another family. What is more, in the early part of the eleventh century—that is, during the reign of Suryavarman I (1011–1049)—a number of great priestly families, who had furnished high officials for the administrative apparatus as well, inscribed their "swan song" (to use the expression of Briggs, who studied all the inscriptions relating to these families) and faded from history. The last of these families is the one that left us the inscription of Sdok Kak Thom (1052). This induced Briggs to conclude that Suryavarman I carried out some important religious-administrative reform destined to curb powers that had become excessive. Nevertheless, even though no great priestly families appear after Suryavarman I, the royal *vrah guru* continues to wield great power. We see, in fact, that in 1080 Divakarapandita legitimized the accession to the throne of a usurper, Jayavarman VI, and then consecrated (in 1107) Dharanin-

Angkor Wat: An aerial view, clearly showing the great moat that surrounds the temple and its precincts. The causeway across the moat is on the west approach.

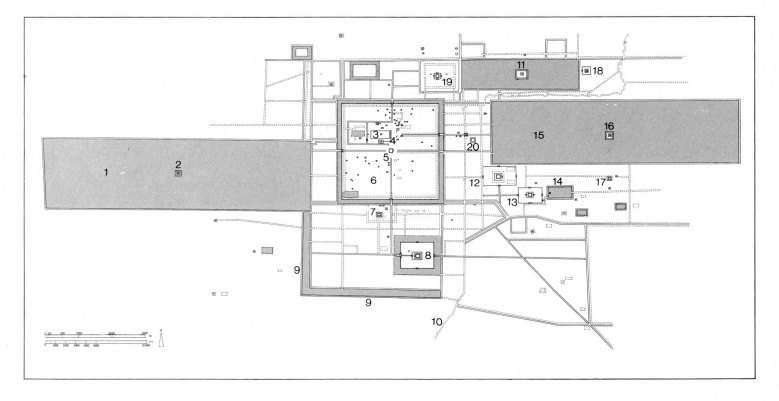

Prasat Kravanh (Angkor): This minor temple, dedicated to Vishnu in 921, is here seen from the east.

THE RESERVOIR OF YASOVARMAN

It was to open up a road for his glory, which had grown too great in this world, toward the nether regions, that he built the vast deep reservoir called Sri Yasodhara.

Inscription at Loe li

Northeast Corner
This king [Yasovarman] . . . also dug this Sri Yasodhara reservoir, which is as lovely as the moon, to refresh living beings.

Northwest Corner
And it was he [Yasovarman] who dug this reservoir equal to this disk of the moon whose substance had become water, reflecting like a mirror the beauties of earth.

Southwest Corner
He [Yasovarman] dug this reservoir similar to the lotus flower in which the creator [Brahma] is born; the restless waves that open up into blades of crystal when they beat the shores are the thousand marvelous petals of the lotus.

Southeast Corner
This king of kings dug this basin whose banks are profuse with trees and flowers. Built on a high level, thanks to a barrier, it is like the river of heaven that flows slowly when it descends from the head of the destroyer of the three fortresses, set in motion by the constant movement of its dance.

Inscription at the East Baray

Angkor: Plan of the capital area, with three of the great reservoirs (indicated in gray, as are moats and other bodies of water).

1 *West Baray*
2 *West Mebon*
3 *Phimeanakas*
4 *Baphuon*
5 *Bayon*
6 *Angkor Thom*
7 *Phnom Bakheng*
8 *Angkor Wat*
9 *Moat of ancient Yasodharapura*
10 *Siemreap River*
11 *Neak Pean*
12 *Ta Prohm*
13 *Banteay Kdei*
14 *Srah Srang*
15 *East Baray*
16 *East Mebon*
17 *Pre Rup*
18 *Ta Som*
19 *Preah Khan*
20 *Ta Keo*

dravarman I, his legitimate successor and brother. Yet Divakarapandita was able to throw his support behind one of Suryavarman I's nephews, who forcibly took the throne in 1133 as Suryavarman II and conferred an exceptionally high title on the *vrah guru* after his consecration.

Among a *vrah guru's* various duties was providing for the education of the heir to the throne. He also presided over the court of justice. The priestly class as a whole enjoyed great economic power, tied, as we shall see, to the control of the temples and, through these, to the exploitation of the produce of the land. We should also remember that the priestly caste was exempt from paying taxes, in that their tribute to the king consisted in part of accumulated "merit." As for the *kshatriya,* or warrior caste, it was essentially represented by the king himself, and as a group it shared political power with the brahmins, or priestly class, while wielding military power. However, it must be pointed out that Khmer epigraphy does not emphasize caste distinctions. The true distinction is between those who exerted some function—that is, representatives of the state apparatus, regardless of how major or minor the post—and those who were without such power.

Two groups who did hold power in the Khmer society deserve at least some mention: those responsible for the administration of justice, and those who made up the military organization. The supreme judicial power was, in fact, held by the king, who exerted it through a central court, presided over by the *vrah guru* and a court in each *visaya,* or province. The legal proceedings we know about involved primarily disputes over property boundaries. Punishment was chiefly corporal, but persons of high rank could have the sentence commuted to a fine. "Celestial judgment," which we discussed in the pre-Angkorean times, was still practiced, at least according to Chou Ta-Kuan, but there is no mention of it in the inscriptions.

The command of the armed forces, meanwhile, was delegated to the *mahasenapati,* who in the official hierarchy came immediately after the king, the royal princes, and the highest ministers of state. We have no way of knowing what system was used for recruiting. An inscription during the reign of Indravarman states: "The supreme king of the land must not press into his own service any of the servants of the Lord Indresvara or of any of the other gods. If an enemy army invades the kingdom, but only in this case, such servants can be called upon to destroy such an army." All indications are that the army was organized on the basis of the subdivision of the territory into provinces.

But of course most people in Khmer society lived out their lives untouched by such structures, and the one that concerned them most, according to Sedov—who studied Angkorean civilization in the light of the concept of "the Asiatic means of production," which we shall be discussing shortly—was the distinction between free men and non-free men, the *khnums.* Sedov deduces this fundamental division in Khmer society from the inscriptions. In bilingual inscriptions, the Khmer word *khnum* corresponds to the Sanskrit term *dasa,* which some scholars translate as "slaves" and others translate as "servants," depending on whether or not they support the view that slavery existed in ancient India. This is hardly the place to cope with such a question. But it should be pointed out that in India, as in Cambodia, although it has been proved that some individuals could not freely dispose of themselves, this relationship has connotations

Above:
Pre Rup (Angkor): Four of the five towers of the center of the temple, here seen from the east. On the left foreground is one of the towers that stand at the front of the temple; on the lower right is a window with small columns. The steps are of laterite, the towers are of brick lined with a thick layer of plaster. The terrace supporting these towers is 40 feet high.

Right:
Pre Rup (Angkor): A closer view of some of the towers that compose the central sanctuary of this temple, dated to 961.

Following pages:
Pre Rup (Angkor): Three of the central towers of the five-towered temple-mountain. In the middle one was the Rajendrabhadresvara *linga;* in the southeast one (left, in photo) Rajendravarmesvara was honored. In the other one (to right) tribute was paid to Visvarupa, mythical ancestor of the king; to Jayadevi, aunt of the king and wife of Jayavarman IV; and to Harshavarman II, son of Jayadevi and predecessor of Rajendravarman on the throne.

completely different from what we in the West today understand by "slavery"—or even by "serfdom" in the Middle Ages.

The *khnums* were almost always donated to the temples together with the land offered to the divinity for the maintenance of the religious foundation. Often the word *khnum* was followed by *vrah*—"that which is sacred." Alongside the name of each *khnum* we find the person's function listed: there are tillers of the rice paddies, but also women who clean the rice, women who grind materials for perfume, gate guards, cooks, musicians, dancers. But in indicating temple staff elsewhere, other terms were also used, such as *anak* (person) or *unvak* (member of a group); in other contexts, such words designate people who were unquestionably free.

It is true that the *khnums* were the object of various transactions: several inscriptions indicate who purchased them and at what price. But these were not "private" transactions. In the Phnom Chisor inscription, which can be dated to early in the eleventh century, one reads that in order to purchase a *khnum* needed at an *ashrama*, it was necessary to have the consent of the village elder *(gramavrddi)* and the inspector of the population *(trvac vala)*. Furthermore, the obligation of some *khnums* to contribute measures of rice to the temple periodically indicates that at least some of them enjoyed the fruits of a plot of land. Meanwhile, the stele of Prasat Trapeang Run (1006) lists two *khnums* among the village elders who acted as witnesses to the marking out of the confines of a sanctuary. Lastly, an inscription from a locality near Sambor, dated to 1001, was the work of an *khnum tem*—an expression Coedès translates as "former servant"—who seems to have been a person of some standing. His descendants *(santana)* were assigned to supervise the temple staff and to supply offerings annually. He asks the king for confirmation of these privileges for himself and his family.

As a result of such findings, it may be said that it is something of a distortion to translate *khnum* as "slave." On a specific basis, we might better use such expressions as "persons assigned to rice paddies" or "persons assigned to temples." In the latter case, we often find alongside the word *khnum* (as also alongside *anak*) the term *ple* (which in modern Cambodian is *phle*, "fruit"), followed by the name of the village of origin, as if what was involved was this territory's "fruit"—or, to put it in context, the tribute of manpower to the temple. And although a different translation for *khnum ple sruk* has also been suggested, the meaning behind the offerings of these persons to the temple remains constant: it was a human tribute that the village community set aside for the temple, along with the foods and objects of worship conscientiously listed in the inscriptions.

Also worthy of note is the fact that, contrary to usage in India, the farm produce to be handed over to religious foundations was never indicated in percentages. Perhaps this resulted from the fact that the full control exerted over irrigation made it possible to obtain a regular output, no longer dependent on the abundance of rain or the length of the dry season, and freed from the danger of floods. And it is possible to draw from the inscriptions a considerable quantity of data on the cultivation of land in common. Of the various terms that appear, some—such as *kule* (family), *santana* (descendants)—stand for blood relationships. Others—such as *vargga* and *varna*—designate persons acting in the interests of a common goal or who are engaged in the same activity (although this latter type, as we have seen in discussing the *varna,* was hereditary). All these words, by the way, are of Sanskrit derivation, reminding us once more of the strong Indian current in Khmer religious and social life. The relationship among these various groups, the exact meaning of some of these words in Khmer society, and whether or not some can be used as synonyms of others, can be established only after a strict comparative study. For the moment, we shall note only that Sedov believes that *vargga* refers to a farming commune.

IV. There was once a king, Sri Harshavarman, who possessed as an ornament the science of good conduct and whose feet, like a fine tree sprang out of the heads of kings, these mountains that reach forth all the way to the sea.
VI. Capable of pleasing creatures with his strength, he mastered the powerful, making the bitter sweet and that which is as small as an atom into a thing of great size, as the sun eclipses fire, the moon, and the stars.
VIII. With its luminosity, the fire of his warlike ardor ceaselessly illuminated the battle night with the lighted lamps that were his burning enemies, as if to render victory visible.
IX. Capable in following the rule, although he was cruel with the partisans of his adversaries, he satiated the crows and the other birds with the flesh of his enemies.
X. He had a courageous, honest dignitary with a hereditary post, who took pleasure in practicing the virtues of a dignitary, head of the third of the four royal storehouses.
XII. He received from the king the hereditary name beginning with Sri Nrapatindra and ending with -*varman*.
XIV. By order of the king Sri Harshavarman, in this city endowed with a new life, where he had installed a group of his relatives, he erected, in accordance with the rites, a two-cubit *linga*, as well as images of the immortal Vishnu and Bhava.

Inscription of Prasat Sralan (Chap. 782)

Pre Rup (Angkor): The entrance pavilions *(gopuras)* of the first and second enclosures, east side, seen from the sanctuary. Popular tradition has attributed a funeral function to the rectangular pit in the foreground, but this has never been confirmed; one scholar believes that it was used as a pedestal, perhaps for a statue of Nandi, Shiva's "vehicle." Similar pits, their length varying from 2 to 4 yards, are also found at other Pre Rup and Koh Ker style monuments, always near the main entrance and within the enclosure.

ANGKOREAN MODES OF PRODUCTION

The cultivation of the land entrusted, within the framework of the village community, to members of the same family *(kule)* gathered together in larger *ganas,* clearly stemmed from the ancient tribal structure. But now the various communities were integrated into a broader community that enabled them to achieve a higher degree of cooperation and therefore a more thorough exploitation of natural resources and more abundant crops. The organizer of production and cooperation, and at the same time the beneficiary of these, was now the larger state, acting through the bureaucratic apparatus. The various communities were absorbed by the state, which thus formed the "superior unity," summed up and expressed by the person of the king.

It would be useful to clarify the relationship between the functionaries of the central administration distributed in the provinces and the notables and elders of the villages. Chances are that the sovereign tended to shift the "natural leaders" from one place to another in order to exert a more direct control over the villages (as Chesneaux has suggested, although not specifically for Cambodia). In any event, the tie between the court functionaries and their native regions remained a strong one.

"The compensation for the economic functions carried out by the state," Chesneaux went on to say, "is the surplus demanded by the state and its agents. For the most part, this surplus is paid in kind, but at times it takes the form of labor on public works, offered free of charge by the inhabitants of the villages." The surplus products were taken to the public warehouses; part was stored, part was earmarked for public works—particularly those concerning irrigation or similar "prestige" projects. These latter were not, as has been charged, an expression of the "megalomania" of the kings, but rather the tangible representation of the "superior unity." The temple-mountains and the Khmer cities are nothing more than the substantiation of the ideology this society represented, an ideology that Chesneaux has summed up as a "feeling of the immutable order of the world." Springing from this sentiment is a representation of the ideal community, the creation of the corresponding terrain of the cosmic city, which precisely through its unchanging order guaranteed the preservation of the conditions on which life itself is based.

Another portion of the surplus production was assigned to the support of the army, some was transformed into merchandise—a matter to be discussed later—and a portion was redistributed to functionaries and royal foundations. The web of relationships surrounding royalty and religious foundations is highly complex. We shall describe it only briefly. There are numerous inscriptions where a dignitary informs the king that he intends to establish a religious foundation and requests permission to dedicate to the foundation's support the proceeds of the lands the king has granted him as payment for his work—or that he has acquired with just such a foundation in mind. The king is asked to confirm this offer, or possibly to grant a plot of vacant land so that the foundation can become a reality, and at the same time to assign to the donor's family or some specific members the care of the foundation and the exclusive right to exploit the land in question.

Once this request was granted, the land was marked off in the presence of several officials and a stele was set up certifying the family's exclusive rights. (And we might well recall the "cadastral stones" that in still more ancient times were set up in Cambodia to make it clear that a piece of land belonged to some group.) The persons receiving such land thus became "intermediaries" between the community and the religious foundation. Those who set up foundations, at least from a certain period on, would ask that they be proclaimed "royal foundations." This would bring substantial advantages in that the royal foundations were not only exempt from paying tribute but received food from the royal warehouses and

KAUNDINYA'S LINEAGE

IV. May Sambhu protect you with the greatest vigor, he who, although free from all passions and unshakable in yoga, nonetheless allowed himself to be seduced by the vivid looks from Gauri, and as a result reduced love to ashes.

VI. He was a king whose toenails had become dazzlingly shiny from having repeatedly rubbed against the sparkling crests of the king's jewels. Although being Baladitya [a rising sun], he was incomparable as a moon that closes the lotuses of hostile races. Born of the line of Soma and Kaundinya, he was the receptacle of all virtues to which the refulgence of his glory served as a parasol and that in Aminditapura, illuminated by his powerful arm, constituted the happiness of. royal Fortune.

VII. Like the sun greeted by the Siddhas, by the throngs of *apsaras,* by the most perfect Brahmans and the Kinnaras, he was incessantly adored by the most powerful kings, whose brows glittered with the dazzling redness of the dust from his feet.

X. He brought together in his person the courage of the lion, the force of the wind, the depth of the ocean, the sovereignty of Indra...the fortune of Hari, an energy superior to that of Kumara, the generosity of the lord of the Daityas, the intelligence of the lord of the gods.

XI. "Love burned, deprived of his members. It was with this thought that the Creator rendered this Lord invincible, eminent for his beauty.

XII. The dust raised by his army on the march. The sun held back, as if out of fear of being devoured by Rahu.

XXXIV. Descrying victory, which, terrorized by the point of his threatening sword and all red with the blood gushing forth from the torn chests of his enemies, hung on her neck, Glory went off as if enraged to the end of the world, and tenderly fond of her though he was, never again appeared before him.

XXXVI. Having abandoned the lotus of Hari, which was withered by the fire that had sprung from the inflamed mass of the poison vomited by the breath of the king of the serpents, as the bee abandons the yellow, dry, torn lotus that will never again revive, radiant Fortune appeared with joy in its resplendent visage, this other unblemished lotus, receptacle of all virtues, lovable flower, whose open petals are formed by its surpassing glory, whose pollen is its grace, whose honey is its smile.

XXXVII. Frightened by the smoke from its holocausts, which darkened all the regions, the lords of these latter took refuge in the woods, reduced to seeking their nourishment in the forest fruits.

XXXVIII. His arm was the dam of justice across the ocean of filth of the Kali, the serpent serving to agitate the treasures of the three worlds, the abode of this other Lakshmi that is his fame, the tree of desires, refuge of gods and sages, the support of the earth, Vishnu's arm itself.

XLI. Divakara has the ready intelligence, knowing the *Samaveda.* He destroyed by means of formulas the coils of serpents.

XLIII. Moreover, having erected, in accordance with the rules, an image of Vishnu in the city of Dvijendrapura of his dear Indralaksmi, the Indra of the Brahmans installed there a seminary for the most illustrious Hindus.

XLVIII. Having made Dvijendrapura an *asrama* here, participating with the god residing at Madhukanana, he prescribed the following services:

Following pages:
Banteay Srei: The approach to the temple and its main entrance pavilion (dated 967). Within the enclosure are three towers and, at left and right, the east pediments of the two "libraries." The low pillars lining the approach are not found at all temples; but they began to be used at some in the Preah Ko period.

other temples. Even when this was not the case, one could still obtain through a religious foundation confirmation of the exclusive right, for oneself and one's family, to farm a given piece of land. This right did not expire with the death of the person who had set up the foundation. However, when there were no direct descendants—and apparently as well in the case where all children were married and had already received their dowries—it was customary for the land to revert to the king.

The donation of precious objects to the temple—and we possess long lists of these objects, whose quantity certainly outstripped the needs of worship—was probably a means of saving surplus production. Lastly, we must not lose sight of the prestige element connected with the founding of a sacred image or a temple, an element that must certainly have played a crucial role in prompting a person to such a foundation. Particularly after the eleventh century, we see that there was one after the other; obviously the state thus controlled more extensive territory.

Unfortunately we have only scanty information regarding the unpaid labor imposed on the people in digging the reservoirs and canals and the construction of temples (what in European feudal societies was designated as *corvée*). Sahai, who conducted a study of the inscriptions in an effort to reproduce the administrative and political structure of the Khmer state, points to two inscriptions as proof of the fact that the *corvé* was carried out by the inhabitants of the villages. A number of elements can also be found in inscriptions showing that certain religious foundations were granted tax exemptions; inscriptions also state expressly that the temple staff is exonerated from the *corvée*. The same was true for the inhabitants of territories devoted exclusively to supplying some product or another to the royal warehouses, an example being a locality on the Plain of Reeds that furnished honey and wax.

The reference to these latter two products raises the question of the exchange of merchandise. Chou Ju-Qua, who left us a description of Chinese trade in the twelfth and thirteenth centuries, places Cambodia second only to Srivijaya (Java) as a producer of wax. Nevertheless, the country's commercial activity, which had been one of the main resources of Funan previously, seems to have become marginal by then. Chou Ta-Kuan reported at the end of the thirteenth century that Cambodia imported cloth from Malaysia and "the West" (probably a reference to India) and exported luxury products (particularly fragrant woods) to China. But the inscriptions give no significant details on such matters, and Angkor, as we have seen, took little part in commercial activities: its role was predominantly ceremonial, symbolic even.

With this admittedly, and necessarily sketchy, account of Angkorean economic life, let us see if this society between the ninth and twelfth centuries might be considered an instance of the "Asiatic means of production," a concept proposed by Karl Marx. He used this term specifically to define the means of production typical of several Oriental civilizations, but it has not been limited to these societies; the concept has been extended to include several states of Africa and, by some, even to the protohistory of the Mediterranean: All the characteristics pointed out by Marx as typical of this Asiatic means of production would also seem to be found in the civilization centered at Angkor. The economic structure was based on the village community, with its "indestructible" autarchy—rendered indestructible by the nonseparation between agriculture and handicrafts. The various communities were integrated into the "superior unity," the state as personified by the king and acting through the bureaucratic apparatus. The king was, as we have seen, the sole proprietor of the land, which he doled out to this person or that family, although their possession was never separate from the public function carried out. Surplus production, appropriated by the state through taxation, was used primarily in connection with the construction of great hydraulic works.

Above:
Banteay Srei: The inner sanctuary, viewed from the west. In the background, left, is the north "library," its tympanum decorated with a sculpture depicting the slaying of Kamsa by Krishna. (See close-up on page 80.) Tribhuvanamahesvara ("great lord Shiva, master of the three worlds") was venerated in the middle shrine. Worthy of note is the difference between the many-lobed pediments of the tower and those of the library. The former, which hark back to earlier styles, end on top in a more restrained curve; the latter give considerable emphasis to the undulating profile. Most of the temple of Banteay Srei was built of sandstone; only the vaulted roof of the portico of the central sanctuary is of brick. The proportions of this sanctuary are of such modest scale that it might really be thought of as a miniature temple; the doors seen here are only about 4 feet, 4 inches high.

Left:
Banteay Srei: East entry pavilion (gopura) of the outer enclosure. The triangular pediment calls to mind buildings with wooden roofs (Koh Ker, for example). The decoration of the tympanum is made up of floral elements that are in turn derived from a head of Kala, a mythical monster (lower middle portion).

In this regard, we might point out that there is serious doubt as to the inevitable tie between a "hydraulic society" and despotic power, as claimed by Wittfogel, who in the 1950s revived the question of the Asiatic production system, distorting it, however, for polemical ends. It has been shown, for example, that in Ceylon and Polynesia great hydraulic works were carried out either by groups of specialized workers connected with the monasteries (in Ceylon) or through promptings from an aristocracy (in Polynesia); but neither society gave rise to a centralized form of government. Nor, for that matter, are the "great works" undertaken by highly centralized governments always connected with irrigation projects.

What, then, was the fundamental class contradiction in an Asian society such as the Khmers? Perhaps it has been best expressed by one student of the subject, Tökei:

> In the states organized in this fashion, and which were always despotic, men were now divided into two great groups: those who themselves produced nothing but who in the name of the ever-larger communities collected taxes and appropriated surpluses; and the direct producers, the peasants in the village communities. These two groups, the first of which felt that it was a class apart from the other, adopting an increasingly aristocratic attitude, have different relationships with the means of production—above all, with the land. The peasants till the soil, while the aristocracy of functionaries acts, through the appropriation of the surpluses, as owners of the

land, as monopolizers of the means of production. Obviously one cannot speak of private ownership of the land; even the aristocracy acts as proprietor only in its totality, as the state. Membership in the 'community' is thus an essential basis of this group's behavior, too. But even these two forms of patriarchal possession are determined by two ways of belonging to the community. The peasants have the right to possess and till the land merely because they belong to the community; the aristocracy of the functionaries possess rights not only because they belong to the community but because they represent and personify it.

Alongside this distinction, which is the fundamental class conflict, Chesneaux has cited another, what he calls "structural," and it is this that he sets up against the "superior community," which springs from the combination of the "integrated" village communities and the state bureaucracy, the forces inclined toward the private appropriation of land. In Angkorean society, these forces were represented, as we have seen, by those functionaries who act as intermediaries between the community and the religious foundations. Nevertheless, according to Sedov's definition, "one cannot speak of private ownership of the land, as a general system, unless the person in possession of the land farms it for his own benefit, free from the interference of the state or that of the higher proprietor (the feudal lord). In the juridical sense, this independence of private property is represented most completely by the right *not* to farm one's own land."

At Angkor, such a thing was unthinkable, at least in the period we have considered: the state remained the supreme authority in this field and the greatest beneficiary. And what is more, the very basis of the economy, the village with its production-consumption unit, was in no way transformed or affected. This is why any forces inclined to appropriate land exclusively for their own benefit were defeated before they started. As we shall see, this society was to undergo a transformation in the second half of the twelfth century, but in this particular period, this system prevailed.

THE EVOLUTION OF THE TEMPLE-MOUNTAIN

Meanwhile, during the tenth and eleventh centuries, Khmer architecture was going through its own transformations. The key to understanding these changes are, of course, the great temple-mountains; the crucial work on this subject include the studies of Stern, Mme. de Coral Remusat, and Boisselier. One of the prime examples of what may be synthesized in a temple-mountain structure is to be seen in the Baksei Chamkrong (see page 61). This is a small building, made up of three laterite levels or terraces, with four axial stairways cutting up through them to the coronation sanctuary; this latter edifice stands on a high platform decorated with molding. We note the absence of the corner pillars that, except for the minor towers of the Bakheng, had heretofore never been missing from outside the chamber. The inscription on the pilasters, engraved in 948 during the reign of Rajendravarman II, records the main foundations of the first kings of Angkor, and then states; "In order to increase the *dharma* [merit] of his parents, he [Harshavarman I] followed the custom and erected these golden images of the two Isvaras [Shiva and Uma] and here at the foot of the Indradri [Indra's mountain] the images of the enemy of Mura [Vishnu] and of the two Devis."

This passage has led scholars to conclude that Harshavarman I, son and successor to Yarsovarman I, had initiated the construction of the Baksei Chamkrong, which was later to be completed by Rajendravarman II (to whom the inscription attributes "the splendor of this stucco-lined tower"). Only if we can identify the Indradri with the Baksei Chamkrong could we attribute this edifice, at least its lower part, to Harshavarman.

But other identifications have been proposed, and in his most recent translation of this inscription, Coedès, makes a sharp distinction between "here" and "Indradri." The fact remains that we know of no other temple-mountain that can be attributed to Harshavarman I; we would also have to consider that, if the building was erected entirely by Rajendravarman II, we would then have to ascribe to him no less than three temple-mountains. And, it is tempting to think that Rajendravarman, having completed the temple of a king who had preceded him on the throne of Angkor, united for the first time in one sole edifice the characteristics of the temple-mountain and those of the funeral temple.

But this is no more than guesswork. Until some enlightening new elements emerge, we must confine ourselves to stating that Harshavarman I certainly made a foundation in honor of his parents at the place where the Baksei Chamkrong stands, and that Rajendravarman built the crowning tower. This latter was made of brick, except for the cornice of the door and the three false doors, which were of sandstone and which therefore functioned as buttressing elements. Their decoration, based on floral motifs, calls to mind the craftsmanship usually associated with woodwork. The roof of the tower is made up of three diminishing tiers, each of which reproduces, in smaller proportions, the main body. On each of the tower's three tiers, at the base and at the crown, we again see the same molding as on the tower's platform. Compared to the temple-mountains examined earlier, Baksei Chamkrong exhibits a clear-cut tendency toward verticality.

Above, left:
Banteay Srei: The edge of a pediment from the east entrance pavilion. The arch's curved border ends in a lion's head, its jaws disgorging a many-headed *naga*.

Above, right:
Banteay Srei: Another pediment edge, this one with a *makara* head with a jewel dropping from its jaws. The *makara* was an imaginary crocodilelike beast, an emblem of water widely used in India and Southeast Asia.

Right:
Banteay Srei: A close-up of the east pediment of the north "library." This library stands before the tower with an inscription stating it was dedicated to Vishnu; thus the library's pediments are decorated with reliefs inspired by Vishnuite legends, particularly the cycle of Krishna, one of Vishnu's incarnations. At the top is the god Indra, the sky god, riding in a chariot drawn by a three-headed elephant and surrounded by winds. The rain coming down from Indra is rendered by the double ranks of diverging oblique lines. In the lower part of the relief is the Vrindavana forest: in the middle, Krishna and his foster brother Balarama are seen surrounded by a number of animals. The composition of this pediment's relief is exceptionally vivacious.

HYMN TO THE GODS

I. Honor to Shiva, whose powerful light spreads afar, brightening the darkness, as does ether in living beings and goodness in things.
II. Honor to Dhruva, support of the two heptahedrons of the world, at whose sparkling feet the bending gods are fixed, and who wears the half-moon on his diadem.
III. Victorious on the head of Hara, the waves surge and swell: undulated members of the divinity Ganges, donated by the generous ocean and the like to ten million young moons.
IV. Sparkling are the arms of Vishnu, which have adorned the Fortune of the three worlds, and which seem to be the four good rules of conduct, incarnate portions of their own image.
V. May the sounds of the *Veda*, murmured by the mouth of the four-faced Brahma, protect you from illusion, as from the threat of Yoganidra in the murder of the enemy.
VI. I greet Uma, into which the half moon, seeing that her face was a full moon, entered as if for shame into the fire of the heavy chignon of Shiva.
VII. Bharati, of the thin, pale body and the white breasts, shines like the Ganges, whose surfacing sandbars gild themselves in the stamens of the lotus.
VIII. I sing Kambu, who created all the kings of Cambodia, humiliating, with the glory of the families of the sun and the moon, the creations of the creators.
IX. The rulers of the land of Sri Kambu, who have conquered the world with their heroism and defeated the enemies of the Bull, glow like the long arms of Krishna, bearer of the disk.

Inscription at the Prasat Andon of Koh Ker
(Chap. 675)

The same "striving" upward, and made more imposing by the edifice's larger dimensions, appears in the temple complex of Prasat Thom, built at Koh Ker, a locality some 45 miles northwest of Angkor, where in 921 Jayavarman IV, brother of Yasovarman I and usurper of the throne, set up his capital. He was evidently obliged to settle here because the legitimate descendants of Yasovarman continued to reign at Angkor. (We know, in fact, that in 922 Isanavarman II succeeded his brother Harshavarman I—both being sons of Yasovarman I—but his reign lasted only to 928, when Jayavarman IV definitely got the upper hand.) The Prasat Thom is made up of six levels of sandstone; the largest measures some 205 feet and 210 feet; the height surviving today is some 115 feet. The temple culminated in a single tower-sanctuary; only the lower part of this remains, but the pedestal of its linga is still in place. There is only one stairway, and it is on the east side, by which one approaches the temple along a monumental way—some elements of which seem to have been built before the temple itself, although all are the work of Jayavarman IV.

The layout of the Prasat Thom complex (see plan, page 86) now requires us to consider the two basic types of sacred complexes of the Angkorean period. One was the "central design"—the pure temple-mountain. The other was the "longitudinal design"—the complex strung along an axis, such as the Prasat Thom. This latter type was almost obligatory when a religious complex was sited on the side of a hill, for the various "stages" then corresponded to the successive levels of the natural hillside (Wat Phu being an example of this). But as Prasat Thom indicates, the plan was also used on a flat area. In any case, it is worthwhile investigating this complex in some detail, since it brought out several new elements that were to lead to later developments of the first magnitude and that were to become characteristic of Khmer architecture.

One of these new developments was represented by the galleries, which appeared as prolongations of the north and south wings of the main entrance pavilions (gopuras). Their east side—which was, in almost all cases, the side by which religious edifices were to be approached—is made up of an unbroken wall, while that to the west is made up of a row of pillars. Judging by the sockets to be seen both in the wall and in the pillars, the roof must have been made of tiles fitted over a wooden frame. This is confirmed by "sketches" of buildings of perishable materials seen on bas-reliefs of a slightly later period. At Prasat Thom, two such galleries face each other on the axial causeway that, crossing over the moat, leads to the main complex. Here one encounters first a double set of walls, followed in the intervening space by a virtually uninterrupted row of buildings in the form of elongated rectangles, those on the north being linked by short galleries. This "chain" of edifices most likely set the precedent for the peripheral galleries that we shall see develop in the temple complexes of the last quarter of the century, attaining their maximum at Angkor Wat.

Rectangular buildings are also used in the Prasat Thom for that part we might call the "approach" to the temple. On the west side, in fact, two of them flank the galleries that prolong the main entrance pavilion. At the eastern entrance to the complex, lastly, we find both to the north and south of the approach a group of so-called "palaces"—four buildings on each side, laid out in a quadrangle to form a sort of courtyard. The name "palaces" is merely conventional and has nothing to do with the use of the buildings themselves, which is unknown to us. It is believed that this pattern was later to give rise to the cruciform courtyards found at Preah Vihear and Wat Phu. At Prasat Thom, as at the Preah Ko (page 53), the entrance pavilions of the outer enclosures are cruciform in shape; elsewhere the pavilions are simpler, in the form of rectangular rooms. Particularly noteworthy at the Prasat Thom is the entrance pavilion of the enclosure around the outer rim of the moat—the third: it was the custom, in fact, to number the enclosures from the inside out—which is a full-fledged tower (Prasat Kraham) and is the first significant example of the gopura's tendency to transform itself into a prasat, a tendency that was to come into its own in a later period.

In the central complex of Prasat Thom we see a series of towers laid out in two rows. Altogether there are nine towers: five in the first row, and four, somewhat larger, in the second, staggered slightly in relation to the first row. The one in the middle of the first row is preceded by a fore-structure, in which we can distinguish—in keeping with the rules and nomenclature of traditional Indian sacred architecture—the mandapa, a rectangular room; the antarala, a vestibule joining the mandapa with the sanctuary; and lastly, a pillared portico. This type of tower-sanctuary, which was to undergo further developments while becoming a common feature of Khmer temples, first emerges here at Koh Ker.

The platform with the nine towers is surrounded by twelve minor towers and preceded by two "libraries." This latter name, like that of the "palaces," is purely conventional, for in reality we have no idea what this type of building was used for. Such "libraries" have been found dating

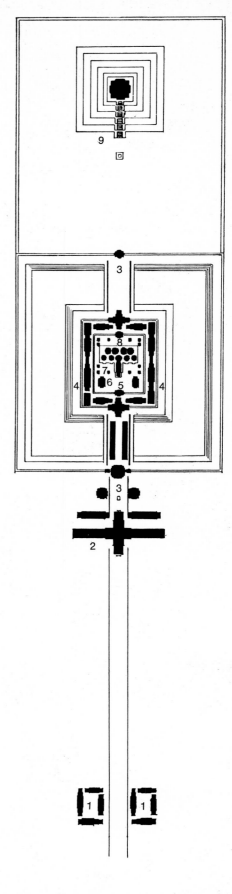

Prasat Thom of Koh Ker: Plan of the temple:
1 *"Palaces"*
2 *Main entrance pavilion*
3 *Entrance pavilions of the third enclosure (the east one is the Prasat Khraham)*
4 *Entrance pavilions of the second enclosure*
5 *Entrance pavilion of the first enclosure*
6 *"Libraries"*
7 *Twelve minor towers*
8 *Central complex with nine sanctuaries*
9 *Temple-mountain (known as "Prang")*

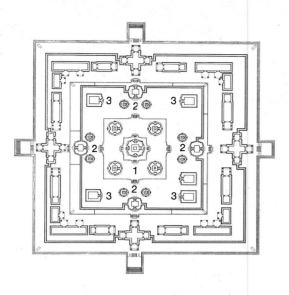

East Mebon (Angkor): Ground plan of temple:
1 Central shrine formed by five towers
2 Eight minor towers
3 "Libraries"

back as far as the Preah Ko period. Built of brick (except in the Bakheng, where they were of sandstone), they were square in shape, at least at the outset, and had one door only, plus a number of small windows. Such "libraries" were usually placed in front of the central sanctuary. In the Prasat Thom, a square shape was employed, but it was varied with a short extension. The materials of these Prasat Thom "libraries" are laterite, sandstone, and brick.

The causeway over the moat of the Prasat Thom complex, as at the Bakong, is flanked with a balustrade made of a quite realistically rendered body of a *naga,* or serpent-deity. Elsewhere at the Prasat Thom, the *garuda* motif was used extensively, both in the decoration of the lintel and in the figures in the round. The most outstanding characteristic of the sculpture here at Koh Ker is the predilection for completely free-standing figures, whether shown in movement—such as the two monkey-kings, Valin and Surgiva, locked in furious battle, found at the Prasat Chen, or the fine fragment, also representing two personages locked in battle, from the Prasat Thom—or static images of monumental proportions, such as the Sadashiva, found at the Prasat Kraham in fragments. Except for these examples, we need only say of the other sculptural elements at the Prasat Thom that on the lintels, a small scene occasionally appears in place of the frontal divinity.

The extremely short reign (942–944) of Harshavarman II, son of Jayavarman IV, appears to have produced no royal foundations. Harshavarman II was succeeded by his cousin Rajendravarman, whose foundations we know through three important inscriptions: at Baksei Chamkrong (948), at East Mebon (952), and at Pre Rup (961). All of these are, of course, at the Angkor site, to which Rajendravarman returned the capital. "He restored the sacred city of Yasodharapura, which had long remained empty," says the inscription at Bat Chum. At first the cult of royalty was celebrated on the island in the middle of the East Baray, where as early as four years before the completion of the Mebon temple, a *linga* and a number of statues had been placed. From the inscription of the East Mebon, we learn that the Rejendresvara *linga* was venerated there, which Rajendravarman had set up to "attain heaven and release."

The East Mebon unquestionably had the design of a temple-mountain, with the superimposition of diminishing levels (although there are only two); on the upper level were the eight towers, the eight bodies of Shiva, the constituent elements of the universe. The central sanctuary with its five towers was built on the terrace in the middle of the upper level. For the first time, a temple is supported by an entirely artificial construction—as opposed to any natural eminence. Perhaps this was what was behind the limitation of the number of levels; also, the temple was erected on artificially filled land. But the towers of the East Mebon were built of brick, and therefore lighter than those of the Bakheng, which were entirely of stone.

In building the East Mebon in the middle of the great reservoir dug by Yasovarman, Rajendravarman reaffirmed his own descent from this sovereign and at the same time "echoed" his work: Yasovarman, recall, had erected his ancestor temple, the Lolei, in the middle of Indravarman's reservoir, the Indratataka. Such factors—the analogy with the Lolei temple, the passage of the foundation inscription that mentions the images of Shiva and Parvati, erected "in honor" of and "in resemblance" to the parents of Rajendravarman, and the consideration that the "rhythm" of the Khmer sovereigns gave top priority to building the ancestor-temple—all these factors induce one to recognize in the East Mebon several of the characteristics of this type of temple. But what was the reason for joining the fundamental characteristics of both the ancestor-temple and the temple-mountain in one edifice? The difficulty in providing a satisfactory answer indicates how limited and fragmentary is our knowledge of the meanings and uses of the Khmer temples.

Ta Keo (Angkor): The main side of the temple, with its peripheral gallery's "false windows" (most of the columns that filled the windows having collapsed). The temple rises to a height (at the middle tower) of 126 feet, and measures some 400 by 330 feet along its base sides; the peripheral gallery measures some 320 by 300 feet.

It may well be that a solution to this problem could also explain the reason behind the building of two temple-mountains, for in 961 Rajendravarman consecrated Pre Rup, south of the East Baray. The Pre Rup temple is built on landfill and surrounded by a double rectangular enclosure. Between the first and second enclosure on three sides stands a succession of rectangular buildings with porticoes on their short sides. In the front of the temple—the east, of course—is a row of five great towers that originally were to have been joined by a sixth. The unbroken succession of rectangular edifices resumes in the inner enclosure. The central body is made up of two levels that support the terrace with the five-towered sanctuary, with twelve minor towers encircling the first level.

The inscriptions tell us in whose honor the five-towered sanctuary was erected. In the middle one was the *linga* of Rajendrabhadresvara, a name that unites that of the king and that of an aspect of Shiva, Bhadesvara, a dynastic divinity whose worship had been particularly widespread in Cambodia since pre-Angkorean times. In the southeast tower, the second in the order of importance, "he [Rajendravarman] set up this Isvara Rajendravarmesvara for his own prosperity, as if it were his own royal substance." In this instance, the name of the king maintains, while merging with that of Shiva, its ending in *-varman,* as opposed to what was usually the case with the middle *linga* of a temple-mountain. The *-varman* ending is kept, however, when a tower is dedicated to a king by his successor—in other words, in connection with a funeral rite. Coedès has raised the question, therefore—among other reasons, in consideration of the fact that the other three sanctuaries are dedicated to the royal ancestors—as to whether Rajendravarman did not dedicate this southeast sanctuary to himself, turning Pre Rup into a mausoleum.

Two temple-mountains were built in the time between the Pre Rup and the Baphuon (itself not built until the middle of the eleventh century): the Ta Keo and the Phimeanakas. The problem of their chronology has

Pre Rup (Angkor): Ground plan of the temple:
1 Central shrine formed by five towers
2 Twelve minor towers
3 "Libraries": The clear parts indicate the original construction; the dark parts indicate the later additions.

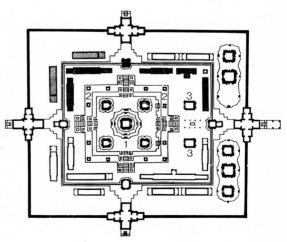

Part of a bronze statue of Vishnu Anantasayin, probably to be identified with one found in the West Mebon, in a temple built by Udayadityavarman II in the center of the vast West Baray (middle of the eleventh century). The statue is of grandiose proportions, this fragment alone being 3 feet, 9 inches high and some 7 feet long. (National Museum, Phnom Penh)

THE REBIRTH OF BUDDHISM

Thanks to the efforts of Kiripandita [priest during the reign of Jayavarman V] the law of Buddha reappeared from the darkness, as autumn brings out the moon that up to a short time before had been veiled by the clouds of the rainy season.

In his person the doctrines of emptiness and subjectivity, obscured by the night of false teachings, reappear like the sun that brings back the day.

He reignited the torch of the true law, the *sastra* Madhyavibhaja, and the others, that the destructive gusts of sin had extinguished. He brought in from foreign lands, in order to spread their study, many philosophical books and treatises, such as the Tattvasamgraha commentary.

Inscription at Wat Sithor (Chap. 11)

given rise to a long debate. Both have been identified at times with the temples mentioned in the Ta Keo and Lovek inscriptions, the *Hemasrngagiri* (Golden Horn Mountain) built by Jayavarman V, or the *Hemagiri* (Golden Mountain), whose construction appears to have been completed by Suryavarman I. It is believed that the Phimeanakas, the lower part of which is laterite, was built before the Ta Keo, dating back to the last quarter of the tenth century. Indications are that it was begun by Jayavarman V and completed by Suryavarman I, who also finished the Ta Keo (which may have been begun by Jayaviravarman).

At this point, a brief description of the political situation between the end of the tenth and the beginning of the eleventh centuries might prove helpful. In 968 Rajendravarman II was succeeded by Jayavarman V, who was still very young. The youth's education was not to be completed until 974, in fact, and it was supervised by Yajnavaraha, the first priest to enjoy the title of *vrah guru* as well as the one who founded the temple of Banteay Srei. Jayavarman V's reign lasted until the end of the century and marked, as we have noted earlier, an increase in the power of the great priestly families.

In 1001, the advent of Udayadityavarman I, who was not a direct descendant of Jayavarman V, unleashed a fight for succession, from which Jayaviravarman and Suryavarman emerged as the leading contenders. These two kings, who were once believed to have been only one man, seem to have reigned at the same time, the former at Angkor, the latter in the kingdom's eastern regions (as is indicated by the location of his inscriptions). But after a nine-year war (1002–1011), Suryavarman finally got the upper hand. His ascent to the throne was sealed by the oath of the *tamrvac* (a type of functionary who acted as messenger and inspector), which was inscribed in the *gopuras* of the royal palace and which bears the date 1011. (Suryavarman I was later to date the beginning of his reign at 1002, which was one reason for confusing him with Jayaviravarman.)

This reconstruction of the first years of the eleventh century (worked out by Coedès) draws on an abundance of inscriptions, partially in Sanskrit and partially in Khmer, of a high technical and linguistic quality. Particularly revealing are those of Suryavarman before 1011, all to be found in the east, and those of Jayaviravarman, who could employ the priests and stone cutters of the capital. The confusing dynastic struggles, moreover, may well provide an explanation of the fact that two temple-mountains were built during this period in successive stages; they may also explain the connection between the various phases and the incompleteness of the Ta Keo.

This temple, despite its grandiose dimensions and despite being lined entirely with sandstone, is devoid of decorations. Or, to be more exact, the decorations are found only in those parts that were usually dressed before being installed—in other words, the finishing stones, the columns supporting the lintels, the diminutive columns of the windows. It was just these few decorated elements that enabled Stern to establish the approximate date of the monument. He decided on a time between the Pre Rup (961) and the Banteay Srei (967), at one end, and the *gopuras* of the royal palace (1011) at the other extreme. Meanwhile, the pediments, unfortunately so rare, have allowed de Coral Remusat to confirm the date between the Banteay Srei and the royal palace *gopuras*. To this we may also add an analysis of two architectural elements—the towers and the "libraries"—conducted by Goloubew, who concluded by assigning the temple to a time "not long before Suryavarman I," as well as Coedès' study of the epigraphic material.

These dates fit perfectly with the study of Ta Keo's structure, which induced Stern to date it between the Pre Rup and the Baphuon. The design is similar to that of the Pre Rup: two rectangular terraces, the upper one supporting the three-level square base of the five-towered sanctuary. There are, however, several differences between the Ta Keo and the Pre Rup. Although both, for instance, have a central mass made up of three superimposed levels, in the Pre Rup there is a clear distinction between the two lower ones, simply square in shape, and the upper one, which is carved and is thus to be viewed as a full-fledged base of the five-towered sanctuary. In the Ta Keo, all the levels are carved. And although both the Pre Rup and the Ta Keo have the central sanctuary on a level base, in the Pre Rup it is the traditional kind with one entrance, facing east, while the one in the Ta Keo has four doors, each preceded by a forestructure and a connecting room. The Ta Keo is an example of the cruciform design we shall see again in the Phimeanakas sanctuary.

But the most interesting element at Ta Keo is the unbroken peripheral gallery that must be considered the result of the fusion of the rectangular edifices that were laid out as a "chain" at the Prasat Thom, the East Mebon, and Pre Rup. The gallery does not supplant these edifices altogether, however; two of them appear along the east side of the outer enclosure, and two, of lesser dimensions, run parallel to the gallery itself (also on the east side). Facing outside, the gallery has a series of walled windows, decorated with small columns; facing in, it has genuine windows. The *gopuras* are incorporated into the gallery, and elements appear at the corners that anticipate the development of the corner towers we shall see in the Baphuon and then, more extensively, at Angkor Wat.

The gallery's roof was probably of brick. This type of covering—made by corbeling bricks—had already been employed for the top part of the rectangular-chamber sanctuaries of pre-Angkorean times; later, corbeling was used for the "libraries," the extensions of the entrance pavilions, and the foreparts of the sanctuaries. But all these spaces were more limited than an extended gallery. Galleries of smaller dimensions than those of Ta Keo, with supporting walls of sandstone and brick roofs, had already been used in two buildings erected at virtually the same time as the Banteay Srei (967)—the Prasat Trapeang Khyang (see page 113) and

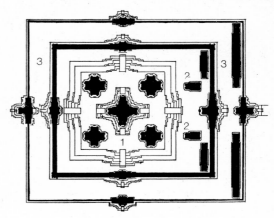

Ta Keo (Angkor): Ground plan of the temple:
1 *Central shrine formed by five towers*
2 *"Libraries"*
3 *Peripheral galleries*

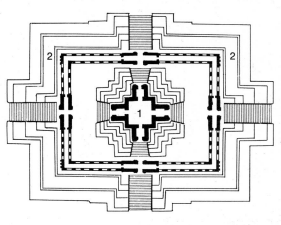

Phimeanakas (Angkor): Ground plan of the temple:
1 Central cruciform tower
2 Peripheral gallery

the Prasat Sek Ta Tuy. Another type of gallery roof, used with success at the Prasat Thom of Koh Ker, was that of tiles built over a wooden frame (again, see the drawing on page 113).

The first gallery built entirely of sandstone was that of Phimeanakas; but it was of smaller dimensions and its height was limited. The blocks of sandstone were laid out in three rows on each side, with a "closing block" to form a pseudovault. The top surface of the roof is bell-shaped and the stone is dressed in such a way as to imitate tiles; the inner part of the blocks is carefully leveled. Perhaps the modest dimensions of the monument (which measures only 115 by 92 feet at the base) encouraged the architects to try their hand at a gallery entirely covered with sandstone and with walls broken by large openings, both inside and out. The three terraces are of laterite, while the gallery, the multiple-stepped base, and the lone cruciform sanctuary were built with reused materials.

The Phimeanakas occupies an area of the royal palace, the only secular building of durable materials that has come down to us. Its construction is assigned to the period running from Rajendravarman to Suryavarman I, but there were many later additions and modifications. In this connection, we quote Boisselier: "The royal palace, as it is to be seen today, and bearing in mind the disappearance of all constructions in light materials, is a rectangular enclosure facing east-west, with a double wall broken by five *gopuras*. In the front part, with its center approximately at the Phimeanakas, there are two reservoirs, plus terraces and shrines. The west side has a complex of courtyards with terraced reservoirs."

THE BAPHUON AND BANTEAY SREI

In the middle of the eleventh century, Suryavarman I was succeeded by Udayadityavarman II, who has been credited with building Angkor's great reservoir, the West Baray; it measures some 5 miles by 1½ miles, and the West Mebon was later built in the middle of it. Udayadityavarman II is also credited with building the Baphuon, the second largest (after Angkor Wat) of the Khmer temple-mountains. An inscription at the Lovek reads: "Having seen the Golden Mountain [Hemadri] looming in the middle of the Jamudvipa, the dwelling of the gods, he [Udayadityavarman II] had a golden mountain built, as if in emulation, in the center of the city. At the very top of this golden mountain in a golden temple, shining with divine splendor, he placed a *linga* of Shiva, to be honored with ablutions in the temples. This king entrusted Sankarapandita, who was well versed in all knowledge, with the office of *guru*, in order to ensure the absolute effectiveness of his sacrifices. Going to the top of this mountain, ornament of the three worlds, on the propitious fifteenth of the month, the protector of the earth named the illustrious sage priest of the golden *linga*."

Coedès tied this inscription in with that of the Preah Nok stele, found at the very foot of the Baphuon. This latter inscription commemorates the offering by General Sangrama of the wealth—received from the king as recompense for his victories—to the golden *linga* "in which resides the invisible and subtle I [self: *suksmantaratman*]" of King Udayadityavarman II. A study of the architectural structure and the decorative elements confirms a date somewhere around the middle of the eleventh century.

The Baphuon is preceded by an elevated approach some 220 yards long, flanked by two rectangular pools. Its design is rectangular, and it is divided into three parts. Situated on the east and west side of the first terrace, which is entirely surrounded by a sandstone gallery with clearly delineated corner towers, is a pair of "libraries," unusual in that they are of cruciform shape. They are connected to one another and have axial *gopuras* like footbridges on low pillars, in accordance with a pattern to be repeated in the cruciform porticoes of Angkor Wat.

The second and third terraces as well are enclosed by a sandstone

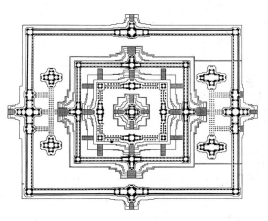

Baphuon (Angkor): Ground plan of the temple.

gallery. We see that for the first time each level is divided into two parts, the upper one being of smaller dimensions (whereas before this design of successively receding levels was confined to the base of the main sanctuary). The gallery of the first terrace presents to the outside an unbroken facade; the interior has a series of windows. The gallery of the second terrace has windows outside as well. The pseudovault of the second gallery is made up of four rows of sandstone blocks, and is closed on the top by two blocks placed close together. The gallery's dimensions are larger than the Phimeanakas': the architects had acquired a greater sureness in constructing stone roofs, even for rooms of considerable length.

Another element that assumed considerable importance in the Baphuon temple—with decorative effects made more effective by the fact that the heights between levels to be surmounted had increased—were the stairways. In addition to the stairways that led from the four axial *gopuras,* between the second and third terrace near each corner, two ramps converged toward the corner towers, proving the importance these latter were acquiring.

But, as Boisselier rightly observes, by reducing the distance between the enclosures, placing the weight of a stone gallery complete with *gopura* and corner towers on each terrace, even that supporting the central sanctuary, on a triple base, and at the same time increasing the height of the three bodies, the architects of the Baphuon "altered the profile's balance" and caused the building's eventual ruin. To be sure, the designers tried to take measures against this danger: it is known that metal crampons were used in the *gopuras* to bind the blocks together, and reinforcing wood beams were widely employed as well. These latter, in accordance with a system already used at Koh Ker, were inserted into blocks of stone especially hollowed out for this purpose and which were not obliged to bear any real weight. At first the method seemed advantageous; in addition to lightening the weight, in fact, it created the long spans necessary for the galleries. Nevertheless, as the centuries went by, the wood used, although of high quality and exceptionally resistant, rotted away; this was all the more serious in that the wood was encased within stone, and this latter was unable to bear the weight now made to rest on it.

Let us turn back to the outset of the tenth century and examine a number of structures that were not founded by kings but through the efforts of dignitaries and priests. In 921, a group of Vishnuite dignitaries dedicated the Prasat Kravanh to Vishnu Trailokyanatha ("Lord of the Three Worlds"). A characteristic element of this building, built of brick, is represented by the reliefs, which contrary to custom are located inside the tower-sanctuary. (As Boisselier has pointed out, however, one might find some point of comparison in a number of statues placed in grottoes during the tenth and eleventh centuries. Another point of comparison would be the paintings inside the two sanctuaries of the Prasat Neang Khmau, which dates to 928, the only example of the Angkorean period that has survived.) Facing each other inside the middle sanctuary of the Prasat Kravanh is a relief of Vishnu Trivikrama (that is, Vishnu in the act of taking the three steps) and another of Vishnu on Garuda (see page 60). Frontal though they are, these images testify to a quest for rhythm and an intention to represent movement, as opposed to the image on the wall opposite the entrance, an eight-armed Vishnu, rigidly frontal and immobile, flanked by six registers of figures of worshipers (who are also portrayed frontally). This distribution, which is also to be found on a number of steles, corresponds to that of the Prasat Neang Khmau. The attributes Vishnu carries in his hand suggest that this was a cosmic portrait of the god, who summed up in himself all the main divinities. The northern sanctuary, on the other hand, is dedicated to Lakshmi, the Hindu goddess of fortune; she is shown with four arms, and carrying in her hand the *trisula* (a trident, an attribute of Shiva), the *cakra* (the cosmic wheel, attribute of Vishnu), the *padma* (lotus), and the *ankusa* (the hooked

Angkor Wat: Pediment of the gallery on the upper terrace (first half of the twelfth century). This is an example of a tympanum with figures set into the pediment's arch, this latter element decorated with a floral motif and a double row of "pearls."

pole used in guiding elephants). The fact that the goddess carried the attributes both of Shiva and Vishnu testifies to the syncretic nature of Khmer religion.

In the second half of the tenth century, two Shivaite priests founded the temple of Banteay Srei, about 12 miles northeast of Angkor. The founding stele (discovered in 1936 by Marchal) both tells us the date the temple was completed (967) and lists the names of the founders: Yajnavaraha, royal *guru,* and his younger brother, Vishnukumara. Yajnavaraha was *guru* under both Rajendravarman and Jayavarman V; the latter ascended the throne in 968—the date of the inscription itself. It is thus not surprising that alongside the praise of Rajendravarman— the Banteay Srei was built in his reign—we also find praise of his successor.

The design of the Banteay Srei harks back to that of the Prasat Thom of Koh Ker. We find again rectangular buildings lined up along the space running between the first two enclosures, and the cruciform *gopuras* in the second and third enclosures. The towers of the central complex are only three, as compared to the nine of the Prasat Thom, but they are of the same type. The approach to the temple, however, has taken on a greater importance and reflects a more organic development. Two arcades flank it along its entire length, broken about midway by two closed rooms, preceded by porticoes. Perpendicular to these closed rooms, both on the north and on the south, are two elongated buildings that open out with two windows to the east. (Such a complex is nothing more than a variation of the cruciform *gopura,* which at Prasat Thom separated the entrance from the temple area proper.) The buildings that at Koh Ker run parallel on the inner side to the extensions of the north and south

HOMAGE TO SRI JAYAVARMAN

I. Homage to Sambhu, who possesses the attribute of the word, which transcends the perception that fills all, which has forms of space.
II. May Satkhi, daughter of the mountain, ardent, faithful wife, closely united to Shiva, contribute to the happiness of living beings.
III. In the Satanaka tree of the descendants of the kings stemming from Sri Kambu, Sri Jayavarman was son of Rajendravarman.
IV. His subjects, immersed in the uncrossable, deep, and terrible ocean of the unhappiness of the time, having reached him like a high bank, regained their senses.
V. Since all the kings, beginning with that of Cambodia, had bowed before him trustingly, he did not even place his hand on his bow, out of benevolence toward virtuous persons.
XII. This supreme king, of a splendor equal to that of the king of the gods, had a *guru,* a master of Shivaite rites of initiation.
XIII. Son of the daughter of King Harshavarman, who was son of Yasovarman and nephew of Indravarman, he was the foremost of the notables.
XIV. His father was the Brahmin Damodara, an adept of the *Rig Veda,* equal in intelligence and nobility to the chaplain of Indra.
XV. Having attained the one who possesses resplendent beauty, the sciences, luminous by nature, shone sparklingly, like the rays of the sun striking a mirror.
XVI. In a saintly manner, he each day practiced, with the same regularity with which he took his meals, the offering of a garland of eight flowers, the oblations over fire, and the disciplines of yoga.
XVII. Each month, in the four phases of the moon, he generously donated to the Hindus gold, garments, and cows with swelling udders.
XVIII. King Sri Jayavarman, who lived with him, constantly honored this sage with parasols of peacock feathers, gold litters, and other marks of esteem.
XIX. With the help of those who develop the sciences taught in the home, and others, he destroyed in himself as in other people the errors of the weak in spirit.
XX. He was the first in the knowledge of the doctrines of Patanjali, Kanada, Aksapada, Kapila, Buddha, in those of medicine, music, and astronomy.
XXI. In his fatherland he ordered writers to compose brief tales, he who knew various languages and writings and himself wrote dramas.
XXII. With medicines, wealth, and science, he wiped out the suffering of man: illness, injustice, poverty, and error.
XXIII. The poor, the disinherited, the blind, the weak, children, the aged, the ill, and other unfortunate people desirous of crossing the ocean of suffering filled his dwelling every day.
XXVI. At Lingapura and other places he founded numerous *lingas* of Shiva, accompanied by statues, reservoirs of water, and ashrams.

Inscription at Banteay Srei (Chap. 575)

wings of the *gopura* have been duplicated, at least as far as the southern part is concerned. But compared to the Prasat Thom of Koh Ker, the dimensions at Banteay Srei are smaller; we find ourselves facing a veritable "miniature" masterpiece.

After the edifices of laterite that characterized the Angkorean architecture of the tenth century, we find once again extensive use of sandstone. It may be that this had something to do with a desire to connect back with the styles of Preah Ko and the Bakheng, as can also be seen in the decorative elements. This tendency to imitate the monuments of Indravarman and Yasovarman, particularly in the decoration, is also visible in the relief of the East Mebon and the Pre Rup, which were virtually of the same period as the Banteay Srei. But at the Banteay Srei, alongside this contrived archaism, a completely new element takes on an importance: the pediment decorated with a scene in which numerous human figures appear. These pediments—among which those of the "libraries" (see pages 80 and 83) stand out for the richness of their composition—are without precedent in Angkorean art. To explain the great mastery the artist shows in placing figures in space, in representing in a lively fashion both the movement and psychological attitudes of the figures, in balancing the numerous elements without resorting to further subdivisions or to registers, de Coral Remusat puts forth the theory that behind the Banteay Srei relief carving was a pictorial tradition of which, unfortunately, only a few traces have survived. (But we might also note the interest in the portrayal of images immersed in space and in movement that the sculptors of the Prasat Thom had shown.) Portrayed in the northern library are stories of Krishna (an incarnation of Vishnu): on the

east tympanum, the slaying of King Kamsa (narrated in the *Bhagavata Purana* and the *Harivamsa* of India); on the eastern side, the onrush of a tempest in the forest where Krishna and Balarama were sheltered. Stories of Shiva appear in the south library's tympanums, in which the god is shown on the summit of Mount Kailasa. On the west tympanum Shiva is portrayed while the demon Ravana, with its many heads and arms, shakes the mountain; on the east tympanum, Shiva is the target of the god of love, Kama.

The Banteay Srei style is contemporary with both the style of the Pre Rup and that of the Kleangs (two monuments standing east of the royal palace at Angkor). At Banteay Srei analogies with the Pre Rup style are evident in the figures in the round, while the style of the Kleangs is influenced by both the Pre Rup and Banteay Srei. Narrative reliefs were to reappear around the middle of the eleventh century, with the stories of Krishna and Rama on the walls of the *gopuras* of the Baphuon. The composition is divided into superimposed registers, each of which portrays a moment in the unfolding of the legend. The narration is vivacious and flowing, the figures generally lined up in a row, but in a variety of attitudes. Often, smaller figures appear as well in a higher position. The environment is indicated with a few revealing details. Despite the pattern that calls for small rectangles, we find the same "happy touch" in distributing the figures in space that we saw at Banteay Srei. And an examination of the reliefs of the Baphuon reveals that in Cambodia, as in Laos and Burma, a local version of the Hindu epic, the *Ramayana,* took hold.

RELIGIOUS LIFE OF THE KHMERS

We have noted that Hinduism and Buddhism were coexisting in Funan at least by the fifth and sixth centuries. This is not the place to become involved in the details of these two great religions as they originated in India, but we shall consider the various changes and developments they

Above:
Angkor Wat: The long causeway that approaches the west facade, with three of the five towers of the central shrine visible in the background and two small "libraries" (left and right) in the middle distance. (This outer approach causeway and its adjacent areas and structures lie outside the area of the plan of Angkor Wat on page 109.) The name Angkor Wat means something like "the capital monastery," *Angkor* being derived from *nagara,* the Sanskrit word for "city," and *Wat* from the word for "monastery." This is not the name, of course, by which its ancient Khmer builders or users knew it, but was attached to it by later Cambodians.

Right:
Angkor Wat: A view of the temple, focusing on the north end of the west facade. In the foreground, the water is one of the two pools outside the external boundary. (A corner of this same pool is visible at the upper right of the picture on page 99.)

Angkor Wat: A view of the approach and the outer gallery, with the cruciform courtyard in the foreground. The outer gallery has a central entrance pavilion flanked by two smaller side gateways; then comes the long causeway with its *naga* balustrades on the projecting sets of stairs on both sides, and the two free-standing "libraries" alongside the causeway. In the very center of the foreground is the pediment of the center gallery of the cruciform courtyard; not visible (because of the foreshortening of the photograph) is the cruciform platform (No. 2 on the plan on page 109), which sits outside the cruciform courtyard, at the end of the causeway.

KING SRI SURYAVARMAN

I. Homage to Shiva, whose manifest portions, which are called Sarva and other names, must because of the presence in them of the sovereign *atman* and the other attributes be known by those who aspire to release.

II. Homage to Shiva, from whom Isa received the order to free from their bonds, with an exact application of knowledge, those who are bound by the ties of the inner soul.

V. Honor Vishnu, whose adorned breast of the Kaustubha rivals that of Sri, richly studded in the center with rubies and sapphires.

VI. I adore the Non-created [Brahma], who recites the Vedas with all four mouths at the same time, as if to imitate the simultaneous murmur of the four oceans.

VII. There was once a King Suryavarman, with blue lotus eyes, whose virtue, in imitation of the sun, which made the lotus grow, assured the constant prospering of each action undertaken.

XI. Only abode of coolness and warmth, because he united in himself the moon and the sun, he was created by the god born of the lotus [Brahma] to fulfill the duties of the *kshatriya*.

XIII. In the lake of his heart purified by the ambrosia of traditional science, Sarasvati, imitating the gait of the *hamsa*, chose as his residence the lotus of his mouth.

XVIII. On the land darkened under the dust raised by his marching army, all beings were alike, as before the creation.

XIX. The enemy army was like a beautiful young woman, all spotless, presented to him by the Creator for his amusement.

XXIII. When thanks to his skill in battle he would cleave enemies in two like the trunks of banana trees, he would have liked to have had strength enough to split bodies as tough as the thunderbolt of Indra.

XXXIII. The ardor of the kings, after having met up with him, melted away like that of the eclipse before the sun, that of the elephant before the lion, that of the serpents before Garuda, and that of the fire before the forest.

XXXVIII. Having abandoned the kings defeated in battle, Fortune came to him, as to the morning moon, difficult to vanquish, sparkling with a penetrating brightness.

XL. Fickle when she was in the care of kings, less constant than the ocean from which she was born, Fortune became faithful when she came into the custody of the one who was as constant as the ocean itself.

XLVII. During this sovereign's reign, no one had to fear that his possessions would be snatched away from him, not even if they happened to fall asleep in the depths of a forest.

passed through in Cambodia—and whenever possible, clarify the reasons. (Many of our conclusions, by the way, are drawn from the fundamental study of Hinduism in Cambodia, by K. Bhattachary, who carefully examined both the iconography and the epigraphic sources.) As for the Buddhism of Funan, it is impossible to establish whether it was of the Hinayanic ("Small Vehicle") variety—the earliest form, with its emphasis on the doctrine of Buddha—or the Mahayanic ("Great Vehicle") variety—a later form, with emphasis on the worship of a divine Buddha and Bodhisattvas. The first clearly Buddhist inscription that has come down to us, composed during the reign of Rudravarman (514–539), throws no light on this question. And although it has been shown that Mahayanic Buddhism was present on the Malay peninsula at this period, we cannot be certain about Cambodia.

Bhavavarman I and Sitrasena, the Chenla kings who conquered Funan, were fervant Shivaites—which simply means they were of that sect within Hinduism that concentrated on Shiva. Their immediate successors were also Shivaites, yet there are also unquestionable testimonials of donations to Buddhist sanctuaries as well as of foundations by Vishnuites—those Hindus who concentrated their worship on Vishnu. Two inscriptions, one from the end of the seventh and the other from the end of the eighth century, testify to the diffusion of Mahayana Buddhism, while representations of Bodhisattvas such as Lokesvara and Maitreya confirm this. But the Hinayana inscriptions are much more numerous, implying that this school established itself in Chenla before the other.

The only sovereign of the early Angkorean period openly to declare himself to be a Vishnuite (as was his mentor, Srinivasakavi) was Jayavarman III. But we should not lose sight of the fact that, whatever the religion primarily practiced by a sovereign, other sects and faiths flourished simultaneously and even remained under his protection. Yasovarman I, for instance, began his reign (889) by building near the great reservoir that bears his name three *ashramas* (monasteries): one for the Shivaites, one for the Vishnuites, and one for the Buddhists. And this coexistence of different faiths—with Shivaism, admittedly, persisting as the major "state religion"—is what characterizes the religious history of Cambodia. This syncretism in the pre-Angkorean epoch found its most concrete (at least for us) manifestation in the abundance of Harihara statues—he being the deity who combined Shiva and Vishnu in his person. In inscriptions, too, there are constant testimonials to such syncretism. It will suffice to point to the Basak (Romduol) inscription, which invokes Shiva in the first stanza, Vishnu Trivikrama in the third, and addresses itself to Harihara in the second. Such testimonials attract our attention today, of course, because they seem to represent some contamination of two currents. But they must have seemed perfectly normal to the Khmers, who for centuries had been accustomed to worshiping the two major divinities of Hinduism alongside still other deities.

Cambodian epigraphy contains frequent passages recognizing philosophical and religious ideas drawn from the main writings of post-Vedic Hinduism: the *Upanishads,* the *Puranas,* and the *Agamas.* It has been shown that a previous epoch already knew the diffusion of the Vedanta—the movement that took hold in India after the seventh century and that considers ritual as only the first step toward the supreme truth of the doctrine according to which "one is all." This was, of course, a monistic concept: Shiva is identical with *brahma,* the transcendental absolute, the sole reality, and at the same time is perceptible in each and every one of us as an inner light. "It is through his *sakti* (energy) that [Shiva] manifests himself, under different forms, through the infinite unfolding of the three *gunas,*" is how Bhattachary puts it in setting forth the theory of creation according to Shivaism. "The one Shiva thus becomes multiple. The entire creation, which began with Brahma and ended with the grass, resulted from the *sakti* of Shiva. Shiva is the sole cause of the universe, the

XLIX. If an illness, however mild, happened to afflict one of his subjects, it troubled all the joys of this compassionate sovereign, as if it were among the most serious and cruel events.
LX. Full of sympathy for the debtor who had no possessions, he could turn over to his creditor, he generally provided him with the necessary funds to free himself from the debt.
LXII. Possessing a thorough knowledge of the intimate meanings of all the treatises, he marked the religious festivals by making everyone perform the prescribed religious rites, beginning with the worship service.
LXIII. Generous with the poor, he stripped and rendered poor like a guilty person all those who had acquired a great fortune, whether it was the result of an inheritance or loyalty toward himself.
LXV. He usually gave a quantity of wealth to all those who asked for it, while he himself, a rich man thanks to inheritances from previous kings, ate leftovers from a wooden bowl.
LXVI. If one of the tax collectors, whose fortunes should have been used to do good to others did the very opposite, he rejected him like an enemy, even if he was dear to him, so great was his love for generosity.
LXVII. With rich donations he assured his heroic, faithful, glory-covered generals a financial position equal to that of a king.

Inscription of Prasat Khna (Chap. 661)

HOMAGE TO SHIVA

The one whom the sages adore like an inner light, desirous of attaining the supreme state, the absolute Brahma.

The one through whom the practices of mortification, study, and sacrifice, although devoted entirely to Him, procure ineffable fruits, not only for those who are still attached to the acquiring of fruits from these works, but also for those who, detached, have renounced them totally.

The one whose foot is without support, endowed with slenderness and other qualities intrinsic to him, and that are developed through the action of the energies that He personifies, outstripping the power of all thoughts and all words, is known by the sage.

Inscription at Phnom Bayang

Angkor Wat: A close-up of the extrados (exterior curve of a vault) of the galleries that make up the cruciform courtyard. The roofs of the vaulted galleries at Angkor Wat are completely of stone, but as this photograph reveals, they imitate the appearance of tiled roofs, with the characteristic curves and horizontal breaks of tiles. At the ends of these sandstone false tiles are decorative antefixes in the form of a lotus petal or the head of an animal, such as a lion, a *garuda,* or a *naga.*

Angkor Wat: One of the many flights of stairs leading off the long causeway, with the balustrade that ends in the *nagas*. The many-crested serpents curve up at the ends of these balustrades, turning a functional element into a dramatically decorative element.

Left:
Angkor Wat: A view of the inner courtyard gallery, with a "library" in the foreground, the cruciform courtyard in the middle, and the long approach in the background.

beginning and end of beings, the one who himself has neither beginning nor end. The Trinity (Brahma, Vishnu, and Rudra) which fulfills the three cosmic functions—creation, conservation, and dissolution—emanates from him, who returns, at the end of the *yuga* (era), in other words, of the destruction, into his absolute unity." Such a summary is based on a combination of different inscriptions from Cambodia. The image that appears most frequently in the inscriptions of the Angkorean period is that of light in water, which breaks up into a myriad of parts although it remains one: this signifies the immanence of Shiva in a tangible manner. Particularly venerated, too, was the *sakti,* a reflection of the god and his creative energy in terms of a female divinity.

The same monistic tendency that asserted itself in Shivaism was present in Vishnuism, with its emphasis on the transcendency and the immanence of the god, as well as his nature as creator, preserver, and destroyer of the world. "Penetrating all matter, he is the smallest of atoms; absorbing in himself the entire Universe, he is the greatest of the great elements," says the Prasat Trapeang Run inscription. There is therefore a fundamental identity between the two supreme Hindu deities, an identity for that matter already explicitly affirmed in a number of Indian sources such as the *Harivamsa* and the *Vishnu-Purana,* writings well known in

Cambodia—and on which much of the carved motifs in the temples were based. In Vishnuism, greater stress was laid on the devotional aspect, or *bhakti,* the trusting abandonment of self to the god, who alone can be the source of salvation. The theory of *avataras,* the aspects or incarnations Vishnu assumed to succor mankind—including the *Varaha* (boar), *Mrsimha* (man-lion), or *Kurma* (tortoise)—is amply reflected in Khmer iconography, too, particularly in the period of Jayavarman VII.

Khmer syncretism not only involved Shivaism and Vishnuism—which, as we have noted, was favored in sharing an essentially identical nuclear faith—but was also extended to Buddhism. The period with the greatest profusion of testimonials to this phenomenon was the reign of Suryavarman I (1011–1050), who, as we have seen, was probably the promoter of an administrative-religious reform with the aim of limiting the power of the great priestly families. Perhaps it is in this motive that we shall find the cause of the favor accorded by Suryavarman I to Buddhism, and not so much in his supposed Malaysian origin (regarding which the evidence is still too fragile). The posthumous name assumed by this king was Nirvanapada, which would seem significant; yet the name does not rule out a Hindu faith, and in inscriptions Suryavarman I is extolled, among other things, as protector of Shivaism. Certainly the first unquestionably Buddhist sovereign was Dharanindravarman II (1150–1160), father of Jayavarman VII, although it was not until the reign of the latter that Buddhism was installed as the dominant religion of the Khmer state.

One of the more interesting problems that arises in clarifying the reasons why some elements took hold rather then others, in connection with Hinduism in Cambodia, is that concerning the relationship between Hinduism and the autochthonous religion. The autochthonous religious substratum of India and Southeast Asia today draws the attention of scholars, but it has been difficult to distinguish among the various elements. There is no doubt, however, that many of them converged into Shivaism, in which they have been, so to speak, "systematized." This was probably the reason behind the great diffusion of Shivaism in Southeast Asia. The local populations, in fact, recognized in this religion various characteristics that were already part of their own religious patrimony.

One significant testimony to this comes from a Chinese source, *Sui Shu (History of the Shu).* This tells us, in discussing Chenla, that "near the capital there is a mountain called Ling-kia-po-po, atop which stands a temple guarded night and day by a thousand soldiers and consecrated to a spirit called Po-to-li, to which human sacrifices are made. Each year the king goes to this temple to make a human sacrifice in the dead of night." The Ling-kia-po-po (*Lingaparvata* in the Khmer inscriptions) was identified with the mountain overlooking the site of Wat Phu. It was on this mountain that Shiva Bhadresvara was worshiped. All the characteristics of the rite described by this Chinese text, a rite performed on the mountain by the king in person, without the aid of a priest but with the support of a victim, lead back to the religious substratum that was basic to "Asia of the monsoons" (as has been masterfully described by Paul Mus).

As we indicated in the very first section, it was a question of the relationship of a group with the god of the territory (the territory, that is, belonging to that group), a god represented by a stone fixed in the ground. By means of a sacrifice, a bloody one celebrated by the leader of the group, the faithful accorded a momentary support to the divinity. And while the sacrifice was being carried out, it was possible to communicate with the divinity and at the same time to open up a passage to the afterworld. Ancestor worship as well, and even more specifically the worship of the dead king—in that he was buried in the ground and hence became a part of the world with which an attempt was being made to establish contact—leads back to the nucleus of autochthonous beliefs.

In concluding, we might note that "territorial divinities" (*Neakta*) are

Left:
A head of Shiva from Banteay Srei (dated 967). Typical of representations of Shiva is the hairdo, with the hair tightened together in a knot and the third (vertical) eye in the center of the forehead.

Angkor Wat: The stairway leading to the central tower of the temple. (Three saffron-robed Buddhist monks are descending.)

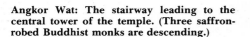

Angkor Wat: A *Buddhapada*, or representation of the imprint of Buddha's foot. This work, which is similar to Siamese images, may perhaps belong to the second half of the sixteenth century, by which time Buddhists had taken over Angkor Wat and converted it into a monastery.

worshiped in Cambodia to this day, bound up with a given territory, the best known being that at Khleang Muong of Pursat. Legend has it that around the end of the sixteenth century the king went to Banteay Chei ("citadel of victory"), a few miles from Pursat. Since the war against the Siamese was going badly, he ordered his men to dig a ditch and to place a quantity of arms in it; then he hurled himself into its depths. A few days later, the Siamese arrived to lay siege to the citadel; but they were soon decimated by the army of the dead whom the sovereign had gone to collect in the world beyond. Each year this victory is marked in the month of *vissakh* (April–May), which precedes the work in the rice paddies, and an agrarian rite has also been added to the celebrations. There is every reason to believe that as such syncretism has persisted to our time, so it once was pervasive throughout ancient Cambodia.

ANGKOR WAT: CULMINATION OF THE TEMPLE-MOUNTAIN

In an imaginary history of the masterpieces created by human genius through the centuries, Angkor Wat would certainly be given its place as the supreme work of the "classical" period of the Khmer civilization. In fact, this is the monument that most effectively sums up the artistic, technical, and spiritual experiences of this people, and then expresses all this most creatively and thoroughly. With Angkor Wat, the Khmer artists reached the point beyond which there could be nothing but excess or repetition or mannerism—in the technical sense, decadence, which is to be understood not as an exclusively negative development but as a period of stagnation, or even expectation, in which the yeast of the next age can ferment and ripen. But Angkor Wat stands before this, a mature classic.

The credit for building this monument must be ascribed to a large group of artists and artisans, not—as some would have it—to the creative genius of one man, royal architect or sovereign or whoever he might be. As for the principal architects, we do not even know the men's names, since all Khmer works of art have come down to us absolutely anonymous. The sovereign who commissioned it, however, was Suryavarman II, who is mentioned in the histories as the protagonist of numerous territorial conquests and extolled by inscriptions as a heroic warrior. Although a usurper of the direct successor, Suryavarman belonged to the dynasty founded in 1080 by Jayavarman VI, a sovereign in connection with whom no inscription or royal foundations have been found, even in Angkor territory. The genealogical data regarding Jayavarman VI is found on steles ordered by his two most authoritative successors, Suryavarman II and Jayavarman VII, and it is through this means that we are familiar with the descendants of the nobility of Mahidharapura and their lack of any kingship ties with sovereigns of previous Angkorean dynasties. (Mahidharapura has been placed as north of the Dangrek Hills, and Jayavarman VI evidently based his capital there for some time.)

It is not unlikely that Jayavarman VI was "elected" sovereign of Cambodia (and was consecrated as such by the priest Divakarapandita) and that he founded the new dynasty while the legitimate sovereign Harshavarman III, or his successor (perhaps Nrpatindravarman) continued to reign at Angkor. In any event, there is no doubt that Divakarapandita made a wise choice in abandoning Harshavarman III for the new sovereign, for not only was the priest loaded with gifts but, as we have

Angkor Wat: The inner courtyard, with a "library" (lower left) and a corner tower (center). Note that the inner wall of the gallery is broken by both real and false windows filled with small columns.

Angkor Wat: A view of an inner courtyard of the middle gallery; the stairway to the gallery on the upper terrace is on the right; on the left is a portico from the cruciform courtyard's gallery, while through it, in the background, is seen a "library."

seen, he remained *vrah guru* to three generations of sovereigns. At an advanced age, he was in a position to commission the inscriptions of Phnom Sandak and Preah Vihear, thanks to which we are familiar with the events of these years.

Jayavarman VI was succeeded for six years by Dharanindravarman I, his younger brother. Then a grandnephew of Jayavarman VI, Suryavarman, "took over the royalty, unifying a double kingdom," as an inscription at Wat Phu puts it. The two kingdoms referred to must have been those of Dharanindravarman I, who ruled at Mahidharapura, and Nrpatindavarman, who belonged to the Angkor dynasty. The road that Suryavarman II took to the throne was probably a difficult one, along which he almost certainly met with stiff opposition. The entire span of his lifetime was characterized by one struggle after the other. He focused his attention first on the east, promoting military campaigns against the Dai Viet with the help of the Chams. When this venture fell through, because of the breakdown of his alliance with the Chams, he turned against Champa itself. The Chams were caught so completely unaware by this sudden shift that they capitulated, and for several years (1145–1149) they had to endure Khmer occupation.

It turned out to be more difficult to realize Suryavarman's territorial ambitions in the west. The *Thai Chronicles* tell of a conflict between the principality of Lavo (Lopburi), which had long been a Khmer possession, and that of Haripunjaya, which was occupied by the Mons. In spite of Khmer victories at the outset, the conflict did not lead to the total defeat of the Mons. The particulars of this episode escape us, the chronology is shaky, and possibly the sources are biased. The fact remains that the

kingdom of Suryavarman II played a significant role in the history of the Khmers, if only because of its great size. But perhaps more important, Suryavarman's kingdom exercised enough political influence for the Emperor of China to confer the title of "great vassal" upon the sovereign. And if all such data suggest the image of an ambitious, powerful monarch continually engaged in grandiose political schemes, it is perhaps the temple of Angkor Wat that best expressed this sovereign's "will to power" and imperial designs.

George Coedès has said of Angkor Wat: "It is a masterpiece of Khmer art, built during the lifetime of the king to serve him afterwards as a funeral temple in which he was to be deified as a statue of Vishnu with the posthumous name of Paramavishnuloka." This says it all succinctly, but behind such a definition lies so much that we must start with a detailed description of the edifice. At the time when he set about building his monumental temple-mountain, Suryavarman II confronted a problem: the finding of a site sufficiently vast to enable him to construct an edifice worthy of his greatness and his aspirations. Whatever the layout of the city of Angkor was at this time, including the areas of ancient Yasodharapura and of the future Angkor Thom, the constructions of the tenth and eleventh centuries occupied a considerable part of the available land. As a result, Suryavarman chose the southeast corner of Yasodharapura, a space evidently free of buildings of durable materials, yet one where he could take advantage of the network of canals laid out by Yasovarman for his capital.

A moat some 650 feet across enclosed a rectangular area roughly one-half mile square. Along its sides a continuous stairway enabled those who lived in the area beyond the moat, as well as those who lived inside the sacred area (and possibly the king himself set his residence there) to draw water from it. Since the temple faced the west, a long crossing on the axis—flanked by a splendid balustrade in the form of a *naga* (whose significance we shall discuss later)—led to the entrance to the first enclosure. Once having arrived at this point, the faithful of the distant past, like the tourist of today, came to a *gopura,* or entrance pavilion, extraordinarily developed lengthwise; it was made up of a middle group of three raised towers, and of two side entrances on the ground level. The constructions are all linked by a vaulted gallery, which on the inside rests atop a solid wall and on the outside atop square pillars. The portico is completed by the addition of a seminave on a lower level, also resting on pillars.

The sacred area proper begins beyond this portal, and the access road, paved with great slabs of stone and flanked by a *naga* balustrade broken by six flights of steps, constitutes the obligatory way of approaching the temple. On the sides, standing free, are two "libraries" and two artificial pools; then comes a broad terrace with, on its west side, a two-story cruciform platform. (This is No. 2 on the plan on page 109.) By now one has reached the entrance to the temple proper.

Angkor Wat, like most of the temple-mountains, is essentially a pyramid produced by superimposing three terraces. The first of these (with dimensions of some 715 by 615 feet) is delineated by a peripheral gallery, broken by the *gopuras* located at the cardinal points and by the small cruciform pavilions in the corners; *gopuras* and corner pavilions are accessible from ample stairways. Continuing on the west-east axis, one passes through the entrance to encounter one of the most unusual Angkorean achievements: the cruciform courtyard (or cloister). From the three units that make up the portal of the peripheral gallery, one comes upon the three parallel galleries leading to the stairways to the upper terrace, these latter also covered with a vaulted gallery. One central gallery subdivides the inner space into four separate sectors—that is, into four courtyards dug out in the middle like swimming pools; originally

Angkor Wat: A view of the southeast corner of the central tower of the main sanctuary. Extending from the tower are the galleries that connected it to the dependent towers located at the four cardinal points; these galleries are composed of one middle vault and two side vaults on pillars. The tower is subdivided into two levels and is richly decorated. The base of the tower has a series of "steps" that make the transition down to the vaulted galleries; they have elegantly carved tympanums with human figures in high relief and pediments ending in *naga* heads. Perched on the corners are great winged *garudas,* the sacred creature that is the "vehicle" of Visnu. The flat surfaces are enlivened with divinities and nymphs set amid luxuriant vegetation.

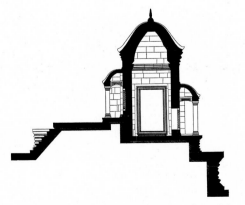

Angkor Wat: Cross section of the west gallery of the first terrace.

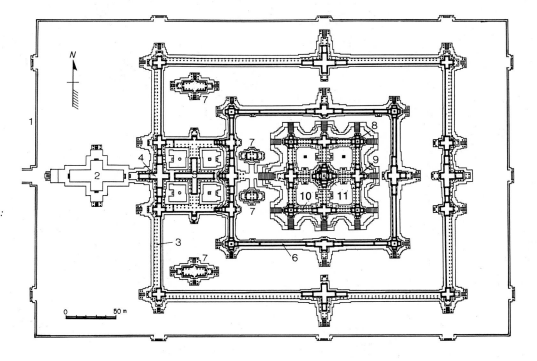

Angkor Wat: Ground plan of the temple-mountain:
1 *Outer enclosure*
2 *Cruciform platform*
3 *Gallery of the first terrace*
4 *Main entrance pavilion*
5 *Cruciform courtyard*
6 *Gallery of the second terrace*
7 *"Libraries"*
8 *Corner tower (one of four) of main sanctuary*
9 *Pavilion of the four cardinal points*
10 *Gallery of main sanctuary*
11 *Central tower*

these must have been used for religious rites. Of the several galleries, the ones on the side present nothing new, whereas the one in the middle is roofed over by a vault and two semivaults on pillars, forming three naves. Freestanding, off to the north and south sides, are two "libraries."

The design of the second terrace (some 380 by 330 feet) by and large repeats that of the first. A three-passage entrance on the west, the axial entrances simplified, the corner pavilions cruciform in design and roofed over with a tower and the peripheral gallery—these are its essential components. The peripheral gallery differs from the lower one, however, in that its outside wall has no openings, one nave only, and an inside wall lightened by rectangular windows, the light from which is reduced by the presence of numerous small columns. In front of the main entrance, a raised horizontal platform connects two relatively small "libraries."

The 42-foot height that separates the third terrace of the pyramid from the second can be climbed by any of the series of steep stairways that lead up to the edifices enclosing the central sanctuary. The upper terrace is perfectly square (measuring some 200 feet on each side). The gallery running all the way around it is supported externally by a wall with silled windows and internally by the usual series of columns. The two galleries on pillars join the central sanctuary with the pavilions raised in line with the cardinal points, thus once more forming the cross motif that characterizes the complex as a whole. As a result, the entire terrace is subdivided into four inner courtyards, as was the case with the lower courtyard.

Angkor Wat: The gallery and courtyard of the second terrace, viewed along the southwest side. Note in the foreground the windows with small columns; when the windows are false, as these are, the columns' only function is to lighten the mass of the stone wall. Probably this style of window was derived from an older type that used bamboo. The uppermost part of the wall, just under the cornice, has a frieze carved in a floral motif.

Angkor Wat: Plan of the "library" in northwest corner of third terrace.

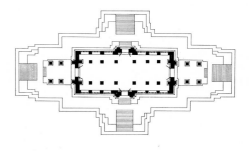

Angkor Wat: *Devatas,* or female divinities, carved on the outer wall of the northwest pavilion; they follow the canons mentioned for the figure on page 95. Most of those seen here, however, wear a special headdress composed of at least three metal plaques—from which several pointed elements protrude—and a few braids. The finesse with which these figures were executed recalls the work of the master goldsmiths whose tradition has been handed down in the countries of Southeast Asia to this day.

ARCHITECTURAL DETAILS OF ANGKOR WAT

Even such a brief description of Angkor Wat's general design and the references to its dimensions will have suggested the gap between this monument and those that preceded it. Yet if we consider on an individual basis some of the elements of the structure, the techniques used, and the expedients adopted, we would have to admit that the new departures here are of minor importance. Even the cruciform courtyard, which we have indicated was an architectural element typical of Angkor Wat, had its roots at Koh Ker's Prasat Thom. As for the building techniques used, the failings we had occasion to point out in the older edifices have not been avoided at Angkor Wat, either. We might single out the problem of the vault. It is known that when the Khmers—like the great builders of India, for that matter—changed over from wood construction to masonry, they were incapable of replacing a wooden roof with a genuine stone vault. Working with bricks, they used the corbeling method, which consisted of superimposing rows of inward-protruding bricks until the closing of the aperture was achieved. Virtually the same method was used for pseudovaults of stone, with stone blocks replacing the bricks; then the uneven stones were cut from within to create the effect of a round vault. This made it possible to elude the problems of statics in that the thrusts were merely vertical, yet a pleasing aesthetic effect was achieved.

Nevertheless, some progress had been made in relation to the initial experiments with temples. Whereas only brick, a relatively light material,

was used in the older vaults, those that followed were of brick and stone; by the twelfth century, sandstone alone would be used. And the acquisition of experience in the use of this new material demanded time and resulted in many unsuccessful attempts. At Phimeanakas, for example, the vault was composed of blocks arranged in three rows, while the Baphuon's vaults used four rows. And where the builders had dared to lighten the supporting walls with apertures (whether windows or pillars), they nevertheless strengthened the galleries with sustaining walls. At Angkor Wat and Banteay Samre, they finally felt confident enough to build a raised vault supported on the outside by a row (or double row) of pillars, and even to put up a three-nave gallery. In fact it is probably fair to say that the conditions laid down by such technical problems influenced the very form of the covered spaces designed, which came down to two types: the square tower and the long rectangular gallery.

The construction of the Khmer temples entailed other problems, of course. With the decline in the use of bricks, which had been held together by strong vegetable glues, the builders turned at first to large stable monoliths; in time, these came to be replaced by normal blocks of stone, which required special devices to keep them solidly connected. But the iron braces and dovetailed joints of carpentry—although highly publicized—were used only in some cases. While utmost care was taken to maintain horizontal alignment, the blocks were at times superimposed without staggering the vertical connections. This would have prevented the widening of the space between blocks and the inevitable collapse.

To this list of "errors" one might also add those of asymmetry between the left and right sides of the same temple, the inadequacy or total lack of foundations, and so on. But this would be wasted breath. What really matters is that the "empiricism" of the Khmer builders enabled them to create a masterpiece like Angkor Wat, where the sense of proportions,

Above, right:
Angkor Wat: An *apsaras,* or nymph, on a pilaster. The headdress has obvious affinities with those of the *devatas* (see photograph on the left). Note the technique with which the work was done—the merest hint of relief.

Above, left:
Angkor Wat: *Devatas* of the outer wall of the west entrance pavilion. The one in the foreground stands on a pilaster entirely decorated with a floral motif. The *devata* in the middle stands in a structure representing a portal with its own pillars and a sinuous pediment in the form of a *naga.*

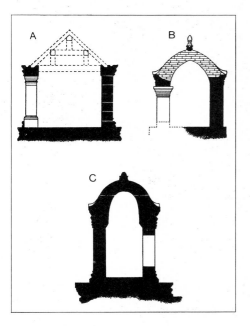

Different types of gallery roofs:
A Wooden roof (Prasat Thom of Koh Ker, Gallery III). The wooden slopes were probably lined with tiles.
B Corbeled brick vault on stone supports (Prasat Trapeang Khyang)
C Stone vault (Preah Vihear, Gallery I)

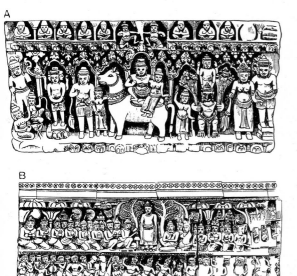

Drawings of lintels:
A Baphuon style, Prasat Prei Thnal, north sanctuary. The supreme triad of Hinduism is represented on the lintel. In the middle is Shiva, accompanied by his consort Parvati; they are seated on Shiva's "vehicle," the bull Nandi. On Shiva's right is Brahma, with four faces. On his left is Vishnu, supported by a garuda, clutching two nagas in its hands.
B Angkor Wat style, Phimai, middle sanctuary. The scene represented shows the adoration of Buddha, on two registers.

precisely in view of the technical shortcomings, is virtually incredible. In observing this monument, we might even gain the impression that the Khmers were familiar with, or at least guessed at, the laws of stereometry and on a basis of those laws made the modifications in symmetry necessary for the creation of a perfect pyramid. Consider a few instances. The road leading up to the temple is almost twice as long as the western facade, a relationship vital for a good perspective observation of the temple. The bases of the three terraces were built progressively higher in order to give the illusion that the upper stories are all of equal height and to prevent the structures on the lower stories from blocking the view of those on the upper levels. In speaking of the harmony of proportions, moreover, one cannot ignore the care taken by the Khmer artists in assuring a flawless balance between vertical and horizontal planes, a care to which Angkor Wat is a significant witness. The galleries and the towers thus alternate adroitly without the former dominating the latter or vice versa, and in such a way as to guarantee the harmony of the whole. For this reason, even the upper structure of the great towers was modified from previous temple-mountains' towers. The roofs of those at Angkor Wat were built up by the superimposition of stories much lower yet much more numerous than in the past; the result is that from a distance the eye perceives a curved line and the whole central sanctuary avoids the conflict between the horizontal and the vertical elements.

From an architectural standpoint, therefore, Angkor Wat is an all-but-flawless work. The same may be said, we feel, of its decorative elements and bas-reliefs. The erection of the various edifices and the creation of their decorations did not proceed hand in hand, though; in fact, the sculptors and stone dressers set to work only when the architects and masons had finished their work. Vast unbroken surfaces were then left to be enlivened by the work of the numerous industrious artisans and artists—some of whom deserve the status of genius—who were later able to set to work with complete freedom of expression. In some of the Khmer structures, this led to an overloading of the surface, but at Angkor Wat, such freedom was still a largely positive force. For example, Angkor Wat's small octagonal or sixteen-faced columns were subdivided horizontally into ten or twelve parts by profusely decorated rings, and the pillars were often entirely covered with a particularly thick floral ornamentation. But thanks to the mastery and lightness of touch of the artist, the ornamentation forms a sort of continuous embroidery in which one can descry traces of a Chinese taste. The same decorative taste is to be found in the details as well, in the molding of the bases and the cornices in the pillars, in the spaces between the pillars, in the windows, on the inner walls, where leaves and lotus petals alternate in lozenge geometrical motifs, or in anthropomorphic motifs done in relief or in the "tapestry" technique. This last-named technique was peculiar to Angkor Wat; it consists of flattening the image as much as possible, undoubtedly in imitation of the brocades and silks that once lined certain walls.

In considering the achievements in sculpture at Angkor Wat, we must grant a position of foremost importance to images of *devatas* (divinities) and *apsaras* (nymphs); sculptured along the walls or on pilasters in great numbers, they enliven their surfaces with the grace of their poses, the beauty of their persons, the refinement of their garments and headdresses. The expression of astonishment, the stereotyped smiles, and the repeated gestures, far from generating a sense of monotony, attract the spectator who is capable of understanding their originality and elegance. And we should realize that the subject is repeated some two thousand times, and that no figure is exactly the same as another.

Other figures—greatly reduced in dimensions, of course—appear on the lintels and in the tympanums that adorn the doors of the *gopuras* and towers of Angkor Wat. We may note that the lintels characteristic of the

Angkor Wat style—for it has inevitably given its name to the style employed in several other monuments of the time—differ little from those of the Baphuon. Like the latter, they are based primarily on floral decoration, and their distinctive characteristic is the dynamic crowd of divinities, animals, and monsters springing up among the leaves, to some degree destroying the clearness and composure of the whole. Exceptionally elegant, however, is the type of lintel appearing at Angkor Wat for the first time, which eliminates the ramifications laid out horizontally and flanks the central motif—which by now has become extraordinarily complex thanks to the inclusion of a monstrous mask and a variety of divinities—with a series of highly stylized vine shoots extending vertically.

The decoration of the tympanums and pediments, which had reached the zenith of its expressive capabilities at Banteay Srei and which later became simpler and simpler, took on a new importance at Angkor Wat. The line of the pediments became undulated as it was decorated with leaves, rosettes, and pendants, while the outside retained the leafy decoration of the preceding styles. Reappearing at the two extremities was the *makara* (the crocodilelike monster), from whose jaws emerged a polycrested *naga*. But at Angkor Wat the *makara* has taken on more the aspect of a dragon, confirming the presence of the aforementioned Chinese influence. Some tympanums were still decorated with mythological scenes that occupy all the available space with a lively narrative tableau. Others are covered by scenes of divinities and faithful in prayer, usually arranged across two superimposed registers. The former style ties in with the tradition of Banteay Srei; the latter anticipates the Bayon style.

Angkor Wat: Three details of the bas-relief frieze along the west side of the outer gallery. These are all scenes from the battle between the Panduidi and Kuruidi (taken from the great Indian epic, the *Mahabharata*). Note the different ways that figures and scenes are treated. Some are rigid, static, hierarchical; others are done with a freedom of movement that transmits a dynamism to everything around them.

Angkor Wat: A close-up of one of the bas-reliefs on the west side of the outer gallery, with a scene taken from the Indian epic, the *Ramayana*. The figure dominating this scene is Ravana, the terrible antagonist of Rama, riding a chariot drawn by imaginary animals. His ten heads and twenty arms, all moving, accentuate the monstrous nature and power of this figure. In the end, though, the scene's drama dissolves in the preciosity of the decorative effects.

DESCRIPTION OF RAVANA

He saw that illustrious king of Lanka resplendent with his dazzling gilt diadem, finely wrought and studded with pearls. He saw him adorned with wondrous golden ornaments, shaped with great art by Visvakarma, crowded with diamonds and other precious gems, clad in a rich garment of fine linen, wearing choice sandalwood and sprayed with various delicate perfumes.

Towering in front of him was the great figure with his ten terrible heads, large and striking, furnished with horrible, sharp, shining teeth, with bright red lips, burning eyes, and a fierce expression, as Mount Mandara towers with its peaks crawling with serpents and other wild creatures. He was resplendent with his arms adorned with bracelets and suffused with sandalwood and with his rotund hands like five-headed serpents.

He was seated on a great noble chair of crystal, profusely adorned and with parts of wrought silver lined with a section of carpet and fanned from every side by women intoxicated with love, ostentatiously dressed and holding furry fans in their hands.

Ramayana (Chap. XLV)

THE VIEW OF LANKA

Thus glittered Lanka in every part, like Amaravati, Indra's city, with its trees all open, born in its wilderness. There were patches of tender, dark-green grass, pleasant wooded regions, blossomed flowers and strong-scented fruits, as men wear ornaments.

That wonder-filled wilderness, florid and delectable in all seasons, like the celestial Nandana, and a favorite haunt of the bees, was resplendent like the wilderness of Ceitraratha. It was a splendid thing to see that great wilderness with its lapwings, peacocks, and water hens frolicking together and its singing cuckoos.

Atop that summit stands the city of Lanka, defended by Ravana. This city is furnished with other gates, resembling white clouds, a portal all of gold and silver, and is nobly adorned with temples and palaces, so that at the end of the hot season the halfway abode of Vishnu is covered with clouds. To be seen in its midst, profusely decorated with its thousand columns, is a royal palace of the impious Ravana, king of the Racsasi, like the peak of the Kailasa and nearly touching the sky, constantly guarded by a full hundred Racsasi.

Ramayana (Chap. XV)

116   ANCIENT CAMBODIA

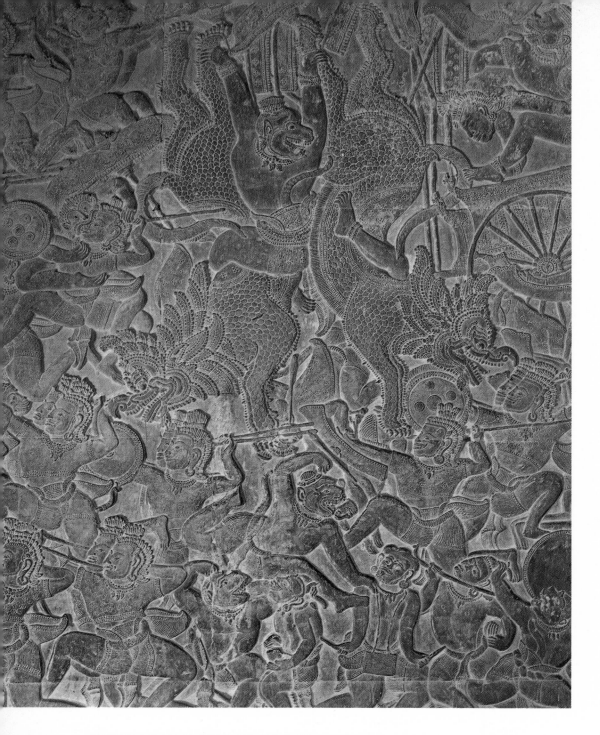

Angkor Wat: A close-up of one of the bas-reliefs on the west side of the outer gallery, this scene being from the Battle of Lanka as recounted in the *Ramayana*. At this moment, the monstrous and fantastic creatures of Ravana's army have the upper hand, and the group in the center is a quite stunning creation; note how the impetus of the scene derives from the upside-down position of the animals' bodies.

Facing page:
Angkor Wat: A close-up of a bas-relief on the west side of the outer gallery, another scene from the Battle of Lanka. Ravana appears as the pivotal element of the composition.

THE BAS-RELIEFS OF ANGKOR WAT

It is perhaps in its bas-reliefs that Angkor Wat attains its pinnacle of artistry, and these made use of mythological, epic, or historical scenes for their subject matter. We meet these bas-reliefs in the galleries around the perimeter of the first level of the temple-mountain. As will be recalled, the entrances corresponding to the cardinal points are connected to the corner pavilions by a gallery subdivided by these edifices into eight parts or wings. The outer wall of this great arcade was formed by pillars, and the reliefs are on the inside of the interior wall where they are bathed by the subtle light that comes through the pillars. All this was obviously part of the master plan from the beginning. And good visibility was essential, for all the figures sculptured along each wing of the gallery formed part of a single tale: these "tales" were supposed to be taken in by the spectator with a single gaze, across an area that might reach as long as 100 yards.

Since Angkor Wat was a temple of the Vishnuite sect, all the episodes represented in the bas-reliefs refer to Vishnu or to his terrestrial incarnations, Krishna and Rama. Starting with the west gallery—that is, the first one meets on entering—the episodes of the two wings flanking the *gopura* are: right (southwest), the battle between the Panduidi and

This being said, that enemy of the king of the Devis climbed onto his chariot drawn by noble, generous steeds, resplendent as flame and dazzling in his lofty company. Honored with the sounds of shells and warlike drums, bellicose acclamations, with the clapping of hands, war cries, and high praises, the great king of the Racsasi started out. Surrounded by his brave warriors, whose bodies were like the mountains and clouds, whose eyes burned like fire and who were flesh-eaters, Ravana marched to battle, like Rudra, lord of the immortals, flanked by hosts of Bhutis.

Having heard Rama's words, Vibhisana, ful king descried the fierce host of Vanaris, ready for battle, armed with rocks and trees and howling like the ocean waves. But catching sight of the ardent army of Racsasi, the magnanimous Rama, the equal of an immortal, climbed atop a hill and spoke as follows to Vibhisana, then standing out impressively among the warriors. "Who is this chieftain leading yon intrepid, indomitable host burdened with so many arms, flags, and standards, bristling with swords, poles, and feathered darts, with disks and crossbows, and accompanied by innumerable elephants similar to King Airavata?"

Having heard Rama's words, Vibhisana, who was equal to Indra in strength, named and sang the praises of the brave indomitable Racsasi, who in that army were the most conspicuous heroes.

"The chieftain riding on yon chariots, brandishing a bow like that of Indra, with a lion as his standard and with curved tusks that make him look like an elephant, that is Indragit, son of the king of the Racsasi.

"That handsome hero, that great warrior, Indra's equal, standing erect in the chariot brandishing a bow with horrible thunder, that is Atikaya, of the towering body.

"That wretch with the tawny eyes the color of the rising sun, who when he mounts a donkey tinkling with harness bells gives out a horrible roar, that is the brave warrior known as Mahodara.

"The one you see mounted on a charger the color of a golden cloud of twilight and adorned from head to foot with a golden harness, brandishing a feathered arrow girt by flashing rays of light, that is Pisaca, who is as impetuous as a stroke of lightning.

"The one armed with a bow and scimitar, clad in mail and wearing a crest and ardent as the end-of-the-world fire, that is Khara's son, Makaraksa.

"The one standing on yon chariot armed with a sword, bow, and arrows, sporting a standard, looking as bright as fire and overflowing with spirit, that is Narantaka, the warrior who fights the summits of mountains.

"That other warrior marching amid a host of fierce-looking beings of every description, with the faces of tigers and camels, elephants and lions, their eyes wild, that is Sudanstra, son of Vigitari.

"That archer, just coming into sight like a great cloud, with a broad solid chest and bearing a great serpent as a standard, holding himself tensely and gripping his bow, that is Kumbha.

"The one brandishing a fearsome, horrid-looking bludgeon studded with gold and diamonds, that is Nikumba, the standard bearer of the army of the Racsasi, a man of fierce, awe-inspiring deeds.

"Over by that sublime white umbrella with golden ribs, glimmering in front of us like a full moon, you see the magnanimous king of the Racsasi approaching like Rudra surrounded by Bhutis. And the one marching so fearlessly, his brow girt with a diadem, radiant, his face aglow, his aspect terrible, an equal of Vindha and the Mahendra, that is the king of the Racsasi, who has already demolished the pride of Indra and Vaivasvata."

Ramayana (Chap. XXXV)

Kuruidi on Mount Kurukshetra; on the left, the battle of Lanka, which has as its principal protagonists Rama and Ravana. The first of these episodes was drawn from the *Mahabharata,* the long Indian poem written by an unknown Hindu who probably lived between the second and fourth centuries A.D. While relating exploits of heroes, the *Mahabharata* also contains many ethical, religious, and judicial teachings that make this *the* book of Hindu culture. The work recounts the vicissitudes of two groups of cousins, the Panduidi and the Kuruidi, who are in constant rivalry among themselves. The rivalry attained its apex at the battle of Mount Kurukshetra, where they met face to face in an open field and where, after many days of fighting, stratagems, supernatural aid (two of the protagonists, Kama and Arjuna, are, respectively, scions of the sun god Surya and of Indra), they fall one after the other, leaving only a few survivors and the womenfolk to give their heroes a worthy burial.

The second episode—on the left of the gallery—like many others in the Angkor Wat cycle of carvings, is drawn from the *Ramayana,* an epic poem of the first century A.D., attributed to Valmiki; the poem relates the adventures and misadventures of Rama in tones of rare poetry—the work has often been compared to Homer. The *Ramayana* tells the story of Prince Rama—himself an incarnation of Vishnu—who is compelled by

will of his stepmother to leave the home of his father and enter the jungle with his faithful wife Sita and his brother Lakshman. The most salient episodes of the poem center around the struggles between Rama and Ravana, a monstrous demon with ten heads. This latter, after abducting Sita, holds her prisoner on the island of Lanka (Ceylon), where Rama manages to reach her and set her free with the help of an army of monkeys and after killing Ravana and his son Indrajit. It is this last episode that is represented in the reliefs of this northwest wing.

The reliefs along the north gallery and in the north wing of the east gallery take as their subject the victories of Vishnu and Krishna over the *asuras* (demons) drawn from the *Harivamsa,* a poem in three parts that was like an "appendix" to the *Mahabharata.* The *Harivamsa* deals with cosmogony and various legends of Krishna. The west wing of the north gallery depicts the struggle between Vishnu and Kalanemi and is a grandiose, extremely lively "group portrait" of all the deities in the Hindu pantheon. On the wall of the east wing of the north gallery, one sees Krishna engaged against the demon Bana, who will be pardoned through the intercession of Shiva. The north wing of the east gallery represents, in its center, Vishnu on his mount, Garuda, while two armies of demons close in on the sides.

In the south wing of the east gallery is represented one of the most interesting episodes—"The Churning of the Sea of Milk"—interesting not only from the iconographic and stylistic viewpoint but also because this scene's repetition on so many pediments, pilasters, and other elements of Khmer monuments attests to its special role in Khmer mythology. The legend was drawn from the *Bhagavata Purana,* still another Indian poem, and relates how the gods *(devas)* and demons *(asuras),* desirous of procuring the good things of life—especially the *amrta,* a liquid like the ambrosia or nectar of the gods in Western mythology, and conferring immortality—whip up the Sea of Milk for some one thousand years. The

Angkor Wat: Three sections of the bas-reliefs on the east side of the outer gallery, all representing the Indian myth of the Churning of the Sea of Milk. Each scene is divided into three levels. The middle one represents the serpent Vasuki being pulled by the *asuras* (demons) and the *devas* (deities). The lower level is filled with a myriad of aquatic animals, either real or imaginary. The upper register is composed of a line of *apsaras*, or nymphs, dancing in a way intended to suggest the celestial world. The figure shown in close-up at the far right is the central subject of the long frieze: Vishnu above his incarnation as the tortoise Kurma, on which rests Mount Mandara, the pivot of the universe, and here being revolved by the demons and deities as they pull back and forth on the serpent, thus churning up the sea from which they hope to extract such good things as the ambrosia that confers immortality.

means of doing this are Mount Mandara, which acts as a sort of vertical shaft; Vishnu, who supports the mountain; Kurma, the tortoise, and incarnation of Vishnu, on which Vishnu sits; and the serpent Vasuki, which is wrapped around the mountain; and the two celestial "teams," which pull the ends of the serpent back and forth and thus revolved Mounta Mandara so that it churns up the sea. Although this myth was probably of Indian-Persian origin, legends dealing with the miraculous powers of intoxicating beverages are found in mythology of virtually all peoples. (Modern psychoanalytical theories of mythology have focused on such miraculous beverages, particularly as they relate to creation myths.) In view of the Khmers' close contacts with Indian culture, their enthusiasm for this motif is not surprising.

In no way connected with mythology, on the other hand, are the two scenes adorning the walls of both wings of the south gallery; they represent the procession of dignitaries and soldiers led by Suryavarman II himself on an elephant, and then of Suryavarman, identified with the god Yama, who judges the just and the wicked, assigning them either to heaven or hell. But even the pavilions erected in the southwest and northwest corners of the enclosure are entirely covered with bas-reliefs depicting such episodes as Krishna and the arjuna tree, Sita's wedding, the Churning of the Sea of Milk, the meeting between Hanuman and Sita, the return of Rama. It is obvious that the inspiration for such sculptures was the same stories of the *Bhagavata Purana,* the *Harivamsa,* and especially the *Ramayana.*

The importance of the decorative elements at Angkor Wat requires us to devote a few words to the techniques used by the sculptors responsible for them. First, we observe that the work was presumably carried out on a "mass production" basis, in the sense that the images were first sketched—that is, scratched onto stone—and then shaped and completed in all their details. In effect, the artists used a system similar to that of the

Angkor Wat: A detail of the bas-reliefs, on the south side of the outer gallery, which represent scenes from Heaven and Hell as envisioned by the Hindus. But the central figure here is Suryavarman II, the Khmer sovereign who built the Angkor Wat complex; he is portrayed as surrounded by some of his faithful followers.

"cartoons" or charcoal sketches so dear to the painters of the Italian Renaissance. This is not surprising: the entire complex of reliefs was probably conceived as a work closer to painting than to sculpture (as evidenced by the importance given to the line and the slight depth of the relief).

The placing of the various elements in the available space follows the two criteria already mentioned for the scenes of the tympanum. There are the panels adorned with only one compositon, in which the figures are placed side by side or one on top of the other, without any dividing lines except for those that play a narrative—or even a "psychological"—role by dividing the various episodes of the story. Then there are the panels laid out in planes of parallel registers, clearly separated from one another. Belonging to the first type are the episodes of Vishnu and Kalanemi, the battle of Lanka, and the battle of Kurukshetra; the second type includes the Churning of the Sea of Milk, the royal procession, and the regions of heaven and hell. The use of one style or the other is significant not only for a technical analysis of the reliefs but also in order to date them. As for the style, there remains little to add to the observations we have been making as we have gone along. The liveliness and finesse of execution are values to be grasped with the first glance, and they enable even the uninitiated to recognize the Angkor Wat reliefs as being among the masterpieces of all cultures. In the scenes with an epic subject, the masses twist and writhe in an orderly tangle of men, animals, and demons. Only from time to time does the artist free himself from his excessive *horror vacui* and set aside a section of the surface for a figure of somewhat larger dimensions—a god, a hero, or a demon.

The dynamism that pervaded the scene, furthermore, was never transformed into drama, for the masses of the bodies never jutted out sufficiently to create violent contrasts of light and shade. Also each figure moves with a rhythm that is its own only in appearance, for in reality all figures resonate with one another. The rigor of this rhythm is self-evident, especially in the register scenes—the interminable lines of warriors and horsemen moving in step, the gods or *apsaras* all alike. But this does not mean that the artist can be accused of a servile observance of iconographic canons. Although his respect for the narrative plot of the myth remained intact, the artist gave his fancy free rein in executing the fabulous fauna of the Sea of Milk or the luxuriant trees of the jungle. In regard to such elements, we might mention the observation of de Coral Remusat, who said that it is precisely from an analysis of this vegetation—now hanging high and ominously overhead, now low and fleeting—that we can deduce an incipient interest in perspective; but this is noted only in the reliefs of the south gallery, and has no subsequent development.

These few stylistic observations are of some importance, as we have indicated, in determining, among other things, the chronology of the monuments. It is not unlikely, in fact, that the reliefs of the two battles and those of Vishnu and Kalanemi are contemporaneous with the construction of the monument, while the Churning of the Sea of Milk and the scenes involving Suryavarman II were executed after the death of the sovereign. The remaining two reliefs unquestionably date from a later epoch. These deductions are based on stylistic considerations— that is, on the fact that in the evolution of relief portrayal of scenes, the adoption of the registers appears to have come later than the other type (and will find its maximum application in the Bayon) and on the presence (in the last bas-reliefs) of a more marked Chinese influence. But the dating is also based on epigraphic data: the inscriptions under the reliefs in which the sovereign is portrayed designate this latter, as we have seen, with his posthumous name of Paramavishnuloka. A chronological arrangement of the reliefs would in itself be of little importance, of course, in that whatever their sequence they all were executed in a brief span of time.

But such an arrangement would be useful to establish their connection with the life and work of Suryavarman II. In the last analysis, however, the dating of the reliefs of Angkor Wat is necessary to establish a correct interpretation of the monument itself.

THE FUNCTION OF ANGKOR WAT

When the question of the function of Angkor Wat was raised in the 1930s, it was posed in such a way as to ask whether Suryavarman II had constructed it to honor the statue of Vishnu or to be buried there—whether, in other words, the monument was a temple or a tomb. Some scholars favored one theory, some the other, both sides often putting forward sound reasons. The most compelling ideas, in our view, are those set forth by Bosch, which avail themselves of the scene of the bas-reliefs, stressing the elements binding them together (and explaining them) if they are "read" by walking around the gallery from left to right—contrary, that is, to the normal route for encircling funeral monuments. In keeping with the sequence he established, Bosch set up a parallel between the sovereign's career and the mythological episodes linked to Vishnu (as a solar divinity) and to the *avataras,* Krishna and Rama. The walk around the monument must then begin with the Churning of the Sea of Milk, understood as an augury myth both for the god (who draws from the ocean his jewels of good government) and for the sovereign. The struggles between Vishnu or Krishna and the *asuras* symbolize the armed clashes between Suryavarman II and his enemies, struggles that culminate with the battle of Lanka—that is, with an episode extolling the definitive victory of good over evil, of Rama over Ravana, of the king over his opponents. The moment of glory is brief, and is inevitably followed by decline. Coming not long afterwards, in fact, is the battle of Kurukshetra, in which there were neither winners nor losers, and the sole master of the situation was death. On the south wall, lastly, the sovereign appears with the sumptuousness befitting his royal dignity, but as can easily be seen it is no longer Suryavarman but Paramavishnuloka who is heading, together with his court, toward the kingdom in the afterworld where, deified at last in the figure of Yama, he is to set himself up as supreme judge.

But such a reading is premised on the claim that the Angkor Wat complex was built for funeral purposes—the very claim that remains to be demonstrated. Was it a temple or a tomb? This is the question examined by Coedès, whose ideas are now highly regarded on this subject. Virtually the only element backing up the temple theory is the structure of the monument—the traditional temple-mountain built by a sovereign while still alive. We have already considered the meaning of the temple-mountain, indicating its political-religious aspects. There is no point in returning to this subject, except for the fact that beginning with a certain period—to be placed between the reigns of Harshavarman I (900–921) and Rajendravarman II (944–968)—the distinction between the temple-mountain and the ancestor temple appears to have grown considerably weaker. It was no rarity for a temple-mountain to become the mausoleum of the sovereign who had built it. Thus, it is likely that at the time of Suryavarman II's reign, the type of architectural structure adopted was no longer as important as it had been in the ninth century.

In favor of the tomb thesis, on the other hand, are a good many elements, such as the suggested counterclockwise "reading" of the bas-reliefs we have examined, and the finding of covered clay vessels closely resembling cinerary urns or bone caskets. As for the written sources, the only text we have covering this period is the account by Chou Ta-Kuan of his visit to Angkor in the last thirteenth century; here we can read that Angkor Wat was the tomb of Lu-lan, a Chinese architect of legendary fame who was said to have lived at the time of Confucius. This architect

THE CUSTOMS OF CAMBODIA

The city wall measures about 20 *li* in length. There are five gates, each one flanked by two side doors. The east side has two gates, while all the others have only one. Outside the wall is a great moat, and beyond the moat the various approaches with their great bridges. To be found on either side of the bridges are fifty-four stone genii, calling to mind stone generals, gigantic and terrible. The five gates are identical. The parapets of the bridges are of stone, shaped like serpents with nine heads. The fifty-four genii are holding serpents in their hands and have an air of wanting to prevent them from escaping. The wall gates carry five heads of Buddha in stone, the face turned to the west. In the middle is another one, decorated with gold.

Emerging from the south gate, one finds at a distance of half a *li* the stone tower said to have been erected in only one night by Lu-lan. Lu-Lan's tomb is to be found about one *li* outside the south gate, and its perimeter measures about ten *li*. In this area are several hundred small constructions in stone.

The King's Palace
I have heard that there are many wonderful corners in this palace, but there are many strict rules against entering, and in fact it is impossible to get inside. Among other things, the palace has a gold tower, at the top of which the king sleeps. All the natives maintain that the tower holds the soul of a serpent with nine heads, the lord of all the land in the kingdom. Every night he appeared in the form of a woman. It is with him that the sovereign sleeps and unites. Not even the king's favorites would dare enter. He comes out at the second watch, however, and then can sleep with his wives and concubines. If a night comes when the serpent fails to appear, this means that the time has arrived for the king to die. If the king fails to keep the appointment even once, this brings misfortune.

The Functionaries
In this country there are counselors, generals, astronomers, and so on, and beneath them, all types of low-ranking employees, differing from our own only in names. The dignitaries with the highest rank use a canopy with a golden pole and four parasols with gold handles. Those that follow have a canopy with a golden pole and a parasol with a gold handle; then come those with only a parasol with a gold handle: then come those with simply a parasol with a silver handle; and finally a certain number with a canopy with a silver pole.

certainly had nothing to do with Suryavarman II, but the author perhaps fell into this error because of a legend (disclosed by much later sources, but evidently already widespread in the thirteenth century) according to which the temple had been built by the divine architect Visvakarman (Brah Bisnula) for the sovereign Ketumala (Brah Kat Mala). It is possible that hearsay had also indicated that the monument was the tomb of a sovereign and that this gave rise to a mix-up that was understandable enough in a foreigner who gathered his data here and there with great enthusiasm and curiosity, but certainly without scholarly scruples.

On the other hand, no so-called proof is altogether convincing. Much has been made of the fact that the entrance is on the west side—unlike virtually all the other Khmer temples, which face east. But however exceptional this might be for Cambodia, similar examples are to be found in the funeral monuments of Java and Bali (both drawing on the same religious inspiration). And perhaps there is a simple explanation: once the choice was made to locate the temple-mountain of Angkor Wat in a large space in the southeast corner of the city, its design was dictated by the need to draw its water supply from the Siemreap canal.

As for the funeral urns, two basic observations must be made. The first is that none of these urns was found *in situ,* hence it is impossible to determine beyond doubt that they were contemporaneous to the monument. The other point is the scarcity of data on the funeral rites of this period. The testimony of Chinese sources (mentioned earlier) refers to more ancient times. Chou Ta-Kuan found that the rites calling for the exposure of the dead body to wild animals and for incineration were both still being employed, although the practice of such rites did not include the court—or at least, not the sovereign, who was "buried in a tower." Unfortunately, however, the author was not in a position to specify the form of burial adopted. That the urns in question, too small to contain the remains of an adult, were sarcophaguses, seems beyond question. But it is fairly probable that, in the case of the sovereign, custom called for a casket containing his bones to be interred inside a tower.

The question we have posed at the outset, then—temple or tomb?—remains unanswered, and it is clear that the terms of the problem must be shifted. What we must try to discover instead is the exact meaning of the words "temple" and "tomb" in the Khmer period in question. This was the view taken by Coedès, who rightly notes that the Hindu temple was not a place where the faithful met frequently to pray or commune with one another (as in the *ecclesia* of the Christian religion of the time). It was, on the contrary, the abode of the god and was visited only on the occasion of periodic ritual festivals. For that matter, even the term "tomb" must be understood as "royal mausoleum," the place where the king was buried but also the place where the presence of his mortal remains made possible the process of deification that had begun the moment he ascended the throne. It appears reasonable, therefore, to accept the position of Coedès, when he states that Angkor Wat is "both temple and tomb . . . the final abode of a being who, when living, had had certain divine prerogatives and that death had made godlike. It is the funeral palace where his mortal remains find repose, but that also houses the statue showing him with the traits of a god." In effect, therefore, Coedès answers the question—"temple or tomb?"—by saying: both.

MONUMENTS CONTEMPORARY WITH ANGKOR WAT

Angkor Wat is the most striking and representative monument of the period that runs from the ascent of Jayavarman VI to the throne (1080) to the capture of Angkor by the Chams (1177). But many other complexes worthy of note were built by the sovereigns of the Mahidharapura dynasty. They also restored, completed, or generally enhanced still others. The first stage of this period includes such monuments as Phnom

The Inhabitants
The inhabitants of this land are crude and extremely dark. Whether they live in the far-off villages on the islands in the sea or along the busiest roads, it is all the same. One must examine the persons who live in the palaces or the women of noble families in order to find women white as jade, which is probably explained by the fact that they never see the rays of the sun. In general, the women wear nothing more than a strip of cloth around their loins, like the men, leaving their milk-white abdomens uncovered. They wear their hair in a chignon, and go barefoot. And this is true of the sovereign's wives as well. The sovereign has five wives, one for his private apartment itself, and four for the cardinal points. As for his concubines and the palace women, the figure has been put at from three thousand to five thousand. They are divided into numerous classes but they rarely cross the threshold of the palace.

Writings
For ordinary writing as for all official texts, deerskin or buckskin or other types of hide are used, dyed black. Most of the characters strikingly resemble those of the Uighurs. One writes from left to right, and not from the bottom up. I have been told that their letters are pronounced almost like those of the Mongols. Only two or three are different. There was a time when they had no seals.

Celestial Justice
There was a time when there was no such thing as corporal punishment, but only pecuniary fines. In the most serious cases, they neither decapitated nor strangled. Instead, they dug a hole outside the west gate and placed the criminal in it, covering him over with well-pressed earth and stones. There is also another excellent procedure. When someone cannot find some object and suspects one of his neighbors, and this neighbor pleads innocent, a potful of oil is heated until it boils. Then the suspect dips his hand into it. If he is guilty, his hand will be burnt all over. Otherwise, nothing will happen to it. This is the way the barbarians proceed in such cases.

It sometimes happens that two families have a falling out, without it being clear which is in the right and which is in the wrong. In front of the palace are twelve small stone towers. Each of the adversaries take up a position on one of these towers. At the foot of the two towers, the respective families keep an eye on each other. After one, two, three, or four days, the one who is in the wrong ends by manifesting it in one way or another, such as coming down with ulcers, catarrh, or malignant fever. The one who is in the right has nothing wrong with him. This is how they decide who is just and who is unjust. They call this "celestial justice."

The Dead
Once they arrive in the open country outside the city walls they put down the body and leave it. They wait for the vultures or the dogs to come and devour it. Nowadays there are a few—all descendants of Chinese—who burn their dead. The king is buried in a tower, but I don't know whether they bury his entire body or just his bones.

CHOU TA-KUAN: *Recollections on the Customs of Cambodia*

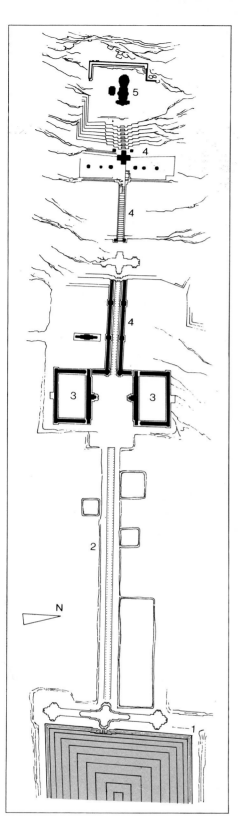

Wat Phu: Ground plan of the temple and its approach:
1 *Reservoir*
2 *Approach way*
3 *Palaces*
4 *Three-flight stairway, broken by platforms with pavilions*
5 *Main sanctuary*

Sandak and, in its more recent aspect, Wat Phu, situated in the northeast part of the kingdom. It also included Phimai, in what is today a part of Thailand. The fact that these monuments were located outside the immediate Angkor region should not be surprising if we recall the events that characterized the history of the reigns of Jayavarman VI and Suryavarman II. Likewise, these monuments' architecture will call to mind many details that caught our attention at Angkor Wat. It is for this reason that such monuments, with those ordered built by Suryavarman and his dignitaries inside Angkor proper (Beng Mealea, Banteay Samre, Thommanon, and Chau Say Tevoda, to mention the major ones), are usually grouped together as belonging to the Angkor Wat style.

Preah Vihear, one of these monuments, is located in the Dangrek Hills; its construction covers a long period, from Suryavarman I to Suryavarman II; it is a significant example of the axial type of temple complex. It is made up of long monumental approaches, enlivened by stairways and terraces. The main *gopura* presents an extension of the wings and the parallel structures, as in the Prasat Thom of Koh Ker. The sandstone sanctuary is composed of a square cell with four porticoes, preceded on the south side by a vestibule that is prolonged into a nave with vaulted roof. Running all the way around the sanctuary, with a vault entirely of sandstone, is a rectangular gallery, which is very similar to that of the Phimeanakas, although of greater dimensions. While the inside wall is solid, the outside one is lightened by a number of rectangular windows. In the two galleries flanking the space in front of the sanctuary, however, the wall interspersed with windows is supported by monolithic pillars. As a result, we find in one and the same monument examples of two successive stages in perfecting technically the vaulted galleries, the process that was to reach its apex at Angkor Wat.

At Wat Phu, the construction design is substantially the same: terraces, stairways, and approach lanes leading to the main sanctuary. This latter, however, is a less linear structure than Preah Vihear because it was built bit by bit, the foundation of the temple dating to the pre-Angkorean period. The final phase, dating to the time of Suryavarman II, extended the nave over the front of the cell, transforming it into a rectangular room with central vault on two rows of pillars and side semivaults resting on outer walls; this renovation almost totally suffocated the preexistent structure. Along the main axis (east-west)—that is, along the approach—a number of terraces and *gopuras* are to be found, while on the sides one sees several ponds or pools as well as two large constructions known as "palaces." Another characteristic of Wat Phu is the reservoir ordered by the *vrah guru* Divakara, at the entrance of the long approach; this reservoir is some 2,000 feet long.

The other basic type of temple—that of the central design—is represented at Phimai (see page 128), where the sanctuary is comprised of a central cell with four doors, each of which has a portico. The facade that corresponds with the principal axis extends into a rectangular construction that is wider than the narrow antechamber of the temples already described. The central sanctuary of this temple is set within a series of three successive enclosures, the first of which has a vaulted gallery, with balustrade windows outside and false windows inside, as well as four entrance pavilions on the sanctuary's main axes. At Phimai, the south *gopura* of the second enclosure is preceded by an approach lane lined with pillars; this latter detail is worthy of note in that such an approach is not usually considered part of the pattern of the central-design type of temple. The third enclosure, a sandstone wall that closed in a vast area and that opened out on four sides with gigantic *gopuras,* was not completed. And lastly at Phimai, as at Wat Phu, the complex was endowed with a reservoir, the Srah Phleng, evidently designed to furnish water to all those who lived or worked inside the temple area.

The Phimai complex is considered a jewel of harmonious proportions and an interesting example of a sanctuary with a marked prevalence of Buddhist statues; this was not to become normal until the reign of Jayavarman VII. The sanctuary pattern we have described for Phimai is fairly simple and linear, yet at the same time it is typical because it was used again in all the constructions of this kind. The major variation came in the apertures—the choice, that is, between real or false doors and windows—and the entrances, with more or less spectacular stairways. In practice, the temples that were built in this period at the Angkor site—Chau Say Tevoda, Thommanon, and even Banteay Samre, the most original and meticulously built Khmer monument after Angkor Wat—followed this pattern more or less faithfully. The most outstanding features at Banteay Samre are the enclosures, which in addition to four vaulted galleries in limonite stone have a paved platform running along the entire perimeter of the inner area. In the second enclosure, the platform is enhanced by a series of pillars, no doubt destined to support a roof of perishable materials, which made it a veritable arcade.

Also belonging to this group is the temple of Beng Mealea, the subject of several studies owing to its resemblance to Angkor Wat. The designs of these two monuments, when compared, in fact reveal a number of remarkable analogies. At Beng Mealea as at Angkor Wat the main facade of the third enclosure has a cruciform platform, a particularly long *gopura*, and cruciform corner edifices. One finds the same cruciform design in the inner courtyard (although it is less complex than the one at Angkor Wat), and to the two side "libraries." The central group of the Beng Mealea, however, made up of the last two enclosures and the sanctuary proper, differs somewhat from that of Angkor Wat. At Beng Mealea, in fact, the last two enclosures are connected by axial *gopuras* that start from the galleries of the facade. The design of the sanctuary proper is similar to that of axial temples, with a central cell, porticoes, and the east nave extended to the entrance standing before them. The most significant differences between Angkor Wat and Beng Mealea, however, are in the height of the two edifices and in their orientation. Beng Mealea is built on a single level, and hence is not a temple-mountain; and it faces east, like the majority of the Khmer temples not intended for funeral functions.

These and other observations have induced specialists to consider Beng Mealea as an undertaking realized in the years immediately preceding the conception of Angkor Wat—in short, a "dress rehearsal" before the construction of the more important complex. Not long ago, however, Boisselier was able to demonstrate that such a chronology does not find sufficient confirmation in an analysis of the architectural elements of Beng Mealea; indeed, it is now accepted that the building of this latter was undertaken after that of Angkor Wat. Probably, however, the Beng Mealea complex was completed in a shorter time, because of its lesser dimensions and especially because of the proximity of a quarry and the flatness of the terrain, which facilitated the transport and assembling of the material.

The group of monuments we have been considering provide the characteristics of the Angkor Wat style, and not only from the standpoint of their architecture but also from that of architectural decoration and sculpture. As for the paintings that once decorated so many of these temples, there is little that can be said. In fact, it should be mentioned that the absence of pictorial reproductions in a book of this kind is not accidental but results from the meagerness of the examples that have come down to us. This should not lead us to think, however, that the Khmer artists were unfamiliar with the art of painting, for we have examples of pictorial decoration in the Bakong and the Beng Mealea. Moreover, the techniques used in the bas-reliefs testify to an experience that cannot but be related to painting.

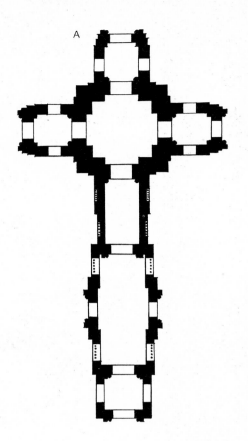

Plans of sanctuaries in the style of Angkor Wat:
A Phimai: central sanctuary
B Banteay Samre

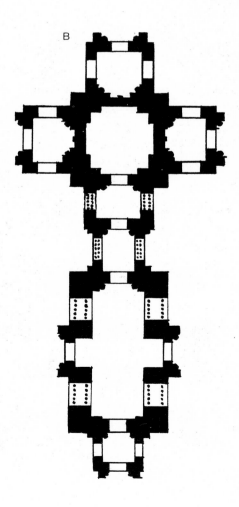

Banteay Samre (Angkor): The main entrance to the temple.

Following page:
Banteay Samre (Angkor): A pediment decorated with figures of divinities, characteristic of the second phase of the Bayon style.

The splendor of the reign of Suryavarman II, which was no longer matched by a solid state organization, came to an end even before the sovereign himself had died—probably around 1150. The last few years of his reign remain obscure, disrupted by rebellions such as those of his two successors, Dharanindravarman II and Yasovarman II. An unstable and weak internal situation was what was most apt to generate in the enemies of the Khmers the hope of waging a successful attack against "the colossus with the clay feet." Jaya Indravarman, king of the Chams, was the first to grasp the situation, and with a brilliant strategic ploy he managed to overrun Angkor in 1177 and sack the city. But dramatic though the capture of the kingdom's capital was, the episode took on a much more far-reaching significance. Coming at the end of a troubled, chaotic period, the event was a serious blow to the Khmer empire, a tragedy that foreshadowed the end, and which the advent of a sovereign like Jayavarman VII, however capable, could only postpone for a time. Meanwhile, the end of Suryavarman II brings down the curtain on an epoch, but one that will be eternally recalled through his masterwork, Angkor Wat.

The Last Phase at Angkor

THE BAYON STYLE: FIRST PHASE

Jayavarman VII, the last great Khmer sovereign, did not ascend to the throne immediately after the death of his father, Dharanindravarman II. Inscriptions tell us that the latter was overthrown by a usurper, Yasovarman II, who after a short reign (1160–1166) was himself killed by a servant. Then a Tribhuvanadityavarman evidently ruled at Angkor for some years—until 1181—until Jayavarman could take over control of the kingdom. It was during the reign of Tribhuvanadityavarman that the Chams sacked Angkor—1177—and Jayavarman VII must have played some part in clearing the Chams out of Cambodia. No inscription from the reign of Dharanindravarman II has come down to us, but his son Jayavarman VII celebrates him as a Buddhist. The construction of the Buddhist temple of Preah Palilay is perhaps to be attributed to him, along with the Hindu temples of Banteay Samre and possibly Beng Mealea (whose decoration includes Buddhist themes).

The last inscription from Jayavarman VII's reign that we know of is dated 1201, and for a long time it was believed that his reign was limited to twenty years. Coedès believes, however, that it actually extended up to 1219. The rhythm of the foundations ordained by the Khmer sovereigns—the public works first, the ancestor temple next, and then the temple-mountain—was maintained by Jayavarman VII. We learn from the Ta Prohm inscription that by 1186—only five years after the official beginning of his reign—102 hospitals had been built in various provinces. The Preah Khan inscription tells us that in 1191 the so-called "houses with a fire" for travelers numbered 121, distributed along the main roads: these were halting places where travelers could put up free of charge and refresh themselves during a trip. The administrative centers of hospitals and the "houses with a fire" were at Angkor, located near the temples of Ta Prohm and Preah Khan. All that has come down to us of these buildings, which were evidently made of wood, like private homes, are the stone "chapels," or annexes, and these date from a later epoch. Unquestionably to be included among the public works of Jayavarman VII were the improvements in the city's water system.

The consecration of the temple of Ta Prohm, which was dedicated to Jayavarman VII's mother, took place in 1186; that of the Preah Khan, built in tribute to his father, in 1191. The sovereign's parents were identified with the Prajnaparamita (a Buddhist divinity, the personification of Wisdom), and with Lokesvara, the Bodhisattva of compassion. The holy triad is completed by Buddha, to whom the Banteay Kdei temple is dedicated.

The monuments erected during the reign of Jayavarman VII have been analyzed by Stern (who in 1965 published a study fundamental to understanding this period). The method adopted consisted of following each motif separately and of tracing its evolution by using a number of fixed points of comparison furnished by those monuments dated with certainty (thanks to inscriptions); then the various elements were compared with one another so as to throw light on what they have in common. At the same time, each monument was studied in its entirety. It was thus possible to establish a minute chronology of the monuments, a chronology that represents a precious working tool and the definitive classification of a period heretofore so controversial.

Preah Palilay (Angkor): The east entrance pavilion, with an image of Buddha seated before it. This temple was evidently built by Dharanindravarman II, father of Jayavarman VII, and its iconography appears to have been inspired by Hinayana ("Small Vehicle") Buddhism rather than by Mahayana ("Large Vehicle") Buddhism. The seated statue of Buddha shows him in the attitude of meditation. Note the standing image of Buddha, surrounded by worshipers, in the multilobed pediment over the entrance to the pavilion. This is the only Buddhist monument at Angkor in which the images of Buddha were not destroyed during the Hindu reaction that followed the reign of Jayavarman VII.

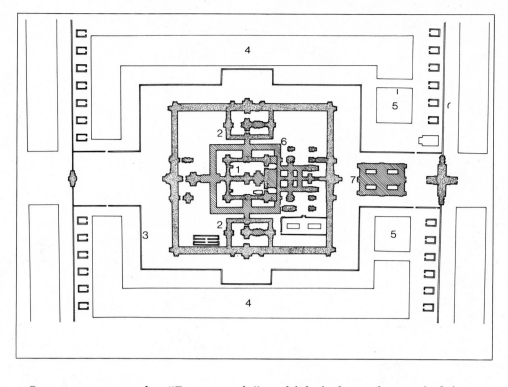

Stern separates the "Bayon style"—which is how the period is now known—into three phases. The first runs from the very outset of Jayavarman VII's reign to the consecration of the Preah Khan (1191) and is centered on the two great temples in honor of his parents. The second phase coincides with the great religious reform and with the introduction of elements of great significance: the long lines of *devas* (deities) and *asuras* (demons) holding up *nagas* outside the gates of the city and the doorways to a number of temples; the great *garudas* with their arms upraised along the walls; pediments decorated with the likeness of Lokesvara; and later on, towers with the four gigantic faces of the Bodhisattva and corner motifs linked with royalty. Also belonging to this phase is the addition of enclosures to a number of monuments of the preceding phase; the building of the stone wall around the city; the first nucleus of the Bayon; and lastly, outside Angkor, the Banteay Chmar temple. The third and final phase was completely centered on the Bayon itself, which absorbed the entire creative effort that had been splintered in the preceding phases.

Among the various guiding elements that made it possible to distinguish these phases, a place of particular importance is occupied by the *devata,* a minor female divinity. This figure's oldest version was characterized by several elements: the absence of a smile; a conical hairdo; a garment with two wide strips of material appearing on the sides (and although one of these panels may appear in front, the rigid stylization is maintained) or completely smooth; and the absence of jewelry. Often one hand is lifted to the waist, in memory of the gesture made by those in the temple of Angkor Wat in raising the edge of their vestments. The figure is framed in a trilobate (three-lobed) arch.

Set against this type of *devata* is the more recent type with a smiling face; a triangle-shaped hairdo, with pointed elements at times enhanced by disks; garments with a triangular panel in the center, wider at the waist and curved at the edge; and an abundance of jewels. The gesture of the hand at the waist is not part of this phase; one of the hands is usually raised, however, or else it holds a scarf-garland at the side. The figure is framed by a sinuous arch, formed by a number of branches with leaves. (In addition to the two types of *devatas* with well-defined characteristics, there is also a transitional type.)

In monumental architecture, the first phase of the Bayon style can be

Ta Prohm (Angkor): The tympanum of this doorway is framed by the bodies of two *nagas*, while within the tympanum is a row of worshipers under an image of Buddha. But the figure of the Buddha was cut away during the reaction that followed the end of Jayavarman VII's reign. This temple (dated 1186) has intentionally been left (at least for now) in the grip of the vegetation, such as this giant silk-cotton tree.

summed up in the construction of the Ta Prohm, the Preah Khan of Angkor, and the Banteay Kdei. This last-named lacks both the characteristics that link the Ta Prohm to the Angkor Wat style and the elements at Preah Khan foreshadowing the later development of the style. There is good reason to date Banteay Kdei's construction after the beginning of Ta Prohm, yet before the completion of the Preah Khan. Stern, in fact, has considered the Banteay Kdei a "model structure" due to the simplicity of its original design and because of the ease with which one distinguishes the more recent parts—nearly all belong to the third phase.

The original design (page 140) of the Banteay Kdei included a central cruciform sanctuary, a gallery with eight towers, four set at the corners, four at the *gopuras,* and a passageway that, by extending the east arm of the cross, connected it to the peripheral gallery, an enclosure surrounded by a moat. Added later was the enclosure wall that Stern calls the *enceinte de domaine*—and which we shall henceforth call the "outer enclosure."

Srah Srang Reservoir (Angkor): In the foreground is the west landing in this reservoir, adjacent to the Banteay Kdei temple. The *naga* balustrades end in the figures of *garudas,* represented with arms upraised.

Banteay Kdei (Angkor): A section of the east wall of the central complex (front dated 1186, rear dated 1191). The type of *devatas* here indicates that the wall is an addition to an earlier structure, having probably been added during the third phase of the Bayon style. Just visible through a window to the right are pillars with figures of paired dancing girls carved in extremely low relief.

Following pages:
Preah Khan (Angkor): The approach to the sanctuary (dated 1191). On both sides in the foreground are pillars; the carvings originally in the upper niches have been removed; in the lower panel is Garuda.

The first outer enclosure with clearly defined characteristics was that at Angkor Wat. Most likely put up to mark off the living quarters (built of perishable materials) of those assigned to maintaining the temples, this wall enclosed an area larger than that of the temple. The fact that the outer enclosure at Banteay Kdei was added at a later date is shown by the moat, which surrounds the temple enclosure; by the presence in the *gopuras* of the towers with the faces of the Bodhisattva; and the great corner *garudas*, characteristic, as mentioned, of the Bayon style's second phase. These elements are lacking in the towers of the inner enclosure. Indications are that the same period—that is, when the second phase was beginning to take hold—saw the addition of the outer enclosures at Ta Prohm, Ta Som, and Ta Nei (the last two being temples counted among the edifices annexed to the Preah Khan of Angkor).

The other rooms added to the Banteay Kdei belong to the third phase and include a connection to the west peripheral gallery (short connecting

units with the north and south galleries having been built earlier), so that the four wings of the central sanctuary were now joined with the gallery. Also, the east passageway was extended and connected with the "libraries." We see here at Banteay Kdei what has been called an "intermediate gallery," closely surrounding the gallery further within with its four towers, to which it is linked. Completely outside the intermediate gallery, on the main axis of the temple to the east, is a rectangular room called "the hall of the dancing girls," not because of the use it was put to (of which nothing is known) but because it was decorated with rows of dancing figures. Such a hall was included in many temple complexes belonging to the second phase of the Bayon style. We also find such halls in the Ta Prohm and in the Preah Khan of Angkor, alongside another edifice that is a characteristic second-phase addition, a two-story rectangular structure with a quadruple row of columns.

The reasons behind such "additions"—which alter the balance of the various parts of a temple, disrupt the original plan, and obstruct the perspectives—may perhaps lie in a desire to add other roofed rooms to hold the statues of deified human beings. The "personality cults" that, as we have seen, were initially conferred upon the royal family and later upon the top representatives of the great priestly families, the bureaucracy, or the nobility, were particularly widespread during the reign of Jayavarman VII. The Preah Khan stele indicates that the temple held no fewer than 430 statues. This same inscription, in fact, records the total number of images or statues in the kingdom as 20,400. In the Phimeanakas inscription, Jayavarman VII's wife, Indradevi, says of her younger sister, Jayarajadevi, the king's first wife: "In every conceivable nook she placed images of her father, mother, brothers, sisters, friends, relatives, people she had known or only heard of." The numerous inscriptions on the chapel walls or on the statues themselves provide the names of the princes and dignitaries who had been deified. The only break with tradition was the fact that private citizens had begun placing numerous images in royal foundations.

The Phimeanakas stele adds that Indradevi "put up numerous images of Sri Jayarajadevi with the images of the king and of herself in every city." These statues probably represent the first portraits of Khmer art. Some of the statues, singled out by Coedès (see page 176), present clear-cut resemblances to the portrayal of Jayavarman VII in the Bayon and the Banteay Chmar reliefs, which relate the battles against the Chams. As a result, they can be considered portraits of Jayavarman VII. A female figure kneeling as in the manifestation of Prajanaparamita, and known in four examples, could well be the portrait of Queen Jayarajadevi (see pages 143 and 170). The fact that she is represented as a divinity, while Jayavarman has no divine attributes, may stem from the circumstance that, since the queen was dead by the time the statues were made, she had become identified with the divine realm.

We cannot take the time to describe the Ta Prohm or the Preah Khan, whose structures are similar to the Banteay Kdei's, although their dimensions are larger and there is greater profusion of the elements we have observed in the Banteay Kdei. In fact, the structures that Stern classifies as "courtyard galleries" are basically temples with the same design as the Banteay Kdei—that is, a central cruciform sanctuary connected with the peripheral gallery of the eight towers along the east-west axis. Such courtyard galleries were placed alongside—as at the Ta Prohm—or all around—as at Preah Khan—the main temple. At Ta Prohm they were perhaps built in honor of the guru, one dedicated to Shiva and the other to Vishnu. Once again, the name "courtyard" or "cloister" gallery says nothing about the function of the structure; it merely refers to a type of gallery surrounding a sanctuary, to which it was connected only at some later date. (Obviously the cruciform courtyard at Angkor Wat is a different matter.)

Preah Khan (Angkor): This *asura*, or demon, has many heads and arms and is here shown clutching the neck of a many-headed *naga*. This is the last *asura* of the row that extends from the temple's outer wall and across the causeway over the moat.

Banteay Kdei (Angkor): Plan of the temple
1 *Central cruciform sanctuary*
2 *Inner enclosure*
3 *Intermediate enclosure*
4 *"Libraries"*
5 *"Hall of the dancing girls"*
The light parts correspond to the original construction, the dark ones to the later additions.

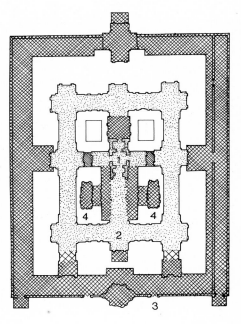

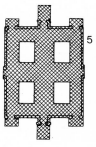

THE BAYON STYLE: SECOND PHASE

The outer enclosure of the Preah Khan of Angkor, completed prior to the consecration of the temple, presents an important innovation: the causeway over the moat (which is outside the enclosure) carries—in place of the traditional double balustrade of *nagas*—two rows, left and right respectively, of deities *(devas)* and demons *(asuras)* supporting the *nagas*. Mus claims that the balustrade of *nagas* is the symbol of the rainbow, an element connecting the divine world to the human. Coedès holds that the two rows of deities and demons supporting *nagas* must be considered as representing the Churning of the Sea of Milk myth, with the temple symbolizing in this instance Mount Meru. In any case, this sculptural complex, which appears for the first time at the Preah Khan enclosure, is repeated in front of each of the five doors of the Angkor Thom wall. (The first stone wall, by the way: heretofore the Angkorean city was surrounded by a moat and by a mound of earth, presumably reinforced by a palisade of wood.) At Angkor Thom, Mount Meru would be symbolized by the Bayon, which is at the very center of Angkor Thom.

In the four inscriptions placed at the four corners of Angkor Thom's boundary wall, this latter is compared to the chain of mountains that shut

This statue of Prajnaparamita ("supreme wisdom") was found at the Preah Khan at Angkor. It is thought that it portrays the features of Queen Jayarajadevi, first wife of Jayavarman VII. Three similar statues have been found (one of which is shown on page 170).

THE NEAK PEAN

In Jayasri [the Preak Khan of Angkor] the king has established the Jayatataka [the reservoir of the Preak Khan] like a wealth-reflecting mirror. In the middle there is an eminent island that draws its beauty from the reservoir, which cleans the dirt of sins from those who come in contact with it, because it serves as a vessel to cross the ocean of existence.

Inscription on Preah Khan Stele

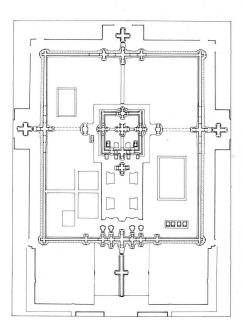

Preah Khan of Kompong Thom: Plan of the main temple.

Preah Khan (Angkor): Plan of the main temple.

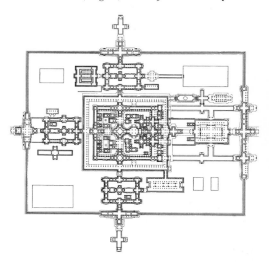

in the universe and the moat to the ocean that surrounds it. "The one touched with its summit the resplendent sky and the other reached, with its unfathomable depths, the world of serpents. This victory mountain (*jayagiri*) and this victory ocean (*jayasundhu*) built by this king imitated the span of his immense glory." The doorways in the Angkor Thom wall—one in the middle of each side, and a fifth in the north end of the east side, an approach to the royal palace and to the Phimeanakas—are surmounted by towers that turn the gigantic countenance of Lokesvara toward each cardinal point. Lokesvara is one of the major Bodhisattvas—a kind of intermediary Buddha—and was particularly associated with healing and compassion. What is involved here, under a different (that is, Buddhist) guise, is the concept of the four visages of Tumburu (Shiva)—mentioned in connection with the royal consecration in the Sdok Kak Thom inscription—of the *cakravartin,* the sun-wheel symbolic of the universal sovereign that dominates the four corners of the world. The visage of the Bodhisattva, embracing all space with his gaze, protects the city and ensures the kingdom's stability.

The first Khmer monument that had a tower with four visages seems to have been the Prasat Preah Stung, in the Preah Khan complex at Kompong Thom. This monument is situated some 60 miles east of Angkor, and it is worthwhile taking a brief detour to examine it. The Preah Khan must have been considered a temple of particular importance, for the

Neak Pean (Angkor): This miniature temple (end of the twelfth century) rose in the center of the basin adjacent to the Preah Khan, a symbolic version of the mythical Lake Anavatapta. Three of the temple's doors were closed off in a later building phase, and a large statue of Bodhisattva Lokesvara was sculptured on each doorway. Visible on the outer walls of the basin are two of the four small shrines added during the rebuilding.

Neak Pean (Angkor): A detail of the free-standing sculpture that is visible on the right of the photograph on the opposite page. It represents a Bodhisattva in the aspect of a winged horse, Balaha, towing to safety a number of merchants who were about to be devoured by an ogress on an island (in an incident from a Buddhist tale).

road leading to it is studded with "houses of fire" built of sandstone (while other structures of this type are of the less durable laterite). The shape of the edifice (page 143) discloses the characteristics of the Angkor Wat style, and at the same time it reveals strong analogies with the Preah Khan of Angkor. There are even reasons to believe the former was the "model" of the Preah Khan at Kompong Thom. In any case, this latter was probably built by Dharanindravarman II, father of Jayavarman VII; Stern even claims that Jayavarman lived there during the "waiting period" (1166–1181). The discovery in the Preah Khan of Kompong Thom of a head closely resembling what are believed to be portraits of Jayavarman VII, although with more youthful features, might be considered confirmation of this.

At the outset of the second phase of the Bayon style, an important complex was built around the Preah Khan of Kompong Thom, composed of buildings that are definitely contemporaneous. These buildings include the "outer enclosure" of a cruciform edifice inside the temple (similar to the one in the Preah Khan at Angkor) and three temples connected to the reservoir: Prasat Preah Stung on the west bank, Preah Thkol in the middle, and Preah Damrei on the east bank. Although built later, the "outer enclosure" closely resembles the Preah Khan of Angkor. (There had already been a change in the type of *devatas,* perhaps caused by an observation of the *devatas* of the Angkor Wat period.)

Left:
Angkor Thom: The south gate (second phase of the Bayon style, end of the twelfth century), viewed from the entrance to the causeway. On the left is a row of *devas* (deities) and on the right a row of *asuras* (demons), all holding onto *nagas*. One theory claims that the serpent is Vasuki, representing a motif from the myth of the Churning of the Sea of Milk. (See the bas-reliefs at Angkor Wat, pages 120–21, for another representation of this story.)

Left, below:
Angkor Thom: A close-up of some of the *devas* holding up the serpent along the approach to the south gate. These deities are distinguished from the demons on the other side by their conical headdress, their eyes, and their expression.

Right:
Angkor Thom: The south gate, topped by three towers carved to represent the head of Bodhisattva Lokesvara (a fourth face looks inward).

Pages 148–49:
Angkor Thom: A close-up of the Bodhisattva Lokesvara in the middle of the tower over the south gate. Visible around the base of the head are the tops of minor divinities.

Pages 150–51:
The Bayon (Angkor Thom): The great central mass and a section of the enclosure gallery; this latter is also topped by towers carved to represent four heads of the Bodhisattva. What is seen here belongs to the third phase of the Bayon style, dated to the outset of the thirteenth century.

It was probably in the Prasat Preah Stung—which, because of the number of identical decorative motifs, appears to be more or less contemporaneous to the "outer enclosure"—that the tower with four faces first appeared. It should be remembered that up to this time such towers had never been seen. Henceforward, however, they were to be found in all outer enclosures. Of special interest was the discovery not far from the temple of a pedestal of a gigantic statue of Buddha with four faces (only one of which was in a condition that allowed for reconstruction). Undoubtedly, though, the culmination of the four-faced tower was to come in the Bayon itself, during the style's third phase.

BUDDHISM AND ROYALTY

Another characteristic element, along with the enclosure approached by rows of deities and demons supporting *nagas,* was the pediment with a statue of Lokesvara. And one of the most interesting examples of this development is the Neak Pean, the small sanctuary standing in the middle of the great reservoir known as the North Baray, adjacent to the Preah Kahn of Angkor. At the time the Lokesvara motif took hold, the four pediments of this sanctuary were already occupied with reliefs representing episodes from the life of Buddha. Three of the doors were therefore filled in and they were then used for representations—in larger dimensions, of course, than the pediments would have allowed—of the Bodhisattva of compassion, Lokesvara.

Also built after the sanctuary of Neak Pean were the four small chapels at the cardinal points of its enclosure, and these also include standing Lokesvaras. These four little shrines have been valuable in interpreting the symbolism connected with the Neak Pean itself, for also discovered in them were sculptures representing: north, the head of an elephant with its trunk lifted; east, a male with a diadem; and west, the head of a horse. All of these were obviously fountain "gargoyles" from whose mouths water spouted. The Buddhist texts (as Finot and Goloubew have pointed out) mention a "great sacred lake in the Himalaya region where the Buddhas, the Bodhisattvas, the *Arhat* (saints), and the *Rishi* (hermits) were accustomed to bathe—Lake Anavatapta. Originating in this lake were four rivers that flowed from its four sides as mouths of a lion, an elephant, a horse, and an ox. This sequence was not strictly applied to the images at the Neak Pean (where a human head was substituted for at least one); nevertheless, the coincidence is too striking to be fortuitous, and the existence of some variant is not unlikely." The two French scholars find further confirmation for this theory in the description by the Chinese pilgrim Hsiuan Tsang of a thermal spring he saw in India, near Rajagriha, where there was also a link with Lake Anavatapta.

We have already indicated that the outset of the Bayon style's second phase coincided with a religious reform that manifested itself through a great diffusion of Lokesvara images, and later through the appearance of the four-faced towers. It may be said that virtually every pediment of the style's second phase—including those of the chapels annexed to the "hospitals" or to the "houses of fire," the *gopuras* of the outer enclosures or those of the city walls—is decorated with the image of Lokesvara. Corresponding to this profusion of images from Mahayana Buddhism are the inscriptions recording the king's claims of protection of his subjects. "He suffered from the illnesses of his subjects more than from his own, for the king's pain is that suffered by the public at large and not his own," says the stele of the hospital. Another stele (that of Preah Khan) states: "Having tirelessly carried out a number of exceptional, meritorious actions on behalf of all living beings, this king, doing his pious work on behalf of his father, for whom he professed great devotion, took this oath: 'So that through these good works . . . my father might rejoice in the enlighten-

ment that others failed to achieve, with the aim of helping others cross the ocean of existence.' "

Now, as we have clearly established, Buddhism, present in Cambodia since pre-Angkorean times, coexisted with Hinduism if perhaps alternating some periods of eclipse along with times of success. During the reign of Suryavarman II and that of his successor, Dharanindravarman II, Buddhist themes in the decoration of temples multiplied. Thus it may be said that the favor accorded to Buddhism by Jayavarman VII was undoubtedly prepared for by preceding periods and represented no drastic change. What may be considered a new departure, however, was the widespread dissemination of Mahayana Buddhism, which was in a sense "propagandized" through the sharp increase, in the various buildings erected, of iconographic elements based on this particular school. The theory has been advanced that Jayavarman VII went out of his way to promote Buddhism in order to check the Hindu priestly class that had become inordinately strong and which, thanks to the fact that it "initiated" the king, wielded great power. In effect, Jayavarman VII was the first to supplant the royal image of the *linga,* which joined the name of the king and of Shiva, with the Buddharaja—that is, an image joining in itself both Buddha and the king. In fact, after the Sdok Tak Thom inscription (1052), we hear nothing more of the worship of the *devaraja.* But indications are that it continued to be observed until Jayavarman VII, as noted, replaced it with worship of the Buddharaja.

It was not by chance that at the outset of the second phase of the Bayon style, side by side with the widespread use of themes from Mahayana Buddhism, elements came to the fore that were closely connected with cosmic symbolism and royalty. Among these were the long procession of deities and demons before the gates of the city to represent the Churning of the Sea of Milk (a creation myth, but also a symbol of the well-being the king procured for his subjects) and the corner motifs that in their most complete forms present a procession from earth to heaven—the three-headed elephants (the "vehicle" of Indra, king of the gods), the lion, Garuda, and Hamsa (the goose), all closely connected in India with the representation of the throne. But the element in which the synthesis of the cosmic symbolism and Mahayana religiosity is most clearly achieved is without doubt the four-faced tower, with the Bodhisattva facing the four cardinal points of the universe.

We have previously observed, in examining the Bakheng, that even the number of towers at a temple had a cosmological significance. And when we come to examine the Bayon we shall note that other symbolism is at work. Thus, the very alternation of light and shade on the four faces must relate to the rotation of day and night, to the movements of the sun and stars (as perceived by Khmers, that is). And the Bodhisattva "whose gaze goes everywhere"spreads his protection through the entire sweep of space. Whether or not we accept the theory that the innumerable images appearing on the towers at the Bayon are portraits of Jayavarman VII, their symbolic significance changes little: the Bodhisattva remains the custodian of the established order, an order whose guarantor is the king.

At this point, we might consider the changes Khmer society had undergone since the period previously investigated. Bureaucracy was still widespread. A reading of the inscriptions of the great royal foundations may give some idea of the persons frequenting the temples, now transformed into full-fledged monasteries. In the Ta Prohm inscription, for instance, we read: "Here are 400 men, 18 great priests, 2,740 officials, 2,232 assistants, including 615 dancing girls: altogether 12,640 persons, including those entitled to lodgings. 66,625 men and women carry out the service of the gods, totaling 79,365 with the Burmese, the Chams . . . while 439 religious saints are fed each day in the Royal Palace, and 970 persons reside with the reader, totaling 1,409." In the Preah

The Bayon (Angkor Thom): A view of the central mass (upper right) rising from an inner courtyard.

The Bayon (Angkor Thom): Several of the face-towers of the central sanctuary. These heads of the Bodhisattva are also symbolic of the universal radiance of the king, a symbolism made explicit in the light and shadow effects resulting from the changing hours of the day.

The Bayon (Angkor Thom): North-south cross section of the main part of the Bayon:
1 Central sanctuary
2 Cruciform towers
3 Sunken shaft
4 Cruciform galleries

Khan inscription we read: "The king and the proprietors of the villages have piously donated 5,324 villages, a total of 97,840 men and women . . . 444 chiefs, 4,606 men assigned to the temple cooks and others, 2,298 assistants assigned to the temples, 1,000 of whom were dancing girls; 47,436 persons who have made an offering."

Somewhat further on, this same inscription points out that numerous other foundations were under the jurisdiction of Preah Khan. The custom of joining two or three foundations together that had begun in preceding centuries now led to the merger of many foundations under the direction of one temple. We also note the appearance of the expression, "the proprietors of the villages": this was perhaps an indication of the fact that those who worked toward the private appropriation of land had been at least partly successful. Meanwhile, those who had taken up the role of intermediaries between the state and the temples evidently succeeded in achieving such a strong position that the king now had to limit their power. Obviously the great priestly families were gravely disturbed by the religious reforms of Jayavarman VII. Proof of this is the violence of the Hindu reaction when his reign came to an end, with the destruction of many of the images of Buddha. This reaction was even more unusual in that Buddha had for centuries been venerated alongside the gods of Hinduism.

Another basic monument in the Bayon style's second phase was the Banteay Chmar, dedicated, apparently, to Jayavarman VII's son who had died in battle. (At present it is in ruins.) The Banteay Chmar is made up of a sanctuary surrounded by a rectangular gallery, which is flanked on either side, east and west, by two similar complexes. To the west, this development along a longitudinal axis is completed by a minor sanctuary surrounded by a courtyard gallery, and to the east by the "hall of dancing girls." On the north and south sides two other minor sanctuaries are found, both surrounded by galleries. A rectangular gallery, with triple *gopura* and sanctuaries at the corners, runs all the way around the complex, which also includes numerous reservoirs. As for the decoration, the Banteay Chmar is the sole monument that enables us to follow the evolution of the *devatas* between the first and second types. Many of the bas-reliefs at Banteay Chmar represent everyday activities of the Khmers, while those in the outside gallery show scenes of the war against the Chams. The outside enclosure is surrounded by a moat. The causeways across it are flanked by long rows of deities and demons supporting *nagas*. Extending in front of the temple is a great reservoir with a tower in its middle. The whole complex is surrounded by the boundary wall of a city.

The Bayon (Angkor Thom): Some of the towers with the four faces of Bodhisattva. In the foreground is a balustrade of a *naga*. The curved roof of a gallery (lower right) shows how the stones were worked to imitate tiles.

THE BAYON

Also belonging to the second phase of the Bayon style is the basic nucleus of the Bayon itself; this cannot be seen any longer, however, as it has been incorporated into subsequent constructions. All indications are that this first structure was also a temple-mountain. It marked the center of Angkor Thom, in fact, and according to the cosmological symbolism connected with Khmer cities it would therefore have to be a temple-mountain. The middle part was later widened so much that it comes close to touching the finely shaped gallery that surrounds it. Yet even this gallery must have been included in the original plan; its inner wall, for one thing, shows decorations that, because of the lack of space, cannot have been executed after the enlargement of the middle mass. Still distinguishable among the decorations is a Lokesvara of large proportions. The pediment with a Lokesvara figure is a characteristic elements of the style's second phase; indeed, there is no trace of such in the first phase, and it was extremely rare in the third.

In the third phase at the Bayon, the gallery was completed by four corner rooms, in order to bring the design back into quadrilateral form. A number of connecting rooms are mentioned in the inscriptions, and Parmentier found traces of them on the ground. There must have been sixteen of these rooms connecting the outer gallery with the innermost one, four on each side, thus creating sixteen small courtyards. But shortly after the end of Jayavarman VII's reign, they were demolished. But this

The Bayon (Angkor Thom): The lintel across this south entrance holds three dancing figures amid floral elements; the relief carving has worn down considerably over the centuries.

Right:
The Bayon (Angkor Thom): A doorway into the intermediate gallery. The *devatas* that flank the two door guards belong to the third phase of the Bayon style.

Left:
The Bayon (Angkor Thom): A section of the north wing of the outer gallery. Clearly visible here are some reliefs that depict (on the left) a number of armies on the march and (on the right) battle scenes. The composition is divided into two registers, but this rigid arrangement does not prevent several of them from being shown frontally rather than in profile. Greater movement may be noted in the battle scenes, but it always exemplifies an orderly rhythm.

The Bayon (Angkor Thom): Plan of the temple

Below:
The Bayon (Angkor Thom): A close-up of a relief on the outer gallery, representing the army of the Chams on the march.

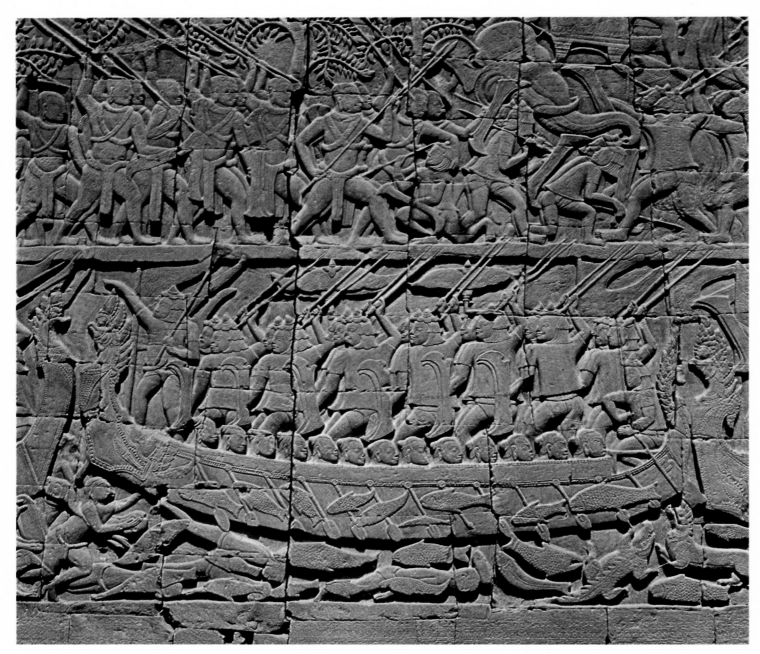

third phase at the Bayon is marked by the multiplication of the small galleries and connecting rooms, although the fundamental characteristics of the temple remain: the middle mass bristling with towers bearing the four smiling visages, an increase in the number of towers, and a generous use of carved reliefs in the galleries. And as with the reliefs at Banteay Chmar, we find not only battle scenes but true "genre" scenes—episodes from everyday life. In those of the Bayon we see lively scenes of markets, fishing, work in the fields; we see the antics of acrobats and cockfights and dogfights. Human beings, no longer arranged in rows, are put into the existing space with variety and liveliness of demeanor, their individual features often carefully portrayed.

Fitting in with this new emphasis on reproducing everyday reality and individual physiognomies is the portrayal of the kings, no longer in impersonal images but with full-blown portraits. But in the outer gallery of the Bayon, the reliefs are ascribed to the second quarter of the thirteenth century, after the end of the true Bayon style: once again we are confronted with stereotypes and once again there is a tendency to arrange human figures in rows.

The dating of the Bayon has been a highly complex process, and it represents an example of how it is possible, through coordinated research, to weed out errors and, piece by piece, establish a correct

The Bayon (Angkor Thom): A relief in two registers, representing (above) a battle in the forest, and (below) the Chams' army traveling in boats. The representation of the marine fauna is full of life, and calls to mind the similar scene from the Churning of the Sea of Milk relief at Angkor Wat (pages 120–21).

chronology. In the beginning, because the dense vegetation that had invaded the city of Angkor Thom made it difficult to obtain exact measurements, it was not even realized that the Bayon was at the center of the city. It was thought, in fact, that the center was marked by the Baphuon or the Phimeanakas (both, in fact, to the north of center). When it was ascertained in 1908 that the Bayon coincided with the center of the city, it was then erroneously identified with the temple-mountain of Yasovarman I and so assigned to the ninth century. (At this time, it was thought that the walls of Angkor Thom marked the perimeter of Yasovarman I's city; it was not until 1933–1934 that Goloubew established the true outlines of his city and identified its "central mountain" as the Bakheng.) And once the Bayon had been dated to the end of the ninth century, other monuments in the same style had to be assigned to later dates, for if the Bayon was the center of Yasovarman I's city, which inscriptions clearly described as the first in the Angkor site, this same place could hold no older edifices.

The monuments were thus for long dated in an inverse order with respect to the true one, and gradually the Bayon came to be treated as the pivot around which the entire chronology of the Angkorean period was made to rotate. Despite the fact that grave contradictions emerged—such as the contemporaneousness of the Preah Ko and the Bakong (the dates

The Bayon (Angkor Thom): The relief (from the outer gallery) representing the celebration of a victory. The scene is spread along three registers. In the middle one, two persons, one of whom wears a garment decorated with flowers, hold up two human heads. The space where the scene unfolds appears to be a pavilion with curtains; some of the latter's decorations are meticulously reproduced; note, too, on the left, the roof of a pavilion, with a hint of tiles (or their imitation in stone). The upper register holds a scene that is yet to be identified: two persons are the object of homage by others, but nothing else is clear. One of these persons (left) is carried on a palanquin; up into the beginning of our own century this same type of palanquin was still in use throughout Indochina. The carving of this relief is very low, with figures close together so as to leave as much space as possible empty. The arrangement in registers, with the people paired off, does not seem to diminish the liveliness of the scene, despite its rigidity.

KHMER PALANQUINS

The palanquins are made with a piece of wood that curves high in the middle and also curves up at the ends, where there are carved floral motifs. Near the ends of this wooden frame are attached metal hooks, with two cords hanging down between them; a large piece of material is folded over these cords in hammocklike fashion. The person then sits on this material, and two men carry the palanquin.

Chou Ta-Kuan: *Recollections on the Customs of Cambodia*

of which were known through inscriptions) with the Bayon, obviously quite different—the date of the Bayon was considered beyond question. When Philippe Stern, still a young man in the 1920s, undertook a stylistic analysis of Khmer sculpture that led him to place the Bayon alongside the Angkor Wat (which by then was correctly assigned to the twelfth century) the first thing Stern did was to question the validity of his own methods! But eventually Stern, encouraged by Coedès and Hadkin, set about to revise the date of the Bayon. In 1927 he stated his conclusions in his first work, *Le Bayon d'Angkor et l'évolution de l'art khmer,* finding the courage to shift the date from the ninth to the twelfth century and placing it alongside the Angkor Wat, although in a somewhat earlier period. The next step was taken by Coedès, who the following year correctly assigned the Bayon to the period of Jayavarman VII. We might add that in the beginning, because it was assigned to the reign of Yasovarman I, the Bayon was considered a Shivaite temple; it was only in 1925 that Finot, thanks to the discovery of the pediment with a sculpture of Lokesvara on the inner face of the cruciform gallery, managed to establish the fact that it was a Buddhist monument.

But other problems still remain, such as the symbolic meaning of the number of towers at the Bayon. This has been debated for years, yet there has never been a study that resolves the matter. Inside the temple we find inscriptions and sculptures that allude to other major Khmer sanctuaries: the Bayon, therefore, was considered the center and microcosm of the entire kingdom. But although that much is accepted, many of the details of the symbolism are still in question.

The Bayon (Angkor Thom): A relief with genre scenes from the south wing of the outer gallery. On the right corner of the lower register is the cockfight shown in close-up on page 20. Alongside it is a market scene, with vendors weighing merchandise on a scale; a girl selling fish; turtles and geese walking amid the feet of shoppers. Visible above is a boat with a number of dignitaries in the middle section—evidently giving orders. On a higher plane a group of fishermen are laying their nets, while one of them releases a hawk (see the small boat at the upper right).

Right:
The Bayon (Angkor Thom): A section of a relief representing Khmer warriors engaged in a navel battle. Along the bottom are genre scenes; note especially the small hut on the left, where a woman is in the act of giving birth.

The Bayon (Angkor Thom): Three *asparas*, or nymphs, dancing, from the pilaster of the outer gallery. The figures of dancing girls were among the favorite subjects of the Bayon period; annexed to the major temples were halls decorated with long lines of dancing figures.

THE DECLINE OF THE KHMERS

Built some time after the Bayon—and perhaps after the reign of Jayavarman VII—were the so-called royal terraces. These were located near the entrance to the royal palace in Angkor Thom, and represented in relief on the outside are a number of *garudas* with their arms uplifted. Coedès holds that the intention was to signify that the wooden structures these terraces once supported were "celestial palaces." The best known of the terraces are the "Terrace of the Elephants" and the "Terrace of the Leper King." In both we note a multiplication and increased heaviness of decorative elements. In the latter, the presence of infernal scenes hidden by other carvings induced Coedès to put forward the theory, based on an analogy with the Barabudur of Java, that these were scenes of the afterworld that someone wanted to hide. The discovery of more reliefs similarly hidden by others at the Elephant Terrace—even though the first ones did not deal with afterworld scenes—throws doubt on this explanation.

After its initial phase, we may say, the Bayon style was characterized by a feverish multiplication of rooms, by hasty constructions—even added to temples of previous periods, such as at Phimai and Beng Mealea—and by the erection of grandiose edifices beyond all proportion. It is clear that the simplification of some elements (for example, the abandonment of the window with small columns, or the simplification of the columns supporting the lintels), the abandonment of techniques demanding great time (such as the insertion of wooden beams into blocks of stone), a

The Bayon (Angkor Thom): A *devata* carved on the intermediate gallery, a figure typical of the third phase of the Bayon style. The distinctive characteristics are: headdress with pointed elements and disks placed in a triangular pattern; the left hand raised to shoulder height to hold a flower while the right hand holds a long scarf-garland; and the style of garment. The arch serving as a frame is formed of floral elements.

carelessness in fitting stone blocks together, and a crudeness in connecting elements when new rooms were added—all this resulted from the haste and size of the works, which were concentrated into a relatively brief period of time. Moreover, the grandiose constructions of the Angkor Wat period, all of sandstone, had almost completely exhausted the nearby quarries. It became necessary to resort to poorer grades of sandstone, and when possible the still less durable laterite was used. Statues of exceptional proportions were frequently built of different blocks, one fitted against the other, with the various parts joined by tenons and grooves.

In 1296, approximately seventy-five years after the end of the reign of Jayavarman VII, Angkor was visited by the Chinese Chou Ta-Kuan, who has left us a priceless description of it. The city was still flourishing, he reported, the irrigation network was still fully functioning. (Thanks to the irrigation techniques, in fact, there were said to be three or even four harvests a year.) Chou Ta-Kuan also noted the spread of Theravada Buddhism, a form of the "Small Vehicle" Buddhism that seems to have originated in Ceylon and Burma and spread to Cambodia through Siam; its distinctive element was a fatalism that discouraged so many of man's activities. In particular, Theravada Buddhism undermined Hinduism, and as more and more of the people adopted Buddhism, a split grew between the population at large and the king and his court (who were to remain Hindus up to modern times). The spreading of Theravada Buddhism is borne out by the inscriptions, in which Pali, an Indian lan-

Above:
The Bayon (Angkor Thom): A statue of Buddha sitting on a coiled *naga*. A similar statue, probably reproducing the features of Jayavarman VII, was found in the central sanctuary of the Bayon, but broken to pieces in the bottom of the central shaft. Both statues perhaps represent the Bayon's main divinity, Jayabuddha, whose name joined that of the king and Buddha.

The Bayon (Angkor Thom): Plan of the water-circulation system of the Bayon. The basin in front with the continuous line is the one where the water flows in the open air; the basin indicated by a broken line is the one where the water was under cover. The arrows indicate exits, entrances and direction of the flow.

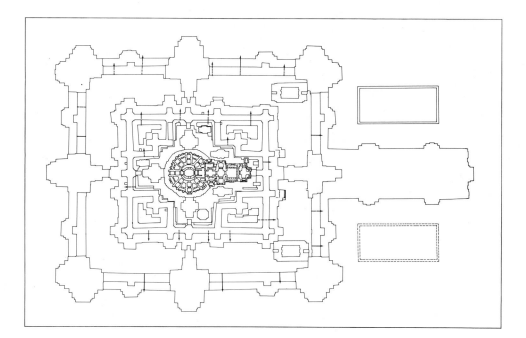

A statue of Prajnaparamita ("supreme wisdom") from the Preah Khan at Angkor, similar to the one shown on page 143. Like that, too, it probably portrays the features of Jayarajadevi, first wife of Jayavarman VII. (Guimet Museum, Paris)

The Elephant Terrace (Angkor Thom): This many-headed elephant is a symbol of the earth, with which the elephant was often linked. Visible in the photographs are the plants that are being sucked up by the trunks. Beginning with the second phase of the Bayon style, this figure group was often represented, particularly as a corner element. Thirteenth century.

The Elephant Terrace (Angkor Thom): A detail of the relief showing people riding on the backs of elephants.

Royal Terrace (Angkor): This figure clinging to the trunk of an elephant is carved completely in the round, which further enhances the sense of spiraling movement.

Following pages:
Terrace of the Leper King (Angkor Thom): This terrace is named after a mythical king (whom later Cambodians sometimes credited with building Angkor). This is but one section of the walls with endless rows of divinities sculptured in a frontal position of meditation. Beginning of the thirteenth century.

guage used by Buddhists, began to take the place of Sanskrit, the language of Hinduism. The last known inscription in Sanskrit, which was that of Kapilapura, is dated 1327. The first in Pali is dated 1309 and was the work of King Sindravarman, who because of his Buddhist faith was compelled to abdicate. No temple-mountain was erected after the end of Jayavarman VII's reign, nor have monuments of stone from that period been discovered except for the temple of Mangalartha, the work of a priestly family dating from the end of the thirteenth century.

In the fourteenth century, although kings continued to reign at Angkor, their powers were waning and the kingdom was collapsing on all sides. To the east, the Chams freed themselves; to the north, a new threat appeared—the Thais. The Thais had originally come from the basin of the Yangtze River in China and founded a kingdom of Nan-chao in Yunan, China, in the seventh century. Later they moved still farther south and settled in the northern sections of what are now Laos, Thailand, and Burma, where they merged with the native populations and converted to Buddhism. But now, in the fourteenth century, with the Khmers weakening, the Thai armies made their way down into Cambodia—on two occasions (1335 and 1353) actually conquering Angkor. Then, in 1431, they sacked Angkor and drove the Khmers into full retreat. The Khmers moved toward the southeast, into territories formerly part of ancient Chenla, but each time they set up a new capital the Thais forced them to retreat and move on again. It was a sad way to conduct a kingdom once based in the great city of Angkor.

Many theories have been formulated to explain the reasons behind the decline of Angkor and the Khmer kingdom, but they come down to two main causes. On the one hand, there was the weakening of the central

power, in turn undermining the entire organization of the Khmer state. On the other hand, there was the pressure from the Thais, who were able to strengthen their position precisely because of the internal weakness of the Khmers. A close analysis of the inscriptions with a view to pinning down the causes of the deterioration of the Khmer state has yet to be made, but we may state with some certainty that two determinant factors were the dragging weight of the great bureaucratic apparatus and the emergence of the "village proprietors," no longer responsible to the state bureaucracy but virtual feudal lords.

But there remains still one other factor that many modern students of the Khmer kingdom tend to emphasize. The Khmers had created an elaborate system that permitted the maximum exploitation of the land without impoverishing it, but this system was closely bound up with a vigilant maintenance of the irrigation network. The least neglect, because of the close interactions among the various elements and the ease with which the ditches could become clogged—given the gentle slopes and clayey terrain—would touch off a chain reaction that would in the end inevitably lead to the ruin of the entire system. It is obvious that the weakening of the state organization would quickly affect the work on the irrigation network and thereby cripple agricultural production. Grave difficulties were also created by wars, which caused the evacuation of people for one reason or another. It was, in other words, a vicious circle, in which every element was at one and the same time cause and effect.

Bernard-Philippe Groslier, one of the leading students of Khmer civilization, has pointed out that the entire hydraulic system in the Angkor plain shows signs of an ancient catastrophe: the main dams gave way at the critical point; the ditches were partly clogged; some of the rivers opened up new beds, disrupting the network of ditches. Yet is is impossible to establish whether this was determined by a breakdown in the system because of some event that, coming on top of some civil disorder, triggered a sudden disequilibrium or whether it was the result of a long period of abandonment. Tradition tells of a disastrous flood at Angkor, linked to a king's slaying of a young Hindu; the first testimonial we have of this dates from the sixteenth century, but it appears to refer to the middle of the fourteenth century—the time of the first devastations of Angkor by the Thais. And it is interesting to note that after the Khmers abandoned Angkor in 1432 they never built anything like that marvelous irrigation system but confined themselves to using the natural water resources. When in the sixteenth and seventeenth centuries some Khmer kings returned for a period to Angkor (see pages 178–79), effort was made to restore the hydraulic system of Angkor Thom, but it was too late: the glories of the Angkorean civilization could not be revived.

Strange as it might at first seem, the post-Angkorean period, although relatively more recent, is the one least known to us today. With but a few exceptions, scholars have concentrated their attention on the "classical" period. And even with that period, the lesser "threads"—those sources of data indispensable for the reweaving of the historical texture—are only now beginning to be unraveled. One thing seems certain, though: however much light comes to be thrown on the Khmers and their civilization, our wonder at and respect for their monuments can only be heightened.

Following page:
This sandstone statue is from Krol Romeas at Angkor; a similar one was found at Phimai, today in Thailand (and on view at the National Museum in Bangkok). In 1934, the French authority George Coedès compared these two statues with the features of Jayavarman VII as he appeared in the reliefs of Banteay Chmar and the Bayon, and found a marked resemblance. There are other heads with similar features, and then there are the statues of Prajnaparamita (see pages 143 and 170), evidently with the features of Queen Jayarajadevi. All would seem to confirm the inscription claiming that Queen Indradevi put up images of the king and his first queen "in all the cities." (National Museum, Phnom Penh)

Appendices

It is the nature of great archaeological sites to give rise to myths, and certainly the remains in Cambodia have inspired their share. Thus anyone today who knows at least a little about the Khmer monuments will probably believe that they were lost to all eyes for many centuries—quite overgrown by the dense vegetation—and that it remained for nineteenth-century Europeans (and a few initiates will even be able to cite the name of Henri Mouhot) to discover and report their existence to the local Cambodians as well as to the world at large. Well, as with all myths, there are seeds of truth here—but also many romantic blossoms. And the full truth is, in fact, far more romantic an epic.

After the abandonment of the capital at Angkor and the decline of the Khmer realm—which, occurred, of course, over many, many decades, but which for convenience' sake is fixed at 1431 when the Thais sacked Angkor—the Khmer people and their leaders lost all focus. There were constant dynastic quarrels, and the capital itself was moved from place to place. During the 150 years after 1431, Angkor was essentially abandoned, although Buddhist monks occupied some of the structures, and Angkor Wat in particular was kept in repair to some extent. But most of the portable works had been carried off by one group or another, and what human beings did not destroy, nature did. So it is fair to say that Angkor and most of the other great monuments of Cambodia did become "lost" in the sense that they ceased to be cared for—or about.

Yet even then we cannot claim that all the structures were totally forgotten. Indeed, King Satha, a Cambodian who reigned in the last quarter of the sixteenth century, actually took his court back to Angkor at one point and tried to restore the temple of Angkor Wat. Satha does not seem to have been able to establish anything like a settlement there, but he did have sculptors finish carving certain details on the frieze (of Galleries E and F). But although succeeding kings (according to Cambodian chronicles) continued to visit the Angkor locality intermittently, none seems to have tried to advance the revival plans of King Satha and none resided there permanently. In the middle of the seventeenth century, King Barom Reachea VI—a convert to Islam—remained there for brief periods. But certainly by the early eighteenth century, Angkor Wat and other monuments of the area joined the more remote sites in being abandoned, and this time they truly became overrun by vegetation.

Again, although the local people abandoned the structures in one sense, there is every reason to believe that many were at least vaguely aware of their existence. Indeed, Angkor Wat temple had acquired considerable fame throughout this part of Southeast Asia, and Buddhist pilgrims had been coming to it from Burma and all over Indochina. (This fact is documented by a number of inscriptions, the last dated 1747.) What we must at least recognize is that these phenomena—the royal revival and the Buddhist pilgrimages, no matter how low-keyed—overlapped with the phenomenon that most concerns us here: the coming of Westerners to Cambodia.

The first to come to Cambodia were the sixteenth-century Portuguese and Spanish missionaries and adventurers, and although they never established anything like the colonial empire of their contemporaries in Latin America, some did try to establish a European "presence" in Cambodia. The first missionary known to have visited Cambodia, however, was a Portuguese monk, Gaspar da Gruz, who was there in 1556 but was only interested in converting the natives, not in looking for antiquities.

Then, during the last quarter of the sixteenth century—the time that King Satha was trying to restore Angkor Wat—another approach was

An engraving by Louis Delaporte showing the east side of Angkor Wat. This (and the two engravings on the following pages) illustrated Delaporte's book, *Voyage au Cambodge: l'architecture khmère,* published in Paris in 1880. Delaporte visited the ruins of Angkor in 1867 in the entourage of Capt. Doudart de Lagrée, the representative of the French government in Cambodia.

taken by two Europeans, the Portuguese Diego Veloso and the Spaniard Blas Ruiz. By supporting King Satha and the claims of his legitimate descendants, these two adventurers obtained the governorship of two provinces, Baphuon and Treang. Since these areas faced one another on opposite sides of the Mekong River, these two Europeans essentially controlled access to Phnom Penh and Srei Santhor, two of Cambodia's principal cities at that time. As "governors," these two men enjoyed an income from their territories for the duration of their rule, but they were not to be allowed to receive lands in the form of feudal estates; that is, the sole proprietor of the land remained the Cambodian king.

Veloso and Ruiz were not satisfied with this arrangement, and they repeatedly solicited the Spaniards based in Manila to intervene—an intervention also advocated by some of the missionaries in Manila—with the prospect of setting up a Spanish protectorate in Cambodia. At last an expedition was organized in 1598, but it was unable to win by force. And while negotiations with the king (no longer Satha, but Barom Reachea II) were dragging on, an incident flared up between the Spaniards and a contingent of Malaysian mercenary troops. It climaxed in the death of Veloso and Ruiz, the flight of Father Maldonado, who commanded the Manila contingent, and the effective end of Spanish influence in Cambodia. A small nucleus of Portuguese and Spaniards did, however, remain in the vicinity of Phnom Penh, where their presence was noted in the seventeenth century. And, incidentally, later versions of Cambodian chronicles refer to Veloso and Ruiz, who are called "two adopted sons of Satha." So it would seem that the first Europeans in Cambodia were absorbed by the local culture; in any case, there is no reason to believe that any of these people had the slightest interest in the monuments of past glory.

Now we know of the doings of these two adventurers, and this whole episode, thanks to one of several sixteenth- and seventeenth-century Portuguese and Spanish who wrote down reports on conditions in this part of the world. In this instance, we are indebted to Diogo do Couto, the official compiler of the chronicles of Portuguese India. He lived for a long time at Goa, the Portuguese colony in India, and although he evidently never went himself to Cambodia, he has left us quite an accurate description of Angkor among his reports. The indications are that do Couto's source was Antonio de Magdalena, a Capuchin friar who visited Angkor about 1585. De Magdalena was one of several missionaries who came from Malacca and entered Cambodia; King Satha did not stop them, and in fact he used them as commercial agents in dealing with Malacca, or as ambassadors to Malacca and Manila in his requests for assistance against the king of Siam.

It was Diogo do Couto who recounted such stories as the episode of Veloso and Ruiz in Cambodia, and also of King Satha's return to Angkor. Obviously, do Couto was totally dependent on traditional accounts, so we cannot be sure he is recording history in the strict sense. But he has preserved some good stories, such as the one about the Cambodian king of the mid-sixteenth century who went elephant hunting.

In the thickest forest in the realm, his servants, beating the bush to open a path for him, suddenly came upon a number of imposing constructions. The vegetation choking the monuments on the inside was so dense that the servants were unable to trample it under their feet and gain entrance. The king, upon being informed of what they had found, hurried to the place himself. Seeing the great length and height of the outer walls, he wanted to get a look at what was on the other side of them, so he at once ordered his men to cut up and burn every last bit of vegetation.

The king remained in this locality, on the banks of a lovely river, while his men—some five or six thousand—carried out his orders. In a short time, the work was done, and the city had been entirely freed, both inside and out and for a considerable area all around, from the exceptionally dense undergrowth and the forest trees that had kept it hidden for so many years. And after everything had been cleared away, the king made his entry, and visiting the entire city he

An engraving by Delaporte showing the Bayon at Angkor Thom.

was astonished by the great size of the constructions. He decided on the spot to transfer his court here, for aside from the fact that the city's layout and general aspect expressed great majesty, it was the finest place imaginable. This region, in fact, is one of the most refreshing in the world, with its woods, rivers, and first-rate springs.

What this king had evidently stumbled on was Angkor Thom, and the description that Diogo do Couto provides is surprisingly accurate. It mentions the five entryways through the outer wall; the wall itself built with such great mastery that the junctures between one stone and another are not visible; and the long lines of "giants"—the *devas* and *asuras* supporting the *nagas* (see page 146). Diogo do Couto, however, had no idea of who was responsible for these works, and attributed them to the inhabitants of Canara, an Indian kingdom of Vijayanagar, to whom he also attributes an inscription reportedly found at Angkor Wat.

Diogo do Couto also provides a detailed description of Angkor Wat, concluding: "In the great plain surrounding the area there are numerous other temples, which appear to have been the tombs of the lords of this kingdom, as the great temple [Angkor Wat] is that of the king who had it built." These words make it clear that the tradition regarding the use of Angkor Wat as a tomb—reported by Chou Ta-Kuan at the end of the thirteenth century—was still alive. (The tradition was to be recorded in the temple itself on an inscription bearing the date 1702—and it has been more or less generally accepted by modern authorities on Khmer culture.) In his account of Angkor Thom, too, do Couto mentions the royal palace and also "one of the most extraordinary temples, in the interior of the city, yet incomplete": this is, of course, the Bayon. And he provides a fine description of the irrigation system of the Bayon complex.

> From every gate of the site [the Bayon] a road as wide as the outer bridges stretched out toward this temple. . . . And reaching forth from either side were exquisite canals filled to overflowing with water from the great moat surrounding the city. The water enters by the two gates on the north and east sides, and then flows back into the moat from the south and east [gates], so that the water in the moat never diminishes, for whatever quantity enters from the two gates returns outside by the other two. As for the great moat, it is always full, since important, well-stocked rivers empty into it. In fact, the excess of water made it necessary to build a number of outlets so that the moat would not run over. So it is that each one of the roads that leaves the gates is flanked by another two [canals] which are used by a multitude of boats. These latter come from the interior of the country along its outer rivers, laden with provisions, firewood, and other commodities that are unloaded at the very doors of houses, which all have two entrances, one on the canal and one on the river. And the city's garbage is removed the same way, hauled outside as far as the moat, so that after the king had discovered the city and transferred his court there, it became the most beautiful, the best served, and cleanest city in the world.

Diogo do Couto's text also gives an account of various practices of the people, such as the rice harvest.

> During a given season, every two years, a great quantity of rice called *bate* [paddy] in India comes up from the bottom of a lake, providing food for the great bulk of the inhabitants of the villages all around. From this description one gathers that this rice springs up under water like seaweed and, when the proper time comes, rises to the surface. And in this period numerous pirogues make their way across the lake gathering in the rice with great celebrations and dances to the sound of musical instruments. The king who discovered this city had its palaces completed at enormous expense, and then set up his court there. He populated the city with persons he brought in from the other cities of the kingdom, donating land to them for their farming, including hereditary plots. There is no question that this kingdom once belonged to the Chinese, and they [the Cambodians] preserve Chinese laws and customs to this day.

Some of the tales that Diogo do Couto reported were handed down by other of the early European reports. But as we read such accounts today, we must realize that most of them did not get read by many people until our own day; they were written in obscure reports that few people read and fewer understood the significance of. (Diogo do Couto's account, for instance, was not published until 1953.) And it is no wonder, either, that these early reporters did not understand the true history of the monuments they were describing. The Spaniard Gabriel Quiroga de San Antonio, for instance, wrote in 1603: "In 1570 a city was brought to light that had never been seen or heard of by the natives." Christoval de Jaque wrote in 1606: "In 1570 a city full of numerous edifices was discovered. . . . King Apramlangara sent a number of his countrymen there because it is situated in the most fertile part of the kingdom." These are obviously retellings of the same story Diogo do Couto told of how the king discovered the vegetation-choked city while on his hunting expedition.

These early accounts, while providing various details that gave their reports an air of history, also began to speculate in a manner that moved the monuments into the realm of myth. Thus Friar Joao dos Santos wrote in 1609:

> Although it may seem that I am digressing from the history of Christianity in Cambodia, which I have been dealing with in this chapter, I will not omit saying a few words about a city that was discovered in this kingdom while I was in those regions. . . . No one knows anything about the founding of this city, nor of the reasons why it was abandoned, and this is astonishing. Still more astonishing is that fact that no stone is to be found in this entire region, so that it was necessary, in order to erect these edifices, to bring it from a distance of thirty leagues.

From such "astonishing" speculations, it was only a short step to more fantastic hypotheses. Thus Bartolome L. de Argensola wrote in 1609:

> And in all this immense city, when the islanders discovered it, there were neither persons nor animals nor living souls, except for that which nature produces in the cracks of ruins. I confess that I hesitated to write this, and I felt I was talking of the fantastic city of Plato's Atlantis or of that of his *Republic*. But there is no thing or event, however wonderful, that does not sooner or later run up against great skepticism. Today the city is inhabited, and our Augustinian and Dominican brothers, serious and reliable and preachers of the gospel in these regions, bear witness to the truth. A person versed in the study of letters might suppose it was the work of Trajan. But although this latter extended his empire further than all his predecessors, I have never heard that he ever arrived as far as Cambodia. If the histories of the Chinese were as well known as our own, they would tell us the reasons why such a large mass of human beings abandoned the city. They would explain the monuments' inscriptions, and everything else the natives know nothing of. Faced with the oblivion and mystery of such a lovely city, I don't know what to say. One finds more to admire there than to reason over.

In this excerpt from de Argensola we may note another element that early entered writing about the monuments of Cambodia: the tendency to attribute them to Westerners—although notice that de Argensola treated this attribution to the Romans with evident caution. Marcello de Ribadeneyra, the author of the oldest published description of Angkor—in 1601—attributed the monuments to Alexander the Great, while Gabriel Quiroga de San Antonio claimed they had been built by Jews settled in China. In effect, they were finding it hard to recognize that the Khmers, or Orientals in general, had the ability to create such great monuments. (Although it should be said that the native Cambodians themselves were ready to attribute them to foreigners.) Only Diogo do Couto attributed the sculptures at Angkor Thom to Indians.

These early reporters of the Cambodian remains concurred in various other details, too—probably because they were often simply repeating each other or the same few sources. One thing they agreed on was that the inhabitants of Cambodia had lost all recollection both of Angkor Thom and its builders. As we have indicated, this is an exaggeration if we are to take it literally and absolutely. Yet once the city ceased to be the capital, no longer playing the role for which it had been built—residence of the king, center of the realm, and symbol of the cosmos—it was inevitable that the monuments should be generally ignored and forgotten. The destruction of the city by the Thais must also have left things in great disarray. Yet the area surrounding the city probably continued to be inhabited, especially if it was true—as various early accounts attest—that it was "among the most fertile," enjoying an abundant supply of water.

After their initial exposure in these early seventeenth-century ac-

An engraving by Delaporte showing the south gate of the outer wall of Angkor Thom.

counts, the monuments of Cambodia tended to fade from the consciousness of even the few Europeans who might have done something about them. For one thing, the Portuguese and Spaniards began to lose influence in this region. Meantime, other foreigners were on the scene. The Japanese seem to have known of at least Angkor Wat by this time; but although they made a plan of the site, they did nothing more to publicize it (and, of course, they deliberately cut themselves off from all foreign contacts by 1640). The English had a commercial mission in Cambodia and even some settlers during the seventeenth century, but none of them ever seems to have heard of Angkor.

The Dutch, on the other hand, were becoming the major European presence in Southeast Asia, although they were not successful in establishing a commercial center in Cambodia. Yet there are a few references in Dutch writings of the seventeenth century, as in the account of Angkor in a letter written in 1656 by Hendrick Indjick. He was a merchant who also "doubled" as a sort of envoy, and he wrote to the Governor-General of the Dutch East Indies: "The king paid a visit to a lovely pleasant place known as Anckoor, which the Portuguese and Castilians call Rome, and which is situated an eight- or ten-day journey from here [Phnom Penh]."

But it was the French who were eventually to have the greatest impact on Angkor, on Cambodia—indeed, on the whole of Indochina. The first Frenchmen to come were the missionaries, starting in the second half of the seventeenth century with the establishment of the Society of Missions in Siam. Some of these missionaries began to write of the legendary remains in the wilds of Cambodia, but despite many references to Angkor, neither it nor the other great monuments were known to Westerners during the eighteenth or first half of the nineteenth centuries. Even when one French missionary, Charles-Emile Bouillevaux, published in 1858 an account of his travels there—and in which he described the ruins of Angkor Wat—no one paid any attention.

The real revelation of Angkor—and by association, all the great Khmer monuments—to the Western world begins with the travels and writings of the French botanist, Henri Mouhot. Between 1858 and 1862, he explored the valleys of the Menam and Mekong rivers, and his diaries were published in book form in 1864 (posthumously: he had died of fever in Laos). His description of Angkor quickly caught the fancy of the world, and soon the site was drawing many travelers of various nationalities and backgrounds. By far the largest number though, were Frenchmen, including such pioneers as Doudart de Lagrée, Garnier, Tissandier, and Louis Delaporte.

The last named was a French explorer-artist, and he published his *Voyage au Cambodge* in Paris in 1880, which included engravings of his fine drawings (three of which are reproduced here). A close look at Delaporte's drawings—and they were done about 1867—reveals that a surprising amount of the stonework stood clear and intact. His work also encouraged the concept of "exotic ruins" that was to color so much of the literature on Angkor—perhaps best exemplified by the French author, Pierre Loti. Although his pages on the ruins (principally in *Un Pèlerin d'Angkor,* Paris, 1912) are unquestionably full of suggestion and provide a good description of the atmosphere that surrounded the temples, submerged in a sea of vegetation, there is total incomprehension of the true significance of the monuments. The British photographer, J. Thomson, who visited Angkor shortly before Delaporte and left the first photographic record of the site—published in *The Antiquities of Cambodia,* Edinburgh, 1867—had surprising flashes of understanding, such as the relationship between the temple-mountain and the Hindus' Mount Meru.

It was in the second half of the nineteenth century, of course, while European colonial expansion was in full swing, that France established itself in the rich territories of Indochina. (Incidentally, in 1794 the Cambodian governor of Battambang, who administered the province of Siemreap, which included the Angkor region, had preferred to pay tribute to the king of Siam [Thailand], so that the Angkor remains were legally a part of Siam from that point on; it was not until a treaty was mediated by France in 1907 that Cambodia was able to regain this territory.) Then, at the turn of this century, the French placed all the remains of Indochina under their control and founded the French School of the Far East *(École Française d'Extreme-Orient)* to supervise their exploration and study. The foundation of this organization was, as one modern Frenchman, Chesneaux, has put it, "an integral part of the Doumer plan [Doumer being the French governor of Indochina at the time], like the creation of the rail network and the state monopolies of opium, salt, and alcohol: in all cases, what was intended was to take solid possession of Indochina for the French." The first director of the school said at this time: "For countries like Annam and Tonkin [Vietnam], imbued with the moral and artistic ideas of China, it is necessary for the missions, to ensure proper administration of these territories, to make an effort to assimilate this complex, profound culture. Only at such a price will this administration obtain from those who are under it an adherence that is not merely physical but also spiritual, thanks to which subjection can become a voluntary collaboration . . . the condition of power is knowledge."

Such sentiments, although expressed about Vietnam, were considered applicable to Cambodia as well. But if these were the reasons behind the founding of the school, it cannot be denied that its staff included scholars who conscientiously carried out the task of investigating and reconstructing the monuments. These scholars left fundamental works that are still useful because of their descriptions of the monuments, even if many of their opinions and interpretations have become outdated. (To cite one, the detailed *Inventaire descriptif des monuments du Cambodge* by E. Lunet de Lajonquière, Paris 1902–1911, remains an invaluable reference work.)

By the early years of the twentieth century, then, the work of study and reconstruction of the great Khmer monuments was well under way, and it may be said that their discovery by the West was inevitable. But it has been only in more recent years that scholars have begun the stratigraphic excavations and study of less monumental elements that are considered indispensable to modern archaeology. For instance, the covered areas that are but annexes to the great temples—invaluable witnesses to understanding the way the Khmers worshiped and the use they made of the great monuments—were brought to light at the Prasat Kravanh by Bernard-Philippe Groslier only in the 1950s; and it was not until 1965 that scholars completed a survey of the upper part of the Bayon temple-mountain. The in-depth investigation, which alone will provide the data for the chronology of the monuments and the daily life of the Khmers, is only now beginning.

Will it ever be completed? This is a question that came to be raised in the early 1970s as several new threats beyond the usual ones of water, vegetation, animal life, and other forces of nature began to endanger the great monuments of Angkor. During the war that swept across Cambodia at this time, the territory of Angkor exchanged hands between the warring parties. The remains were respected by both sides, although there was some artillery damage to the south side of the outer gallery of Angkor Wat. But the vital work of maintenance and restoration came to a half for at least one period; and many of the statues and movable works had to be buried underground for safekeeping—the larger pieces at Angkor itself, the smaller ones in the capital, Phnom Penh.

Perhaps just as appalling have been the assaults made on the sculptures by smugglers, who carry them off and sell them to "art dealers," who in turn sell them to private collectors and museums around the world. The war eventually ended, after all, but the smuggling must be stopped if these monuments are to remain in the hands of their true inheritors.

Do these monuments, in fact, retain such significance for the Cambodians of today? There is no doubt about the answer. Like all peoples who have been subject to colonial domination, the Cambodians tend to look back to their traditional past. In the process of consolidating the new national consciousness, the Khmer monuments—and those of Angkor in particular—have emerged as a symbol of a culture that the Cambodians can recognize as their own and at the same time as a symbol of their independence from the West. It is no coincidence that both sides in the war that fought for Cambodia appealed to Angkor—and included an image of the towers of Angkor Wat in their flags. Prince Norodom Sihanouk, former head of state of Cambodia, while living in exile in Peking, once announced that he would establish the capital of "free Cambodia" at Siemreap, the town near the temples—an obvious bid to identify his side with Cambodia's glorious past. But whichever side prevails in Cambodia, one hopes that the day is not far when all descendants of the Khmers, and the world at large, will be able to enjoy and respect these great monuments.

CHRONOLOGICAL CHART OF THE KHMER CIVILIZATION

DATE	RULERS	EVENTS IN INDOCHINA
B.C. **c. 5000** **1000**		Early people develop Mesolithic and Neolithic cultures
1000 **0**		Metallurgy spreads
A.D. **c. 150**	Unidentified rulers of Funan	Strong Indian influence starts perhaps via trade but spreads through all aspects of life
c. 400–420 **c. 480–514**	*FUNAN KINGS* Kaundinya Jayavarman	Indian influence continues. Funan one of several kingdoms on peninsula
514–539	Rudravarman	
c. 550	*CHENLA KINGS* Bhavavarman I	Unification (to some degree) of Chenla and Funan
c. 600–616 **616–c. 635**	Sitrasena Isanavarman I	
c. 635–656	Bhavavarman II	
657–681	Jayavarman I (Puskaraksa?)	Breakup into Chenla of Land and Chenla of Water
713	Jayadevi ?	Javanese influence (conquest?) during eighth century
802–850	Jayavarman II	Founding of Khmer kingship; capital moves around several sites in Angkor region
850–877	Jayavarman III	
877–889	Indravarman I	Establishment of Khmer power
889–900	Yasovarman I	Capital at Yasodharapura (Angkor)
900–921	Harshavarman I	
921–928	Isanavarman II	
921–941	Jayavarman IV	
942–944 **944–968**	Harshavarman II Rajendravarman II	Khmers conquer Champa
968–1001	Jayavarman V	
1001–1002	Udayadityavarman I	Struggle for succession ends with victory for Suryavarman
1002–1010 **1011–1050**	Jayaviravarman Suryavarman I	
1050–1066	Udayadityavarman II	
1066–1080 **(1080–1113?)** **1080–1107**	Harshavarman III (Nrpatindavarman ?) *MAHIDHARAPURA* *DYNASTY* Jayavarman VI	Possibly division of power and dynastic struggle
1107–1113	Dharanindravarman I	

CITIES & MONUMENTS	STYLES	ARCHITECTURE ELSEWHERE
	Hoabinian	3500–3000: Sumerian pyramid-temples
	Bacsonian	2200–1700: Stonehenge
		1700–1500: Knossos palace
Large stone works	Megalithic	c. 1000: Temple of Jerusalem begun
Bronze works	Dong-son	447–433: Parthenon
		72–80: Colosseum (Rome)
		312: Arch of Constantine
City of Oc-Eo		Gupta art of India (320–600)
City of Angkor Borei		532–7: Hagia Sophia (Constantinople)
Capital at Bhavapura		c. 550: S. Apollinare (Ravenna)
Capital at Isanapura	Sambor	
Lintels; Buddhist bronzes	Prei Kmeng	625–675: Mamallapuram Temples, India
Lintels; Hindu sculptures	Prasat Andet	
		693: Dome of Rock begun in Jerusalem
	Kompong Preah	Great Mosque of Damascus
Damrei Krap		
Rup Arak	Kulen	Barabudur Temple, Java
		873: First cathedral at Cologne (Germany)
Capital at Roluos		
879: Preah Ko	Preah Ko	c. 879: Ibn Tulun Mosque, Cairo
881: Bakeng		
893: Lolei		
Phnom Bakheng	Bakheng	
921: Prasat Kravanh		914: First Cluny Abbey church
(Baksei Chamkrong?)		
Prasat Thom at Koh Ker	Koh Ker	
952: East Mebon		950: Pagoda of Daigo-ji, Kyoto
961: Pre Rup	Pre Rup	963: Earliest recorded London
967: Banteay Srei	Banteay Srei	bridge
Phimeanakas	Kleang	c. 970: Saxon Church of St.
Ta Keo		Lawrence, Bradford-on-Avon, England
Preah Vihear (start)		
Baphuon	Baphuon	1017–37: St. Sophia, Kiev
West Mebon		(first Russian stone church)
		1052–65: Westminster Abbey
Phimai		1094: St. Mark's, Venice (completed)

DATE	RULERS	EVENTS IN INDOCHINA
1113–1150	Suryavarman II	Khmers dominate Malaysia, Siam, and Champa
1150–1160	Dharanindravarman II	
1160–1166	Yasovarman II	
1166–1181	Tribhuvanadityavarman	1177: Chams attack Angkor
1181–1219	Jayavarman VII	Khmers annex Champa
1219–1243	Indravarman II	
1243–1295	Jayavarman VIII	1296: Chou Ta-Kuan visits Angkor Spread of Theravada Buddhism
1296–1434		Decline of Khmers; Thai invasions 1431: Angkor falls to Thais

RECOMMENDED READING

There is now a large and growing literature on the Khmers, their monuments, and their culture. For obvious reasons (see pages 183–85), the bulk of the primary scholarship in this field is in French, and several of these texts are cited throughout this work. But this is a more specialized list, designed for the English speaker who might want to complement various aspects of this volume. The books have also been chosen on the basis of accessibility—their price, their recent publication, and their attempts to communicate with the general public.

Asia House Gallery: *Khmer Sculpture.* (New York, 1961)

Boxer, C. R. (ed.): *South China in the Sixteenth Century.* (London, 1953)

Briggs, Lawrence P.: *The Ancient Khmer Empire.* American Philosophical Society (Philadelphia, 1951)

Cady, John F.: *Southeast Asia: Its Historical Development.* McGraw-Hill (New York, 1964)

Coedès, George: *Angkor: An Introduction* (trans. and ed., Emily Gardiner). Oxford Univ. Press (1963)

Coomaraswamy, A. K.: *The Transformation of Nature in Art.* (New York, 1956)

Edmonds, I. G.: *The Khmers of Cambodia: The Story of a Mysterious People.* Bobbs-Merrill (New York, 1970); (for young people)

Ghosh, Manomohan: *A History of Cambodia.* (Saigon, 1960)

Giteau, Madeleine: *Khmer Sculpture and the Angkor Civilization.* Abrams (New York, 1966)

Groslier, Bernard: *The Art of Indochina.* Crown (New York, 1962)

CITIES AND MONUMENTS	STYLES	ARCHITECTURE ELSEWHERE
Angkor Wat Beng Mealea Chau Say Tevoda Thommanon Banteay Samre Wat Phu (finished) Preah Khan (Kompong Thom)	Angkor Wat	c. 1130: First hall at Alcazar, Seville Many Gothic cathedrals being built throughout Europe 1163: Notre Dame, Paris, begun 1174: Campanile (Leaning Tower) of Pisa
Ta Prohm Banteay Kdei Preah Khan (Angkor) Wall of Angkor Thom Banteay Chmar Bayon Neak Pean Royal Terraces (?)	Bayon	1194–1260: Chartres Cathedral 1246–58: La Sainte-Chapelle, Paris 1296–1434: Florence Cathedral

Groslier, Bernard, and Jacques Arthaud: *Angkor: Art and Civilization.* Praeger (New York, rev. ed., 1966)

Hall, Daniel G.: *A History of South-East Asia.* St. Martin's (New York, 1968)

Lee, Sherman: *Ancient Cambodian Sculpture.* Asia House Gallery–New York Graphic Society (New York, 1969)

LeMay, Reginald: *The Culture of South-East Asia: The Heritage of India.* Humanities Press (New York, 1954)

Macdonald, Malcolm: *Angkor.* (London, 1958)

Malraux, André: *The Royal Way* (trans. Stuart Gilbert). Random House (New York)

Munsterberg, Hugo: *The Art of India and Southeast Asia.* Abrams (New York)

Myrdal, Jan: *Angkor: An Essay on Art and Imperialism* (trans. Paul Austin). Random House (New York, 1971)

Porée, Guy and Eveline Maspéro: *Traditions and Customs of the Khmer.* Yale Univ. Press (New Haven, 1953)

Pym, Christopher: *The Ancient Civilization of Angkor.* Mentor–NAL (New York, 1968)

Pym, Christopher (ed.): *Henri Mouhot's Diary.* Oxford Univ. Press (New York, 1967)

Rowland, Benjamin: *The Art and Architecture of India.* Penguin (Baltimore, 1953)

Sitwell, Osbert: *Escape with Me.* Macmillan (London, 1939)

Steinberg, David J. (ed.): *Cambodia: Its People, Its Society, Its Culture.* Yale Univ. Press (New Haven, 1957)

RECOMMENDED VIEWING

Nothing would make the world of the Khmer seem so real as a visit to the actual sites; failing that, the next best thing is a visit to a museum with a collection Khmer works. Most of these works, of course, are in museums in Phnom Penh or Paris, but there are collections elsewhere. Some of the finest are these:

GREAT BRITAIN:
London: British Museum
Norwich: Sainsbury Centre for Visual Arts, University of East Anglia
    (one outstanding 11th century sculpture)

U.S.A.:
California: The Center of Asian Art and Culture (Brundage and DeYoung Collections), San Francisco
Massachusetts: The Museum of Fine Arts, Boston
New York: The Metropolitan Museum of Art, New York City
Ohio: The Cleveland Museum of Art, Cleveland

There are still other collections of Khmer works in North America, some highly specialized, some more general, but all open — within certain restrictions — to the general public. The list that follows, in conjunction with those singled out above, should allow people everywhere throughout North America to start an acquaintance with this great civilization.

Arizona: Art Museum, Phoenix
Connecticut: Yale University Art Gallery, New Haven
Illinois: Art Institute, Chicago
Massachusetts: Harvard University, Fogg Art Museum, Cambridge
New York: Brooklyn Museum; Asia House Gallery (occasional exhibitions), New York City
Oregon: University of Oregon Museum of Art, Eugene

CANADA:
Royal Ontario Museum, Toronto

CREDITS

The plans and drawings in this volume have been taken, with
the kind permission of the publishers, from the following vol-
umes:
J. Boisselier, Le Cambodge, *Manuel d'archéologie d'Extrême-*
Orient, première partie: Asie du Sud-Est (Paris, J. Picard, 1966) for
those on pages 26, 34, 35, 36, 108, 109, 110, 113[1]. J. Dumarçay,
Atlas et notices des planches (Paris, 1967) for those on pages 156,
161, 171. Parmentier, *L'Art Khmer classique, monuments du quadrant*
nord-est (Paris, Ecole Française d'Extrême Orient 1939) for those
on pages 36[30] and 127. Ph. Stern, *Les monuments khmers du style du*
Bàyon et Jayavarman VII. (Paris, Musée Guimet, 1965) for those on
pages 113[2×3], 128, 134, 140. H. Stierlin, *Angkor* (Fribourg, Office
du Livre, 1970), for those on pages 53, 58, 66, 86, 87, 88, 90, 91,
143.
The redrawing of the plans on pages 26, 30[1], 34; 35[1], 134, 140,
143[1], 156, and 171 was done by Giuliano and Giovanni Battista
Minelli; the maps on pages 12 and 19 are by Marcello Fiorentin;
the drawings on pages 30, 31, 33, 38, and 47 are by Carlo Ranzi.

The literary texts and inscriptions that appear in the margins
are based on material in the following texts, with kind permission
of the authors and publishers:
K. Bhattacharya, *Les religions brahmaniques dans l'ancien Cam-*
bodge (Paris, 1961). J. Boisselier, *Le Cambodge, manuel d'archéologie*
d'Extrême-Orient, première partie: Asie du Sud-Est (Paris, J. Picard,
1966). G. Coedès, *Inscriptions du cambodge, collections de textes et*
documents sur l'Indochine (Paris, Ecole Française d'Extrême-Orient,
1929–66, 8 vols.) B. Ph. Groslier, *Angkor et le Cambodge au XVI*
siècle d'après les sources portugaises et espagnoles (Paris, Presses Universitaires de France, 1958). Innes Miller, *The Spice Trade of the*
Roman Empire, 29 B.C. *to* A.D. *641* (Oxford, 1969). P. Pelliot, *Le*
Fou-Nan (Paris, *Bulletin d'Ecole Française d'Extrême-Orient,* III,
1903). Ph. Stern, *Les monuments Khmer du style du Bàyon et Jayavar-*
man VII (Paris, Presses Universitaires de France, 1965). Tcheon
Ta-Kouan, *Mémoires sur les coutumes du Cambodge,* traduits et an-
notés par P. Pelliot (Paris, *Bulletin d'Ecole Française d'Extrême-*
Orient, 1951). P. Wheatley, *The Golden Khersonese* (Kuala Lampur,
University of Malaya Press, 1961). O. W. Wolters, *Early Indonesian*
Commerce (Ithaca, N.Y., 1967).